MODERN SOUTH ASIA

Drawing on the newest and most sophisticated historical research and scholarship in the field, *Modern South Asia* provides a challenging insight for those with an intellectual curiosity about the region. After sketching the pre-modern history of the subcontinent the book concentrates on the last three centuries. Jointly authored by two leading Indian and Pakistani historians, it offers a rare depth of historical understanding of the politics, cultures, and economies that shape the lives of more than a fifth of humanity.

In this comprehensive study, the authors interpret and debate the striking developments in contemporary South Asian history and historical writing, covering the entire spectrum of the region's modern history – social, economic and political. The book provides new insights into the structure and ideology of the British raj, the meaning of subaltern resistance, the refashioning of social relations along the lines of caste, class, community and gender, the different strands of anti-colonial nationalism and the dynamics of decolonization.

This third edition brings the debate up to the present day, taking account of recent historical research and covering the closer integration of South Asia with the global economy, the impact of developments in Afghanistan on the region as a whole, and the fresh challenges to South Asia's nation-states.

Sugata Bose is Gardiner Professor of History at Harvard University. His publications include *Peasant Labour and Colonial Capital* (1993) and *A Hundred Horizons: The Indian Ocean in the Age of Global Empire* (2006).

Ayesha Jalal is Mary Richardson Professor of History at Tufts University. Her publications include *Self and Sovereignty: Individual and Community in South Asian Islam Since 1850* (2000) and *Partisans of Allah: Jihad in South Asia* (2010).

MODERN SOUTH ASIA

History, Culture, Political Economy

THIRD EDITION

Sugata Bose and Ayesha Jalal

AUG 0 8 2011

PROPERTY OF
SENEGA...
NEWNHAM CAMPUS

WITHDRAWN

Routledge
Taylor & Francis Group

LONDON AND NEW YORK

First published 1997 by Oxford University Press, Delhi
First published by Routledge 1998
Second edition by Routledge 2004
This edition 2011 by Routledge
2 Park Square, Milton Park, Abingdon, Oxon, OX14 4RN

Simultaneously published in the USA and Canada
by Routledge
270 Madison Avenue, New York, NY 10016

Routledge is an imprint of the Taylor & Francis Group, an informa business

© 1997, 1998, 2004, 2011 Sugata Bose and Ayesha Jalal

The right of Sugata Bose and Ayesha Jalal to be identified as authors
of this work has been asserted by them in accordance with sections
77 and 78 of the Copyright, Designs and Patents Act 1988.

Typeset in Sabon by Taylor & Francis Books
Printed and bound in Great Britain by
MPG Books Ltd, Bodmin, Cornwall

All rights reserved. No part of this book may be reprinted or reproduced
or utilised in any form or by any electronic, mechanical, or other
means, now known or hereafter invented, including photocopying and
recording, or in any information storage or retrieval system, without
permission in writing from the publishers.

British Library Cataloguing in Publication Data
A catalogue record for this book is available from the British Library

Library of Congress Catalog-in-Publication Data
Bose, Sugata.
Modern South Asia : history, culture, political economy / Sugata Bose
and Ayesha Jalal. -- 3rd ed.
p. cm.
"Simultaneously published in the USA and Canada"--T.p. verso.
Includes bibliographical references and index.
1. South Asia--History. I. Jalal, Ayesha. II. Title.
DS340.B66 2010
954--dc22
2010031589

ISBN13: 978-0-415-77942-5 (hbk)
ISBN13: 978-0-415-77943-2 (pbk)

FOR

SEHR JALAL
NAIRA MINTO
ASIM JALAL

AIDAN SAMYA BOSE ROSLING (TIPU SULTAN)
KIERAN SHAURYA BOSE ROSLING (TUNKU)
EUAN SHARANYA BOSE ROSLING (PUCHKU)

AND THROUGH THEIR HANDS
TO THE YOUNGER GENERATION

CONTENTS

ILLUSTRATIONS

PREFACE TO THE THIRD EDITION

The inexorable march of history necessitates periodic revisions and new editions of general works of historical scholarship. The changes that need to be taken account of are primarily of two kinds. First, significant recent events need to be assessed in the context of longer-term structures and processes. Second, new knowledge generated by cutting-edge research deserves to find a place in any major work of synthesis and interpretation.

Modern South Asia was first written on the occasion of the fiftieth anniversary of South Asian independence and partition in 1997 and a second, revised edition appeared in 2004. During the six years that have now intervened crucial developments have taken place both in terms of historically significant events and innovative historical scholarship. We had argued in the first edition that the idea of changeless tradition in South Asia was always a myth. While certain structures of material life may be slow moving over time, nothing is a simple 'given' from the past. Traditions with deep roots in the past are always in the process of being reinterpreted. If we consider what might be called a medium-term conjuncture from the late eighteenth century to the early twentieth, South Asia can be seen to be going through a world-historical transformation. In many ways, the region is recovering the global position it had lost in economic, political and cultural terms at the onset of British colonial rule. So far as the history of events is concerned, South Asia has witnessed more than its due share of dramatic assassinations and insurgencies as well as changes of regimes.

The trend that we had noticed in the second edition of new historical scholarship on the formation of regional and religious identities gathered further momentum in the last few years with the publication of insightful first books by younger scholars, some but by no means all being our own former graduate students. The theme of the intricate relationship between religion and politics has engaged our own scholarly interest, as is evident from Ayesha Jalal's *Partisans of Allah: Jihad in South Asia* published in 2008. South Asian history has been placed creatively in the wider context of the inter-regional arena on the Indian Ocean as well as connections of a global scope. Our involvement in the writing of new connective histories is exemplified in Sugata

xi

Bose's *A Hundred Horizons: the Indian Ocean in the Age of Global Empire* that came out in 2006. South Asian historiography has been enriched of late by a renewed interest in the history of economic and political ideas in a transnational frame. Our own work in this field and that of our many colleagues and students find reflection in this revised third edition of *Modern South Asia.*

Our leaves from Harvard and Tufts in the spring semester of 2010 enabled us to complete this work of revision, expansion and refinement of our text. We have put together the third edition in Calcutta and Lahore and we wish to thank our mothers Krishna Bose and Zakia Jalal for their support. We hope the new edition will continue to be the book of choice of teachers and students of modern South Asian history as well as interested non-specialists in the subject.

Sugata Bose and Ayesha Jalal
Summer 2010, in Calcutta and Lahore

PREFACE TO THE SECOND EDITION

The first edition of *Modern South Asia* had been published some six years ago on the occasion of the fiftieth anniversary of the subcontinent's independence and partition. We have been gratified by the enthusiastic response it has received from teachers, students and non-specialist readers with an intelligent interest in South Asia.

There are primarily three reasons for publishing a second, revised edition at this stage. First, the strength of *Modern South Asia* lies in its use of the newest and the most sophisticated historical research and scholarship in the field. In the past six years there has been some excellent new work, particularly on the formation of religious, regional and national identities in South Asia, which is reflected in the new edition. South Asian historiography in this area is moving beyond the dichotomy between statist, 'secular' histories and communitarian, 'subaltern' histories towards a subtler understanding of the place of religion in the public sphere. The second edition of *Modern South Asia* aspires to convey to a general readership the current and cutting-edge state-of-the-art. We are grateful to our former Ph.D. students, now colleagues in the academy, for spurring us to do so. Second, *Modern South Asia* in its first edition had narrated the subcontinent's history up to 1997. Key developments since that date – not least the 1998 nuclear tests, the rise of the BJP to power in India, yet another military regime in Pakistan and new twists and turns in India–Pakistan relations – all suggested that the story needed to be brought up to date in purely chronological terms. Third, we have now had occasion to rethink some of the key issues discussed in the first edition and have received sufficient feedback from our colleagues and students to engage in a chapter by chapter revision. For example, we have rewritten the introduction and shifted the more difficult discussion of historiography to the beginning of the bibliography. In the chapter on the eighteenth century or India between empires we may have leaned a little too far towards the thesis about decentralization rather than decline. We seek to restore the balance somewhat in the second edition on the relationship between region and religion. The chapters on the colonial state have more to say on the raj without losing the general focus on Indian society. We have a few new insights into Gandhi's thought and practice, at variance with existing interpretations, which we bring into play in the chapter on the 1920s. We have added material on Muslim society and politics throughout, including the discussion of partition, and updated chapters 18, 19 and 20. A chronology of key events is supplied at the end of the book.

We wish to record our gratitude to our mothers, Krishna Bose and Zakia Jalal, for their support.

We hope that the second edition, like its predecessor, will help generate discussion and debate about South Asian history. *Modern South Asia* combines a narrative with synthesis and interpretation. We trust that in an improved second edition it will continue to be the book of choice for teachers, students and non-specialist readers searching for the one authoritative and enjoyable book on South Asian history.

Sugata Bose and Ayesha Jalal
April, 2003

PREFACE TO THE FIRST
EDITION

Times of commemoration can occasion fresh ways of rethinking the past. And 1997 seemed as good a moment as any other to bring together the myriad threads of modern South Asian history, pause and reconsider, while taking account of the more important findings of recent historical research. The shifting parameters of scholarly debate on South Asian historiography with the unfolding of the process of decolonization of the mind need to be placed before a broader audience. In deciding to put together a general history of the South Asian subcontinent, the audience we had foremost in our minds was the younger generation of South Asians and students interested in South Asia. That is why we have chosen to dedicate this book to our nieces and nephews and through their hands to the next generation. We hope of course that our book will engage interested non-specialists of whatever generation curious about South Asian history.

Our deepest debt in writing this book is to our students at Columbia University and Tufts University who heard earlier versions of our arguments in the form of lectures. Their queries as well as occasional incomprehension has greatly helped to sharpen and clarify our interpretation of complex historical processes and events. Interactions with our graduate students, Ritu Birla, Semanti Ghosh, Farina Mir, Mridu Rai, Shabum Tejani and Chitralekha Zutshi, have militated against over-implication. Farina Mir and Shabnum Tejani at Columbia and Semanti Ghosh and Chitralekha Zutshi at Tufts have served as our teaching assistants and contributed to the finer points of our text.

We are grateful to a number of our colleagues for reading the manuscript in whole or in part and making invaluable comments. Kumkum Roy cast an eye over our chapter on ancient India while Muzaffar Alam and Mridu Rai scrutinised the three chapters dealing with the period from *c.* 700 to *c.* 1800. Christopher Bayly did a critical reading of the entire manuscript and made a number of apt suggestions. David Washbrook also read the manuscript through and toasted its success even before it was published. We benefited from the comments on our proposal by the four readers of Routledge. The two anonymous readers for Oxford University Press made perhaps the most astute comments on the pages of an earlier version of the manuscript. We would not have got our manuscript ready if not for the prodding encouragement of Rukun Advani of OUP-Delhi who has published some of the best research on modern South Asian history in the last two decades. The enthusiasm of Heather McCallum at Routledge was a source of confidence while Bela Malik at OUP-Delhi competently attended to the editorial task of getting the manuscript ready for the printers.

Once more we have to thank our families for their continued and warming support of our scholarly endeavours. We would like to thank each other for choosing the path of negotiation rather than war when it came to addressing disputes and disagreements in the course of writing this book. It is our hope that this work will encourage more dialogues across the great divide of 1947. Our contribution to the fiftieth anniversary of independence and partition will have been made if it enables the opening of an intellectual and cultural corridor stretching from Lahore to Calcutta.

Sugata Bose and Ayesha Jalal

ACKNOWLEDGEMENTS

The authors and publishers would like to thank the following for granting permission to use copyright material in the volume:

Nehru Memorial Museum and Library (Figures 19, 20 and 29)
Netaji Research Bureau (Figures 22, 23, 24, 27, 28 and 31)
Ananda Bazaar Patrika (Figures 32 and 34)
Information Division, Embassy of Pakistan, Washington, D.C. (Figure 30)
Ayesha Jalal, *The Sole Spokesman* (Cambridge University Press, 1985) (Figures 21 and 26)
C.A. Bayly, The Raj (National Gallery Publications, 1990) (Figures 10 and 15)
'Partition', copyright © 1966 by W.H. Auden, from COLLECTED POEMS OF W.H. AUDEN by W.H. Auden. Used by permission of Random House, Inc and © 1976, 1991 The Estate of W.H. Auden

While every effort has been made to trace and acknowledge ownership of copyright material used in this volume, the publishers will be glad to make suitable arrangements with any copyright holders whom it has not been possible to contact.

1

SOUTH ASIAN HISTORY
An introduction

The very idea of India, and not just its wealth and wisdom, has been the site of fierce historical contestation. G.W.F. Hegel, the famous German philosopher, gave a not untypical nineteenth-century description of India as an object of desire:

> From the most ancient times downwards, all nations have directed their wishes and longings to gaining access to the treasures of this land of marvels, the most costly which the Earth presents; treasures of Nature – pearls, diamonds, perfumes, rose-essences, elephants, lions, etc. – as also treasures of wisdom. The way by which these treasures have passed to the West, has at all times been a matter of World-historical importance, bound up with the fate of nations.

He added approvingly, 'the English, or rather the East-India Company are the lords of the land; for it is the necessary fate of Asiatic Empires to be subjected to Europeans ... '. In the early twentieth century Gandhi lamented in his tract *Hind Swaraj*: 'the English have not taken India; we have given it to them. They are not in India because of their strength but because we keep them ... Recall the Company Bahadur. Who made it Bahadur ... it is truer to say that we gave India to the English than that India was lost'.

The battle to win India back was waged not only on the political plane but also in the realm of ideas. A turn-of-the-century Indian nationalist Bipin Chandra Pal, in his book *The Soul of India*, delved back into ancient history in attempting to question the Western definition of India: ' ... while the stranger called her India, or the land of the Indus, thereby emphasizing only her strange physical features, her own children, from of old, have known and loved her by another name ... that name is Bharatavarsha'. This name deriving from the ancient king of kings Bharata, Pal claimed, was 'not a physical name like India or the Transvaal, nor even a tribal and ethnic name like England or Aryavarta, but a distinct and unmistakable historic name like Rome'. India may have been a name given by foreigners, but its emotive appeal came to be internalized by many inhabitants of this land. The ancient Persians and Arabs referred to the

1

land beyond the river Sindhu or Indus as Al-Hind or Hindustan and the people inhabiting that land as Hindu. The words India and Indian were simply Greek, Roman and finally, English versions of the old Persian terminology. It was only gradually that the term Hindu came to be associated with the followers of a particular religious faith as a matter of convenience since the 'Hindus' did not deploy a single term to define their religion. The leading twentieth-century Muslim poet writing in Urdu had no difficulty celebrating Hindustan as his own. Mohammad Iqbal in his 'Tarana-i-Hindi' (The Anthem of Hind) of 1904 extolled the virtues of his homeland:

> Sarey jahan sey achhaa, ye Hindustan hamara
> Hum bulbulen hain iske, ye gulsitan hamara
> (Better than the whole world, is our Hindustan
> We are its singing birds, it is our garden of delights)

Iqbal later became one of the foremost proponents of a homeland for India's Muslims. On the eve of partition in 1947, Mohammad Ali Jinnah, widely acknowledged as the founder of this homeland, wrote indignantly about 'the wholly unwarranted assumption that Pakistan would be an area seceding from the Indian state', arguing that there could be no union of India without the Muslim-majority areas of the subcontinent. In the sixty-three years since independence and partition the political and ideational contests among its own people for proprietorship over the soul of the subcontinent have, if anything, greatly intensified.

It is not unusual for peoples burdened by history in their own contexts to be transformed into peoples without history in others. Given the tendency towards the 'essentializing' of India by Western orientalists over the past two centuries, it is no surprise that in the Western popular consciousness the Indian subcontinent tended to evoke two contrary images until the late twentieth century. On the one hand, it was lauded as an ancient land of mystery and romance, extraordinary wealth and profound spirituality. On the other, it was denounced for its irrationality and inhumanity and derided for its destitution and squalor. Even after the *maharaja* of old had been reduced to a caricature in the advertisement of India's national airline, television audiences in both Britain and the United States were entranced during the 1980s by the nostalgia of India's final fling with the British raj. Yet one had only to switch from the channel showing the soap opera to the news to find the coveted jewel in the crown portrayed as a veritable crucible of calamity, confusion and chaos. Stark poverty replaced the vision of India's grandeur, religious strife rudely disturbed the calm of other-worldly meditation, and fierce violence unleashed by both man and nature seemed to make a mockery of the peaceful messages of a Buddha or a Gandhi. Both images, whether optimistically fanciful or pejoratively stereotypical, stemmed from an inability to understand or comprehend, far less explain, the enormous complexities of South Asia.

The dawn of the twenty-first century witnessed the rise of a new set of contradictory images. Dynamic economic growth, the emergence of a number of high-profile billionaire entrepreneurs and a booming consumer culture in urban areas, especially but not only in India, seemed to portend 'a rise' alongside China after two centuries of poverty and relative economic decline. By contrast, a Maoist insurgency spreading ominously across India's tribal heartland, coupled with stories of sporadic farmers' suicides, suggested that the problem of inequities and gross disparities had been further compounded in the contemporary phase of globalization. Meanwhile, the turbulence in Pakistan's tribal frontier acquired menacing proportions in the decade following the 11 September 2001 terrorist attacks in the USA and the American military retaliation in Afghanistan. The violence spilled into the metropolitan cities, often in the form of ghastly suicide bombings. Caught as always in the vortex of global opportunities and conflicts, South Asia finds itself at one of the more significant milestones in its history.

The subcontinent defies piecemeal approaches much the same way as the proverbial elephant confounded the blind men in the famous story by the Muslim Sufi poet, Jalaluddin Rumi. When made to touch the different parts of the elephant's anatomy, each of the blind men described it according to the part of the body his hands had touched. So to one blind man the elephant appeared like a throne, to others like a fan, a water pipe and even a pillar. No one could imagine what the whole animal looked like. This book promises to present a view of India and South Asia with the blindfolds off. Recourse to history is indispensable in order to broaden perspective and sharpen focus. A single volume on the complex history of the subcontinent can only offer a glimpse of its richness and nuance, but with a good angle of vision it could be a penetrating and insightful glimpse.

What then is this Indian subcontinent – or South Asia, as it has come to be known in more recent and neutral parlance – whose history will be interpreted in this book? Both South Asia and India are in origin geographical expressions. South Asia is a more recent construction – only six decades old – which today encompasses eight very diverse sovereign states of very different sizes: India, Pakistan, Bangladesh, Sri Lanka, Nepal, Afghanistan, Bhutan and the Maldives. Some would also include Myanmar, which as Burma was a province of British India until 1935. The term India, as we have seen, is of much older origin. What South Asia lacks in historical depth, it makes up for in political neutrality. The terms South Asia and India refer in the first instance to a vast geographical space stretching from the Himalayan mountain ranges in the north to the Indian Ocean in the south and from the valley of the Indus in the west to the plains of the Brahmaputra in the east. This huge geographical expanse has become home to a teeming population of well over a billion people, who account for over a fifth or, to be more precise, 23 per cent of humanity. The subcontinent carries the weight not only of its people but also of their ancient history stretching back five millennia, and a modern history encompassing the experience of British colonialism compressed in tumultuous developments within the past couple of centuries.

It is a commonplace in any introduction to South Asian history to expound on the cliché about the region's unity in diversity. It may be more appropriate to characterize South Asia and its peoples as presenting a picture of diversity in unity, indeed of immense diversity within a very broad contour of unity. The geographical boundaries drawn by the highest mountain ranges in the world and encircling seas and oceans set the whole of the subcontinent apart from the rest of the world. Yet within these boundaries there is great diversity in natural attributes – imposing hills and mountains, lush green river plains, arid deserts and brown plateaus. Peoples inhabiting such a clearly defined, yet diverse, region have evolved a shared cultural ambience, but at the same time are deeply attached to distinctive cultural beliefs and practices. Over the millennia the peoples of the subcontinent have engaged in many cultural exchanges with the outside world and worked out creative accommodations of cultural difference within.

The peoples of South Asia speak at least twenty major languages, and if one includes the more important dialects, the count rises to over two hundred. A panoply of very diverse languages and language families, South Asia has made enormous contributions to world literature from ancient to modern times. It has major accomplishments in the arts and maintains distinguished musical traditions. Adherents to every major world religion are to be found in the subcontinent. It is the source of two of the world's great religions and the home to more devotees of a third than either the Middle East or South-East Asia. Hinduism, with its ancient roots, modern transformations and multiple interpretations, plays a vital part in the culture and politics of the subcontinent. Hindus form the majority of India's population, but are distinguished along lines of language and caste. While the formal adherents to Buddhism may have dwindled in the land of its birth, it continues to flourish in Sri Lanka and the Himalayas as well as in East and South-East Asia. Some of the greatest cultural and political achievements of Islam have taken place in the subcontinent, where almost half a billion of the world's 1.65 billion Muslims live today. Each of the three most populous countries in South Asia – India, Bangladesh and Pakistan – has over a 175 million Muslims, next only to Indonesia as the largest Muslim countries in the world. South Asia also has significant Jain, Zoroastrian, Christian and Sikh minorities.

South Asia today is strategically a vital part of the world that has large implications for the international order at the beginning of the new millennium. With the testing of nuclear devices by India and Pakistan in 1998, the continuing conflict in Kashmir, and the US war in Afghanistan fanning into Pakistan's north-western tribal areas, the subcontinent of late has been attracting more than the usual dose of media attention. The location of one of the most intractable international problems of the past sixty-three years that could still trigger a catastrophic war, South Asia demands a depth of historical understanding. Since the early 1990s South Asia, especially India, has undergone crucial shifts in economic policy, making it important to assess the region's linkages to the global economy, along with an examination of its persistent problems of poverty and inequality. Genuine prospects of peace, democracy and cooperative development vie with disputes such as Kashmir to place South Asia at a decisive crossroads in its history. Flourishing electoral democracy coexists in the region with deep strains of authoritarianism, often within the same country. In spite of very strong and persistent, often localized, traditions, the notion of changeless 'Tradition' in South Asia was always a myth, but perhaps never more so than at the present moment, as South Asians negotiate their place in an arena of global interconnections in the throes of rapid change. How do we begin to address the long and complex history of the peoples of this subcontinent?

Over the millennia South Asia developed rich and complex layers of culture, which during recent centuries had a dramatic historical encounter with the West. This is a book on modern history, concentrating on the problem of change in society, economy and politics from *c.* 1700 to the present in subcontinental South Asia – mainly present-day India, Pakistan and Bangladesh. Three background chapters unravelling the more important features of India's pre-colonial history set the stage for the detailed treatment of British colonialism in India and its aftermath. A focus on the colonial period does not entail missing out on South Asia's pre-colonial heritage, since much of India's 'tradition' was recast, if not re-invented, during the colonial era, a process analysed in some detail in this book. But in order to grasp the issue of continuity and change under colonialism the book shifts the emphasis away from the concerns and imperatives of the imperial masters. Colonial initiatives in and of themselves cannot encapsulate the complex and at times largely autonomous and certainly contestatory dynamics that moulded relationships in Indian society, economy and polity. Colonialism as an agency of historical change is placed in its appropriate social context and studied in its interplay with the culture and politics of anti-colonial resistance.

The enormous difficulty in fashioning a balanced yet insightful approach to the study of modern South Asia is reflected in the yawning gap between a few general histories and the large number of research monographs and scholarly articles published over the last three decades. The general works that do exist are no more than one-dimensional sketches of the metaphorical Indian elephant, while more rigorous and sophisticated research has dissected discrete parts of its complex anatomy. The challenge before us is to find a good perspective for a multi-dimensional, high-definition overview of modern South Asian history in the pages of a single book.

South Asian historiography has achieved a remarkable level of depth and sophistication in the past quarter of a century. This book is a work of synthesis and interpretation covering the entire spectrum of modern South Asian history – cultural, economic, political and social – that seeks to take full account of the striking new developments in the field. A number of major themes have emerged in recent historical research. These need to be placed within a general context. Among these have been the role of intermediate social groups in the construction of the British raj and that of 'subaltern' social groups in anti-colonial resistance; the part played by the colonial state in the re-invention of 'communal' and caste categories; the refashioning of social relations of class by the linking of Indian economic regions to wider capitalist systems; and the impact of the interplay between national, communal and regional levels of politics on the process of decolonization. Various works on these themes have differed in their relative emphasis on the affinities or contradictions of class and caste, religion and language, nation and region, community and gender, economics and politics, and so on. The 'subaltern studies' group, for instance, began with a political conception of class before going on to stress culture and consciousness over economics and politics as explanatory variables. The last decade has seen valuable contributions in at least three areas of South Asian historiography – the formation of regional and religious identities going beyond the dead-end debate between secular statist and subaltern communitarian perspectives; the place of South Asian economy and culture within larger inter-regional and global arenas of interaction; and the articulation and global circulation of economic and political ideas emanating from South Asia. The more insightful contributions of not only schools of historiography but individual scholars need to weighed and placed into a broader and more meaningful framework for the study of modern South Asian history.

A meaningful framework for conceiving the history of modern South Asia on a subcontinental scale may be provided by the twin dialectics of centralism and regionalism and of nationalism and communitarianism, so long as there is a keen awareness of the historically shifting definitions of and relationships between centre, region, nation and community. This is of the essence if we are to establish the contours of both the idea and the structure of India or South Asia on the basis of an analysis of the relationship of its constituent parts to the whole. Once this is done it becomes possible at the central and regional levels, and within the arenas of nation and community, to probe the relations of power along lines of class and gender. As the different parts and the whole of South Asia became more organically linked to a wider capitalist world from the early nineteenth century, critical alterations took place in social relations within the subcontinent. These occurred not only along the axis of class but were also refracted through a myriad of social and cultural relationships, including those of caste and community as well as gender and generation. These social and cultural relationships were not only inheritances from the past but were in the process of constant renegotiation and reformulation during the colonial era. Religious strife in contemporary India, for example, has little to do with any supposed ancient religious divide between Hindu and Muslim and cannot be explained without accounting for the invention of communally defined political categories in the early twentieth century and the historically dynamic dialectic between communitarian and provincial as well as religious and linguistic identities. The history of South Asian nationalisms has unfolded within larger transnational contexts. The interplay of nationalism and universalism is a subject that has received nuanced treatment in recent historical studies. Both the temporal thresholds and spatial boundaries of the subcontinent are in the process of being re-evaluated by historians.

How does our own location in what has been termed the post-modern era shape our perspectives on modern history? Despite our firm rejection of an uncritical celebration of the 'fragment' inherent in a particular brand of post-modernism, we believe it is important to recognize that the march of history has left some of the certitudes of high modernism by the wayside. A modern history of modern South Asia would have confidently tracked the unilinear emergence of the nation-state in the political domain, the teleological path of capitalist (or socialist) development in the economic sphere and the slow but sure triumph of modernity over anachronistic, traditional social bonds and values. The cracking and crumbling of the modern nation-state system, the disintegration of the socialist alternative and the disillusionment with the false promises of capitalism, and the resurgence of redefined social identities thought to have been obliterated by the steam-roller of modernization have all rendered interpretations of the modern era in South Asian and world history much more complex. Along with a greater sensitivity to difference and distinctiveness, the spotlight had been shifting in the late twentieth century towards the fragmentary parts rather than the monolithic whole of modern social, economic and political structures. Yet the intellectual breakaway from modernist dogma may have swung a little too far towards the fissures and away from the fusions which formed an equally important aspect of the historical process. The ties of the subcontinent to the Indian Ocean world and the global context are being freshly recognized as historically significant. A recourse to South Asian history, where the dialectic between union and partition, centripetal and centrifugal tendencies, territorial nationalism and extra-territorial universalism, the secular and the religious are so dramatically played out may well enable a much-needed decentred balance in our current disoriented scholarly predicament.

2

MODERNITY AND ANTIQUITY

Interpretations of ancient India

Rabindranath Tagore, modern India's most celebrated poet, wrote to Mohandas Karamchand Gandhi in 1939 that he could identify only two 'modernists' among India's national leaders. Even these two rare embodiments of 'modernism' were deeply attached to their country's ancient heritage. In his book *The Discovery of India*, Jawaharlal Nehru took solace in 'the continuity of a cultural tradition through five thousand years of history' which made the 180 years of British rule in India seem like 'just one of the unhappy interludes in her long story'. And on the opening page of *The Indian Struggle* Subhas Chandra Bose emphasized two features critical to an understanding of India: first, its history had to be 'reckoned not in decades or in centuries but in thousands of years'; and second, only under British rule India 'for the first time in her history had begun to feel that she had been conquered'. The mission of an independent India, therefore, should be to deliver to the world a rich 'heritage' that had been preserved from past ages.

A 'heritage' more than five millennia old, containing multiple layers and strands of cultural influence and assimilation, was bound to be a very complex one and open to many interpretations. There were many individuals and social groups other than the 'modernist' national leaders ready and eager to offer their versions of India's lengthy and intricate past. Among them were British orientalists and Indian traditionalists and revivalists, Hindu as well as Muslim, each possessing an implicit if not explicit political agenda. Occasionally there were unlikely convergences, as was exemplified by the shared view of some nineteenth-century European scholars like Henry Maine and Gandhian utopians of self-sufficient and happy village communities somewhere in the subcontinent's lost golden age. The plethora of theories and fanciful evocations of tradition undoubtedly complicate the modern historians' task of interpreting South Asia's pre-modern history. The best that can be done is to carefully sift the extant evidence and be alert to the uses made of old evidence by earlier interpreters. What can be discarded straightaway is the undue and ahistorical privileging of religion in the periodization of Indian history adopted by historians of the colonial era. There are no grounds for branding the ancient, medieval and modern phases of the subcontinent's long and complex history as Hindu,

Figure 1 The Presence of the Past. A Hindu village in Punjab, Pakistan (Courtesy Ayesha Jalal)

Muslim and British periods. It may have served James Mill's purpose in the early nineteenth century, as he set about in his *History of British India* to buttress his theory of an ascending order of civilizations. But his lengthy, uninformed digression into India's pre-colonial past as a justification of British colonial rule has by now long outlived its limited utility.

It was in the twentieth century, in 1922 to be exact, that a millennium and a half were suddenly added to the age of Indian history. Archaeological excavations unearthed the ruins of a quite stunning civilization in the Indus valley region with two key urban centres at Harappa and Mohenjodaro. The archaeologist Alexander Cunningham had written a preliminary report on the Indus valley settlements in 1875, but it was during the next half a century that the exciting process of finding these forgotten cities unfolded. The location of the key Indus valley cities in present-day Pakistan has placed the onerous responsibility of preserving the remains of a heritage dated to *c.* 3000 BC on a state just over six decades old. More recent excavations at Mehrgarh in Baluchistan suggest a dating that may be as old as 6000 BC. Drawing subsistence from the rich agricultural tracts of the Indus river, the people of Harappa and Mohenjodaro had achieved a highly sophisticated level of urban culture. The immaculateness of their urban planning of streets and drainage might put some of the modern cities of South Asia to shame. Artefacts found at the excavation sites indicate the existence of long-distance trade with that other great ancient civilization – Mesopotamia in modern-day Iraq. The Indus valley possessed a literate culture. But scholars are still struggling to decipher the script that was used. Images recovered suggest that the people may have worshipped the mother goddess and venerated the bull – both powerful symbols of fertility. Although both these icons reappear in later phases of Indian civilization, no unbroken line of continuity with the Indus valley era can be traced. The prosperity of the region came to an apparently calamitous end well before the civilization of the Vedic age struck roots in the plains of that other great Himalayan river – the Ganga.

Although there is substantial archaeological evidence on neolithic and chalcolithic cultures, especially in central India, relatively little scholarly attention has been given until very recently to the original inhabitants of India outside the Indus valley region until the age of the so-called Aryans, beginning around 1500 BC. The nineteenth-century ethnic definition of the Aryans has been effectively debunked by recent scholarship. They are now more accurately seen to be a linguistic rather than a racial group, whose speech adhered to the common core of Indo-European languages. Clues about the society, economy and politics of these Indo-Aryan settlers are to be found in the Vedas. The first and most important of the Vedas – the *Rig Veda* – was composed before 1000 BC. The great epics – the *Ramayana* and the *Mahabharata* – may contain some references to historical events that occurred between 1000 and 700 BC, but since the versions available to us are dated to the Gupta age (the fourth and fifth centuries of the common era) they need to be cross-checked against other, especially archaeological evidence. It was during the Vedic period that the Indo-Aryans appear to have made the transition from nomadic pastoralism to settled agriculture in the Gangetic plain, even though settled agriculture was practised in different parts of the subcontinent even earlier. The political organization of the early Indo-Aryans appears to have had a strong democratic element, with popular assemblies known as *sabha* and more select gatherings known as *samiti*. Even after the Vedic age republican forms of government seem to have been more pervasive than kingdoms. But with the expansion of political scale there was a noticeable drift towards monarchical forms. Kingdoms arose in the Gangetic heartland, while republics proved to be more resilient along the outer rims of Indo-Aryan settlements.

Vedic society developed and elaborated upon an inherited Indo-European model of a tripartite social structure consisting of warriors, priests and a third large group comprising agriculturists, traders and cattle-raisers. The first mention of the famous caste system that has mesmerized generations of Indologists is to be found in a single reference in the *Rig Veda* which lists four *varna*, literally meaning 'colour', but having an applied meaning closer to social orders. The four castes in order of hierarchy were the Brahmans (priests or the sacerdotal elite), the Kshatriyas (warriors), the Vaishyas (originally encompassing both agricultural and merchant groups) and the Shudras (providers of menial labour). The Purusha Sukta verse in the *Rig Veda* describes the emergence of the Brahmans from the face of purusha, the cosmic man, the Kshatriyas from his arms, the Vaishyas from his thighs and the hapless Shudras from his feet. In time only the traders and richer landowners could aspire to

Vaishya status, while the bulk of the working peasantry fell into the Shudra rank. Caste by *varna* merely provided a theoretical scaffolding to peg different strata of social status. In reality caste by *jati*, literally 'birth', which included numerous sub-castes originally classified by occupation, was more relevant to social practice. Recent research has suggested that the origins of caste in south India did not quite fit into the *varna-jati* scheme elaborated in the north. Early mobility between occupational sub-castes was soon restricted, however, and the *Upanishad*, the teachings appended to the end of the Vedic texts around the eighth and seventh centuries BC, provided an eschatological justification of the rigidity of caste status in the doctrine of *karma*. Caste in the present life was determined in this scheme of things by the quality of actions in a previous incarnation.

On the issue of gender, Indo-Aryan society tended to glorify womanhood in theory but cast women into an inferior role in social practice, generally excluding them from the public domain. There appears to have been a further deterioration of women's position after the Vedic period. In the great epic the *Mahabharata* the main female character, Draupadi, is portrayed as a possession, if not a pawn, in the conflict between two male-dominated clans – the Pandavas and the Kauravas. Only a few passages including a forceful speech delivered by Draupadi when she escapes humiliation through the divine intervention of Krishna suggest that there was some consciousness as well of the inequity and injustice to which women were subjected. In the *Ramayana*, too, the kingdom of Ayodhya is depicted as a patriarchy and Rama's wife Sita, who had been abducted by the demon-king Ravana, finally has to ask Mother Earth, after being rescued, to take her back into her womb to save her from further humiliation by the king's subjects.

The Vedic religion was at one level a sophisticated version of animism. Its pantheon consisted of powerful natural forces – Indra, a thunderbolt-wielding warrior being the king among them – who were all elevated to the status of gods to be placated by mere mortals. But the Vedic texts also had at the very end a mystical and metaphysical section – the *Upanishad* – which clearly enunciates the notion of a Supreme Being, referred to as Brahma. The Upanishadic theory of salvation or moksha expounds on the merging of the individual soul, Atman, with the oversoul, Brahma, a merger that also signifies release from the cycle of rebirths. This philosophy was quite distinct from the much later mythology about the triumvirate – Brahma the creator, Vishnu the preserver and Shiva the destroyer of this universe.

The teachings of the *Upanishad* passed into the realm of high philosophy and became divorced from day-to-day religious and social practices. The Indo-Aryan social order dominated by the Brahman caste came under serious and widespread challenge from the sixth century BC. Gautama Buddha and Mahavira, founders of the Buddhist and Jain faiths respectively, launched two of the most influential social and religious movements of this era. Both had belonged to the Kshatriya caste and came from republics on the periphery of the Gangetic plain. Buddhism and Jainism questioned caste,

11

especially Brahmanical social orthodoxy, and shunned elaborate Vedic rituals. Buddhism, which later spread far and wide from India to other parts of Asia, called for a new ethical conception of human affairs. In the Buddha's view, human life was full of suffering. The only means to escape this suffering was to follow the eightfold path consisting of right views, resolves, speech, conduct, livelihood, effort, recollection and meditation, which together constituted the middle way or a balanced and harmonious way of life. Perfection along this path would finally lead to release from the cycle of rebirths and the attainment of *nirvana*. The Buddhist concept of nirvana is subtly different from the Upanishadic concept of *moksha*. The Buddha made no mention in his teachings of God or a supreme being. So, while moksha represents union with Brahma or a supreme being, nirvana is simply a blissful transcendental state beyond human rebirths.

The Buddhist aversion to individual personality was later qualified when followers of the faith split into two major schools some six hundred years after Buddha had passed from the world. The Theravada or old school, also referred to as Hinayana (the lesser vehicle), was more orthodox and true to the original teachings of the Buddha. The Mahayana (the greater vehicle) school of Buddhism began to venerate the individual personality of the Buddha and also a number of Bodhisattvas, who could be loosely defined as Buddhist saints. The Bodhisattvas were those who had so perfected their lives that they were eligible for nirvana but stopped short at its threshold to reach out a guiding hand to suffering humanity. With the establishment of the Mahayana school, images and statues of the Buddha and Bodhisattvas were made for the first time in the Gandhara region of north-western India. Theravada Buddhism eventually took hold in Sri Lanka, Burma and Thailand, while Mahayana Buddhism spread from Kashmir to China, Japan and northern Vietnam.

The political history of the centuries following the rise of Buddhism and Jainism saw the emergence and consolidation of powerful regional states in northern India. Among the strongest of these was the kingdom of Magadha, with its capital at Pataliputra (near the modern city of Patna). The Magadhan kingdom expanded under the Maurya dynasty in the fourth and third centuries BC to become an empire embracing almost the whole of the subcontinent. Chandragupta Maurya founded the dynasty in 322 BCE, just a few years after Alexander the Great's brief foray into north-western India. The Maurya empire reached its apogee under the reign of Ashoka (268–231 BCE). Early in his reign Ashoka made far-flung military conquests. Legend has it that after a bloody war against Kalinga – present-day Orissa – Ashoka underwent a change of heart and, if Buddhist sources are to be believed, became an ardent Buddhist. He accepted the principle of non-violence, denounced caste and banned Brahmanical rituals. Kings of earlier times generally held an elaborate ceremony known as the Ashwamedha Yagna, involving the sacrifice of horses in a ritual advertisement of their power. Ashoka abolished animal sacrifice and instead chose his patronage of *dhamma*, an ethical way of life, to be the legitimating glory of his empire. A reading of *Arthashastra* by Kautilya, a leading courtier of Ashoka's grandfather Chandragupta, as well as contemporary Greek sources, might suggest, on the face of it, that the Maurya empire developed a centralized bureaucracy and an intricate network of spies and informants. *Arthashastra* literally means 'science of wealth', but reads more like a manual for kings, in the same way as Machiavelli's *Prince*, in so far as it is an amoral analysis of the exercise of power. The *Arthashastra* is no longer regarded by historians of ancient India as a unitary text, and in any case was largely prescriptive and may never have been implemented. Moreover, it is clear that Ashoka was deeply concerned about morality and, especially, the question of imperial legitimacy. His edicts were inscribed on pillars and rocks in all the different regions of his vast empire. While some of his edicts propagated the message of Buddhism, much of his *dhamma* was more universal, preaching the values of mutual respect and tolerance. Ashoka was clearly interested in commanding loyalty from the outlying parts of the empire through means other than coercive control from the centre, but he was not above threatening the forest tribes with the use of force if they proved recalcitrant. His was clearly an agrarian empire drawing revenues mainly from the land. The degree and nature of state intervention, however, was quite different in the Magadhan core and the provincial peripheries.

Not long after Ashoka's death the great Maurya empire underwent a process of decentralization. After the passing of this far-flung empire the fragmented character of Indian polities lasted about five centuries, from *c.* 200 BCE to *c.* 300 CE, even though new settlers established quite strong and prosperous states, such as the Shaka and Kushana kingdoms in western and northern India. The Satavahana dynasty, probably of indigenous tribal origin, consolidated its hold on the north-western part of the Deccan. During the second century BCE a politically disparate India appears to have enjoyed a good deal of economic prosperity and cultural glory. The centuries prior to 300 CE witnessed a thriving coastal trade and long-distance trade with the Roman empire and South-East Asia, as well as the quiet and peaceful assertion of Indian cultural influence in places like modern-day Thailand and Cambodia.

The process of empire building from the Magadhan base was renewed by the Gupta dynasty, which lasted from 320 CE to the early decades of the sixth century. The early emperors, Chandragupta I and Samudragupta, undertook the conquests, while the consolidation of the empire and the major cultural achievements took place during the reign of Chandragupta II. The structure of the Gupta empire was looser than that of their Maurya predecessors. The Guptas did not even attempt to impose centralized control over the distant parts of their domains, even though a marriage alliance between the Guptas and the Vakatakas supplied a north–south linkage. The legitimating glory at the centre stage of the Gupta empire, which was the symbol of their power, was unquestionably Brahmanical in character. Vedic rituals were revived and the horse sacrifice again became an indispensable imperial spectacle. Caste hierarchies once more became rigid and a number of social customs placed renewed emphasis on the inferior status of women. The *Bhagavad Gita*, which represented some-thing of a departure from the Vedas, was quite influential by the Gupta age. Revolutionary and inspirational in its exposition of the way of love and personal devotion to reach the supreme being, its philosophy of *niskama karma* or disinterested action and its message of strength, the *Gita* was not, however, particularly egalitarian in matters to do with caste and gender. As Krishna says at one point in the *Gita:* 'If those who are of base origin, such as women, Vaishyas and Shudras, take refuge in me, even they attain the highest end.'

The revival of Brahmanical legitimation and dominance notwithstanding, the Gupta rulers were tolerant towards other religious and social beliefs and practices. Fa-xian, a Chinese Buddhist pilgrim who visited the Gupta domains early in the fifth century, found Buddhism to be in a very healthy state. The high Brahmanical tradition appears to have coexisted with a more diffuse and popular Shramanik tradition. Historic Hinduism, as we know it today, took recognizable form by about the fifth century. This Hindu religion was at one level a polymorphic monotheism with three major cults – of Shiva, Vishnu/ Krishna and the Mother Goddess (Durga or Kali). In the sophisticated Hindu view, the supreme being was one but could be worshipped in any of these three major forms of manifestation, according to the devotee's preference. Yet in the coexisting Shramanik tradition there could be a much greater multiplicity of deities and enormous variation in beliefs and practices. Hinduism as it evolved historically was, as Romila Thapar puts it, 'not a linear progres-sion from a founder through an organizational system with sects branching off'; it was rather 'the mosaic of distinct cults, deities, sects and ideas and the adjusting, juxtaposing and distancing of these to existing ones, the placement drawing not only on beliefs and ideas but also on the socio-economic reality'.

The greatest strength of the Gupta age, often regarded as a 'classical' era, was a measure of political, social and religious flexibility, despite the resurgence of Brahmanical orthodoxy in certain spheres. The Gupta emperors, of course, could afford such a breadth of outlook. This was at least partly because of general economic prosperity based on an expanding and thriving agriculture and a lucrative long-distance trade across the Arabian sea with Rome and the Mediterranean world and across the Bay of Bengal with South-East Asia. A politically secure and economically prosperous Gupta centre presided over a great literary, scientific and cultural efflorescence. The greatest literary figure of this time was Kalidasa, whose works included the play *Shakuntala* and the poem *Meghaduta* (The Cloud Messenger), the latter renowned for its breathtaking evocation of the natural splendour of India. Aryabhatta, a great mathematician and philosopher, was noted for his scientific achievements, including remarkably accurate calculations of the value of 'pi' (3.141) and the length of the solar year. Of course, he suffered the same sorts of scepticism from the ranks of religious orthodoxy as Galileo and Copernicus were to face much later during the European renaissance. In the fine arts an example of the brilliance of the Gupta era can still be seen in the cave paintings of Ajanta in western India.

The Gupta empire came under a number of stresses and strains from the early sixth century. Defence against a number of Hun invasions in north-western India drained the treasury. Evidence of an economic crisis can be noted in the debased coinage of the later Guptas. The trend towards imperial decentralization, if not disintegration, during the sixth century was briefly reversed in the first half of the seventh century under Harshavardhana, the founder of another short-lived empire in northern India between AD 606 and 647. A record of Harsha's reign is available in his biography, *Harshacharita*, one of the finest expositions of Sanskrit prose, by his court historian Bana Bhatta. The great Buddhist university at Nalanda, founded in the fifth century, was flourishing in the seventh century when the Chinese scholar-pilgrim Xuangzang came to visit. The great mathematicians Brahmagupta and Bhaskara lived further to the west at this time. Some historians have identified the seventh century as the beginning of the early medieval era in India. Underlying the oscillation between the forces of centralization and decentralization, there was a noticeable drift, if not a clear long-term trend, in early medieval India from tribe to caste as the basis for the emergence of regional polities.

From the eighth century onwards many of the new developments in both the higher historic and popular forms of Hinduism, including commentaries,

Figure 2 Descent of the Ganges. Pallava era 7th–8th century wall relief, Mamallapuram (Courtesy Ayesha Jalal)

exegesis and fresh departures in the form of cults, occurred in southern India and the peripheral areas of the north. The best-known Hindu philosopher of this later period was Shankaracharya, who lived in the ninth century and propounded the doctrine of *maya* or the illusoriness of human life. Sixty-three Shaivite saints, known as the Nayanars, and twelve Vaishnavite saints, called the Alwars, had already launched the devotional *bhakti* movement in Tamil Nadu as early as the sixth century. The teachings of the eighth and ninth-century leaders of the Shaivite devotional cults were compiled as the *Tirumurai*, hymns calling Brahmanism into question and celebrating the direct communion of devotee and God. A number of women saints came into prominence, notably Andal, who sang in praise of the god Vishnu.

Politically, too, it was the south that saw the rise of powerful new kingdoms in this period. The most famous of these was the Chola kingdom that flourished from the tenth to the twelfth century. Based in peninsular India, the Cholas made military forays into the north and cast their political, economic and cultural influence over South-East Asia. Rajaraja I conquered Sri Lanka near the end of the tenth century, while his son Rajendra I launched a great northern campaign during 1022–23 which fetched the temples and palaces of the southern kingdom a vast quantity of jewels and gold. Yet Rajendra, an aspirant to universal kingship, desired legitimacy as much as wealth. Having defeated the Pala king, he ordered the princes of Bengal to carry the holy water of the Ganga to his new capital called Gangaikondacholapuram at the mouth of the river Kaveri. In 1026 his navy defeated the forces of the great South-East Asian empire Srivijaya. More important, the Cholas furthered economic and cultural exchange between southern India and South-East Asia.

Indian society, economy and politics from ancient times until the twelfth century displayed a great deal of dynamism that does not accord well with stereotypical images of India's changeless tradition. The very cultural assimilation of influences emanating from a succession of new arrivals – Aryans, Greeks, Scythians, Parthians, Shakas and Huns before the eighth century, as well as the Arabs, Persians, Turks, Afghans and Mongols between the eighth and the twelfth centuries – was a vital and dynamic process. Indigenous tribal groups also played a creative role in processes of state formation. Politically, phases of imperial consolidation were followed by periods of decentralization. But even the empires, far from being centralized despotisms, were typically loosely structured suzerainties. Economically, instead of closed and static village communities, there was mobility and commercial exchange. For long stretches of time the subcontinent played a central role in a vast network of Indian Ocean trade and culture. Socially, there were unique institutions such as caste; but contrary to the stereotypes of hierarchy propagated by scholars trapped in the rigid mould of caste, there was much in Indian society that emphasized equality as a value and in practice. Buddhism and, after the eighth century, Islam represented, at least in part, egalitarian challenges, but even within Hinduism the high Brahmanical tradition was more than counter-balanced by the popular Shramanik one. There

Figure 3 Kali. Chola bronze sculpture, 10th century, in Chennai Museum (Courtesy Sugata Bose)

were undoubtedly many instances of conflict and even internal colonization. But it was the ability to accommodate, if not assimilate, an immense diversity within a very broadly and loosely defined framework of unity that has given Indian cultural tradition its durability and appearance of unbroken continuity. It is to the greatest and most challenging of the many creative accommodations forged in the subcontinent's long history – the fashioning of an Indo-Islamic social and political universe – that we turn in the next chapter.

3

PRE-MODERN ACCOMMODATIONS OF DIFFERENCE

The making of Indo-Islamic cultures

It was in the seventh century, 610 to be precise, that Muhammad, a Meccan merchant given to austere tastes and solitary meditation, had a grand vision which led to the founding of a new world religion in the Arabian peninsula. The first person to accept Muhammad's message as prophetic revelation was his wife, Khadija, giving her a position of pre-eminence in what was to soon become a very large community of the faithful. The role of women in the construction of the community of Islam is quite crucial, but scholars are only now turning their attention to uncovering that veiled reality. The historical spotlight has remained on the spread of the Islamic doctrine through a dramatic expansion of Muslim political power. By the fifteenth century Muslims either ruled or lived in all known corners of the world, presenting one of the greatest challenges to earlier established religions and cultures. But, contrary to stereo-typical distortions of Islam as a religion of the sword and of Muslims as unbending fanatics thriving on hatred and violence against non-believers, the Prophet Muhammad's teachings allowed for tolerance and assimilation of regional and local cultures. One of the most spectacular of these processes of accommodation was the fashioning of an Indo-Islamic cultural tradition in the South Asian subcontinent. Both military conquest and religious conversion in the medieval period need to be understood in historical context.

The first wave of Arab political expansion reached the subcontinent when the Makran coast in north-western India was invaded in 644, towards the end of the caliphate of Umar. Although this and a second raid, during the reign of Ali (656–61), were repulsed, Makran was finally subjugated under the first Ummayid caliph, Muawiya (661–80). The eastern frontier of early Islam was reached when Muhammad bin Qasim conquered Sind in 712. So the Islamic belief in one God and in Muhammad as the final prophet struck very early roots in at least one region of north-western India. From the eighth century onwards, Arab traders also settled on the western coast of India, but they were primarily interested in profits and did not attempt to bring about any large-scale conversions to Islam. There was no further expansion, political or economic, by peoples professing Islam until the Turkish and Afghan invasions from the turn of the eleventh century onwards. Between the seventh and eleventh centuries in politically decentralized northern India the high Brahmanic and more popular Shramanik traditions continued to coexist, with the latter being more pervasive. Far from being a dark age, this was another period in Indian history that saw the consolidation of regional kingdoms presiding over new economic initiatives and cultural achievements. The Tomaras, formerly feudatories of the Pratihara overlords, founded the city of Delhi in 736. The magnificent architecture and sculpture of the Khajuraho temples were executed under the patronage of the Chandellas in the tenth century.

The great Central Asian scholar Al-Beruni, who visited India in 1030, wrote: 'The Hindus believe with regard to God that He is One, Eternal ... this is what educated people believe about God ... if we now pass from the ideas of the educated people to those of the common people, we must say that they present a great variety. Some of them are simply abominable, but similar errors also occur in other religions.' In making this comment Al-Beruni was not simply giving a Muslim view but echoing the Hindu elite's position on monotheism and polytheism. There is little agreement among historians of medieval India about the extent to which the coming of Islam to the sub-continent fomented new processes of cultural accommodation and assimilation. At one extreme is the view that there was a clear distinguishing line between Islamic civilization and the pre-existing corpus of 'Hindu tradition'. This argument is dented not just by the sheer scale of the conversions to Islam among lower-caste Hindus but also by the contiguity of peoples belonging to different religious faiths, which meant that Islam in the subcontinent could not but develop local Indian roots. On the other hand, recent research on Islam in a variety of regional settings has emphasized variants of an argument about 'syncretism' that tends to obscure the issue of religiously informed identity. For example, Richard Eaton's portrayal of Bengali peasants as a 'single undifferentiated mass' with a uniform 'folk culture' neatly erases the problem of difference. With the major historiographical challenge conveniently out of the way, a fanciful cultural argument can then be erected on quicksand-like material evidence from Bengal's agrarian frontier.

Any historical interpretation of the spread of Islam in the subcontinent needs to be attentive to regional specificities in the domains of economy and culture as well as the great variety of Muslims – Turks, Mongols, Persians, Arabs, Afghan and so on – who came from abroad. Taken together, these factors not only explode the myth of a monolithic Islamic community in India but also call into question any general model of Muslim conversions based on a limited understanding of rather scanty evidence from one regional economy and culture. What the available sources do permit is a plausible argument to be advanced that not only were creative Indo-Islamic accommodations of difference worked out at various levels of society and culture, but also India or al-Hind became the metropolitan centre of an Indian Ocean world with a distinctive historical identity that stretched from the Mediterranean to the Indonesian archipelago.

Figure 4 Islam in India. The Qutb Minar, Delhi – a thirteenth-century monument to the Sufi saint Qutbuddin Kaki started by Qutbuddin Aibak and completed by Iltutmish (Source: print from drawing by William Daniell exhibited at the Oriental Annual, 1834, in the private collection of Sugata Bose and Ayesha Jalal)

The emergence of India as the hub of an integrated Indian Ocean economy and culture by the eleventh century preceded the fashioning of Indo-Islamic accommodations within the subcontinent's society and polity in the fourteenth century. Early conversions to Islam were more gradual than sudden, a process carried over a period of time but generally facilitated in regions where a weak

Brahmanical superstructure overlaid a much stronger Buddhistic substratum, as was the case in Sind in the eighth century and in Bengal after the eleventh century. While military action undoubtedly took place in the conquest of these regions, capitulation and submission was the usual norm, followed by the laying down of terms of loyalty and dependence. This was in accordance with the overall theory and practice of conquests in India at the time and explains why wars did not lead to significant political change. In the words of the ninth-century merchant-traveller Sulaiman: 'The Indians sometimes go to war for conquest, but the occasions are rare ... When a king subdues a neighbouring state, he places over it a man belonging to the family of the fallen prince, who carries on the government in the name of the conqueror. The inhabitants would not suffer it otherwise.'

Eighth-century Sind was a typical Indian polity in which sovereignty was shared by different layers of kingly authority. The *Chachnama*, the principal source of information on the Muslim conquest of Sind, elaborates a royal code that demands sensitivity to the fluidity and shifting nature of the real world of politics. This is in contrast to Kautilya's 'classical' and largely theoretical text *Arthashastra*, which advises princes on ways to avoid the dilution of absolute and centralized power. The pardoning of a fallen enemy, described by the *Chachnama*, provided a quick route to legitimacy by renegotiating a balance

Figure 5 Islam in Kashmir. The Jamia Masjid, Srinagar, originally built in 1400 (Courtesy Ayesha Jalal)

between different hierarchically arranged layers of sovereignty. The Arab conquest of Sind, instead of representing a sharp disjuncture, can be seen as a form of adaptation to pre-existing political conditions in India.

Although there were no additional military conquests in India from the north-west until the eleventh century, the India trade became vital to the Islamic world during the eighth and ninth centuries. India's export surplus attracted a steady flow of precious bullion and made it the centre of an Indian Ocean world-economy with West Asia and China as its two poles. It was the prosperity in India and the relative decline in West Asia that provided the context for the next wave of Ghaznavid invasions into the subcontinent, beginning in 997. The accumulated treasure in the palaces and temples of northern India was a prime target of a series of raids (997–1030) by Mahmud of Ghazni into north-western India that, interestingly enough, were roughly coterminous with and not too dissimilar from Rajendra Chola's northern campaigns from his south Indian base. On one of his raids Mahmud of Ghazni looted and smashed the idol in the famous temple at Somnath in Gujarat. The looting raids of this period were motivated as much by hardheaded economic and political motives as by an iconoclastic zeal fired by religion. In the case of Mahmud, a great patron of the letters and the arts, it was partly a need to finance his imperial ambitions in Central Asia that led him to devastate well-endowed religious places of worship in India. The colonial re-interpretation of Mahmud's attack on Somnath stressing religion rather than economics and politics can be traced to the period of the first Anglo-Afghan war of the early 1840s. Mauled in Kabul, the British forces retreated to India via Ghazni and dismantled the doors of Mahmud's tomb, which they mistakenly believed had been taken from Somnath.

It was a similar combination of economic and political imperatives that led Muhammad Ghuri, a Turk, to invade India a century and a half later, in 1192. His defeat of Prithviraj Chauhan, a Rajput chieftain, in the strategic battle of Tarain in northern India paved the way for the establishment of the first Muslim sultanate, with its capital in Delhi, by Qutubuddin Aibak. The Delhi Sultanate lasted from 1206 to 1526 under the leadership of four major dynasties – the Mamluks, Khaljis, Tughlaqs and Lodis. These Turkish and Afghan rulers exercised their sway primarily over northern India but the more powerful Sultans, like Alauddin Khalji (1296–1316) and Muhammad bin Tughlaq (1325–51), made incursions into the Deccan. Southern India in this period boasted two powerful kingdoms – the Hindu kingdom of Vijayanagara founded in 1336 and the Bahmani kingdom founded by a Muslim governor who revolted against the Sultan in 1345.

The Turkish, Persian and Afghan invasions of northern India from the eleventh century onwards injected the Turko-Persian content into the formation of an Indo-Islamic culture. The roots of this variant of the emerging Indo-Islamic accommodations actually preceded the establishment of the Delhi Sultanate and can be traced to the occupation of the Punjab by the Ghaznavids between

1001 and 1186. Lahore was the first centre of a Persianized Indo-Islamic culture until Delhi rose to political pre-eminence and almost became a replica of the ancient Sassanid court of Persia. The symbols of sovereignty, which had been wholly absent in the far more austere Arab Islam of the preceding centuries, became much more ceremonial and ornate. Persian cultural influence was balanced by a strong Turkish slave element in the composition of the nobility and the ruling classes during the first century of the Sultanate. Slavery went into decline in India in the fourteenth century. From the beginning of the fourteenth century onwards, the Turkish Mamluks, or slave aristocracy, were steadily replaced by a new aristocracy of Indian Muslims and Hindus as well as foreign immigrant Muslims of high status. So it was in the fourteenth century that a true Indo-Muslim culture was forged based on Hindu–Muslim alliance building and reciprocity. While northern India witnessed accommodations with the Turkish–Persian variant of Islam, the Arab imprint continued to be indelible in the Malabar coast of western India as well as coastal south India and Sri Lanka. So we find at least two different variants of the Indo-Islamic accommodations in the subcontinent, one straddling the overland belt from Turkey, Persia and northern India to the Deccan and the other bridging the ocean from the Arabian peninsula to coastal southern India and stretching across the Bay of Bengal to Java and Sumatra.

The state structure constructed by the Delhi sultans was based on experiments carried out in West Asia but also elaborated on pre-existing forms in India. While upholding the supremacy of the Islamic *sharia*, the rulers desisted from imposing it on their predominantly non-Muslim subjects, who were allowed to retain their customary and religious laws. A series of imperial edicts complementing the sharia underpinned the day-to-day administration of justice, especially in the domains of criminal and civil law. Modelled on Ummayad and Abbasid rule, the intermeshing of religious and secular law was an intrinsic feature of the pact of dominance established by Muslim sovereigns in India. It had the merit of keeping the *ulema* or Muslim theologians at bay without straining the legitimacy of Muslim rule among the non-believers.

The Delhi sultanate drew its revenues primarily from the land, and its many flourishing towns depended to a large extent on the agrarian surplus. Some of the land revenue was paid directly into the state coffers but most of it was channelled through *iqtadars* or land-grant holders. The *iqta* was a non-hereditary prebendal assignment of revenue devised especially to suit the imperative of paying relatively stable state salaries in the highly monetized and fluctuating economic context of the Indian Ocean world-economy. Generally, iqtadars and provincial governors known as *muqtis* enjoyed a fair amount of autonomy from the Delhi sultan. A few sultans attempted a greater degree of centralized control for brief spells. Alauddin Khalji, for instance, made drastic changes to existing iqtas with a view to reordering the bonds of loyalty between the centre and the provincial peripheries.

The southern kingdom of Vijayanagara drew revenues from land, but was also closely integrated with the broader economy and civilization of the Indian Ocean. Merchants from the Vijayanagara domains engaged in profitable trade with both West Asia and South-East Asia. The Vijayanagara centre was the repository of considerable wealth and glory, but, according to Burton Stein, the state structure was segmented to provide for a substantial division and devolution of powers. After going through a number of vicissitudes the Vijayanagara kingdom recovered its glory under the great ruler Krishnadeva Raya (1509–29), whose reign saw impressive achievements in temple architecture and Telegu literature. In addition to the broad-based sultanates and kingdoms of the north and south, independent sultanates had emerged by the fifteenth century at the extremities of northern India – Kashmir, Bengal and Gujarat – each forging wider contacts of its own. After Taimur's attack on Delhi in 1398 even Jaunpur and Malwa emerged as independent sultanates. The fifteenth century ought to be seen as a period when there were several regional sultanates, since even Delhi was reduced to the status of one of the regional sultanates of north India.

During the era of the Delhi sultanate – its expansion and attrition – northern India developed a distinctive Indo-Islamic culture. Society consisted of three broad classes: the nobility, artisans and peasants. The nobility was drawn substantially though not exclusively from Turkish, Afghan, Persian and Arab immigrants. The great majority of Muslim artisans and peasants were converts from lower-caste Hindus to whom Islam's egalitarian appeal had held

Figure 6 The Feminine Dimension of Islam. Tomb of Bibi Jiwandi in Uchh Sharif, Punjab, present-day Pakistan (Courtesy Ayesha Jalal)

an attraction. Some recent works on early Islam in India have sought to underplay this dimension on grounds that Muslim conversions were more numerous where inequalities within the social structure were not as great as elsewhere. Yet this hardly invalidates the case about an egalitarian appeal, since it is entirely logical that societies with a history of valuing equality would be more amenable to its attractions. The egalitarianism of Islam did not, however, extend equally to women. Both Muslim and Hindu women of the upper social strata were largely restricted in this period to the private domain and were expected to be in purdah or behind a veil. One early Delhi sultan of the Mamluk dynasty – Raziya Sultana – succeeded in becoming the first Muslim woman ruler in the subcontinent. Acknowledged to have been a capable ruler, she was assassinated by male rivals.

The Sunni and Shia sectarian division, which had occurred over differences of opinion on Muhammad's successor to the Khilafat, was reflected in Indian Muslim society. A great majority of Indian Muslims were Sunnis. In parts of Sind and southern Punjab, Multan in particular, Shias had become influential. But they seemed to be at a disadvantage in northern India during the period of the Sunni Delhi sultanate. Yet in a sense the most influential of Muslims in India were the Sufis, who represented the mystical branch of Islam – which had achieved prominence in Persia since the tenth century. Members of the Chishti and Suhrawardy orders carried out many of the conversions to Islam after 1290. The Chishti order made its mark in the environs of Delhi and the Ganga–Jamuna Doab, while the Suhrawardy order developed a strong following in Sind. It was in the Islamic mystical tradition that women played a decisive role. One of the first mystics of Islam was a woman, the chaste and pure lover of God Rabia, who lived in Basra during the eighth century and won the admiration of fellow male Sufis. The names of famous women Sufis are to be found throughout the Islamic world. In all the Muslim-majority regions of the subcontinent, especially Sind and Punjab, there are shrines of women Sufi saints. So the feminine dimension in Islam, closely associated with spirituality, played a part in the peaceful spread of Muhammad's message. Evidence of the Sufi role in facilitating Islam's accommodation with its Indian environment can be seen in the very special mystical appreciation of the feminine in their poetry. While in Persian, and also Arabic, the metaphor of mystical poetry is predominantly male, the imagery is altered in Indian Sufi tradition into a love of the divine in the form of a woman devotee. Drawing upon the Hindu traditions, the soul is described as that of a loving woman seeking union with God, the ultimate Beloved.

There was much in common between the *bhakti* strand in popular Hinduism and the Sufi strand of Islam. Both sought union with God through the way of love and revered pirs and gurus as spiritual leaders and mediators. The Sufi Islamic influence gave a powerful impetus to the bhakti movement in India, strengthening the Shramanik tradition and promoting a few syncretistic cults. Among the prominent leaders of the bhakti devotional movement were

Kabir (1440–1518) in northern India and Chaitanya (1486–1533) in Bengal, while the stream led by Guru Nanak (1469–1539) culminated in the foundation of the new Sikh religious faith in the Punjab. Both Kabir and Nanak rejected the caste system and sought not so much to integrate Islam and Hinduism as to offer alternative views of the Creator. Kabir, when he did not deny the Hindu and Muslim conceptions of God, sought to equate them in eclectic fashion. He claimed himself to be the child of Allah and also of Ram. Nanak went much further in the direction of negating specifically Hindu and Muslim ideas of God while drawing on the mystical strands within both. The more resolute negation of the rituals of Hinduism and Islam by Nanak contributed to the emergence of Sikhism as a distinctive and separate religion after his death. Nanak's teachings were compiled in the *Adi Granth* and were disseminated by nine Gurus who came after him.

Most leaders of the bhakti movement preferred to communicate in regional languages that established the importance of regional dialects and scripts such as Bengali, Assamese, Oriya, Maithili, Gujarati, Rajasthani, Kashmiri, Awadhi and Braj (sometimes referred to as Hindavi). The devotional songs of the famous woman bhakti preacher Mirabai were composed in Rajasthani, but she was influenced by other bhakti composers who developed Awadhi and Braj. Another great woman poet and saint of the fourteenth century was Lal Ded, who did much to promote the Kashmiri language with her simple but powerful verses. The congruence between language and region was clearly drawn in India between the fourteenth and fifteenth centuries, even though Persian remained the court language of the sultanate. Urdu (literally 'the camp language'), borrowing liberally from Hindavi syntax and grammar and Persian and Arabic vocabulary, developed into something of a lingua franca only in the sixteenth and seventeenth centuries.

The half a millennium that stretched from 1000 to 1500 is seen by some scholars, like Sheldon Pollock, as being marked by a process of vernacularization. This process, however, was not entirely state sponsored in most regions, as it appeared to be in the Kannada-speaking region of the south. Devotional poets and preachers led the trend towards vernacularization in Hindustan (north India), Kashmir, Bengal and Gujarat, where they composed their messages in regional languages. The rise of the vernacular did not necessarily entail the decline of the universal, as is sometimes supposed. Islam, while adapting to the regional settings of Kashmir or Bengal, never lost its universal appeal. The growing literary and religious salience of regional languages like Kashmiri or Bengali coexisted with a universal language, Persian, that gained pre-eminence in the domain of statecraft and politics.

The cultural fusion on which Indo-Islamic civilization was coming to be based was frowned upon by certain social groups. Some Muslim ulema, who advised the sultans on issues pertaining to Islamic law, tended to be cultural exclusivists. Their religious bigotry was more than counterbalanced by the pragmatic needs of governance in a scenario where an overwhelming majority of the populace were non-believers. The Islamic doctrine of *jihad*, to struggle in the way of God, continued to be invoked. But it was the discourse and practice of jihad's obverse, *aman*, literally 'peace and protection', which held sway in the Indian context.

The Brahmanical tradition on the Hindu side could be equally exclusivist when it could not absorb and dominate and, consequently, averse to accommodation. One Nrisinghacharya was reputed to have told a congregation of high-caste Hindus at a Kumbha Mela – a great religious fair held at the confluence of the Ganga and the Jamuna – to adopt *kamathabritti* or the habit of a tortoise, in other words withdraw into a shell in order to be impervious to Islamic influences. Indeed, if one reads the *Dharmashastra* or Hindu law books of this period, to the exclusion of other sources, one would not even begin to suspect that there were Muslims in India. Not all upper-caste Hindus, of course, could become tortoises. Some Rajput princes made alliances with the sultanate and a few converted to Islam. These Rajput Muslims could not quite aspire to the *ashraf* (honourable, noble) status of the aristocracy of West Asian origin, but they still enjoyed much higher status than the large numbers of artisans and peasants who became *ajlaf* (commoner) Muslims. Islam, in adapting to the Indian environment, could not, despite its strong egalitarianism, avoid the social imprint of caste. According to one view, the Arab variant of Indo-Islamic culture in the coastal south was less of a hybrid than the fusion that took place in the hinterlands. While it is undeniable that the coastal towns of the Coromandel retained more of a purist Arab imprint than the Indo-Islamic culture of continental India, Hindus, Muslims and Christians of the south came to share, as Susan Bayly has demonstrated, some common religious and social idioms. Many southern mosques contained Hindu decorative features such as lotus columns, replicating the Indo-Islamic accommodations in architectural designs in northern India, where the Turkish-Persian variant of Islam was stronger.

The fourteenth and fifteenth centuries witnessed both a powerful current towards cultural accommodation as well as pockets of stubborn resistance to it. By around 1500 Indo-Islamic cultures, with their creativity and ambiguity, accommodations and tensions, had struck deep roots in the subcontinent. It was at this juncture that a new empire was established in northern India by a ruler of Turkish-Mongol descent. The next chapter turns to this empire and further developments within an Indo-Islamic social and political universe under its aegis.

4

THE MUGHAL EMPIRE

State, economy and society

While unravelling the complex weave of India's pre-modern history we could hardly not have noticed two recurring themes. First, the infusion of new peoples and ideas, sometimes in the form of an invasion from the north-west and, second, temporal cycles of imperial consolidation and decentralization. Invasions were not sharp disjunctures, and were most commonly followed by fresh processes of accommodation, assimilation and cultural fusions. The high points of great imperial epochs were often characterized by political cohesion, social vitality, economic prosperity and cultural glory. But it was also abundantly clear that periods of political decentralization were not necessarily accompanied by social and economic decay. These general observations drawn from a thematic survey of the long term in Indian history can be investigated more closely with reference to the Mughal empire, which was established in 1526, enjoyed expansion and consolidation until about 1707 and survived, even if in drastically attenuated form, until 1857.

Empires in pre-modern India, we have seen, were not based on rigid centralized domination. This has been established by the most insightful of recent historical research, and runs counter to the misperceptions of many nineteenth-century historians and twentieth-century comparative sociologists. Few polities have been subjected to greater misinterpretation by Western comparativists than the Mughal empire, which has been seen as a prime example of 'oriental despotism'. Reading backwards from the twentieth century experience of European totalitarianism, pre-modern Asian states were seen to be all-powerful revenue-extracting machines presiding over passive and pulverized societies lacking not only in dynamism but also processes of relatively autonomous social group formation. The historiography of the Mughal era has been only recently freeing itself from the despotism of orientalist scholarship. While differences remain on the extent of centralization actually achieved, the Mughal empire is beginning to be viewed as a complex, nuanced and loose form of hegemony over a diverse, differentiated and dynamic economy and society.

The founder of the Mughal empire could not have been aware of the enduring legacy that he was to leave in India. Having set up a small kingdom

28

in Farghana in Central Asia at the turn of the sixteenth century, Zahiruddin Babur was initially more interested in conquering Samarkand. After several futile attempts to expand in a northerly direction, Babur settled down to rule the environs of Kabul in modern-day Afghanistan. From there he made a raid into the Punjab, and then in 1526 defeated Ibrahim Lodi, the last of the Delhi sultans, in the first battle of Panipat. Babur's use of Turkish cannon in this battle led some historians to include the empire he founded in the category of 'gun-powder empires'. It is now clear that this sort of technological definition of empires is neither very accurate nor very appropriate. The Mughals in any case were more reliant on cavalry in making their conquests, although artillery was also used in an innovative way for selective purposes. Babur was descended from Taimur (the great Turkish empire builder in Central Asia) on his father's side and Genghis Khan (the great Mongol war leader) on his mother's side. Contemporaries referred to the empire he founded as the Taimurid empire. The choice of the term Mughal, derived from Mongol, appears to have been a nineteenth-century preference. Babur was not particularly attracted to the heat and dust of the plains of northern India where he established his political power. In his introspective and evocative autobiography, the *Baburnama*, he expresses a longing to return to the cool valley of Kabul:

> Hindustan is a country that has few pleasures to recommend it. The people are not handsome. They have no idea of the charms of friendly society, of frankly mixing together, or of familiar intercourse. They have no genius, no comprehension of mind, no politeness of manner, no kindness or fellow-feeling, no ingenuity or mechanical invention in planning or executing their handicraft works, no skill or knowledge in design or architecture; they have no horses, no good flesh, no grapes or musk melons, no good fruits, no ice or cold water, no good food or bread in their bazaars, no baths or colleges, no candles, no torches, not a candlestick.

But there were also passages in the *Baburnama* more appreciative of the charms of Hind:

> The one nice aspect of Hindustan is that it is a large country with lots of gold and money. The weather turns very nice during the monsoon. Sometimes it rains ten, fifteen, or twenty times a day; torrents are formed in an instant, and water flows in places that normally have no water ... Another nice thing is the unlimited numbers of craftsmen and practitioners of every trade. For every labour and every product there is an established group who have been practising their craft or professing that trade for generations ... In Agra alone there were 680 Agra stonemasons at work on my building every day.

Before he could expand or consolidate his Indian domain Babur died suddenly, in 1530. His short reign might have been remarkably uncontroversial, were it not for an accusation that surfaced in the late nineteenth century and achieved political prominence in the late twentieth – that one of his generals, Mir Baqi, had destroyed a Ram temple to build a mosque in Ayodhya, the Babri Masjid, named after Babur. There is no sixteenth-century evidence that any temple had been destroyed to construct this particular mosque.

The newly founded Turkish dynasty's control over north India remained very shaky and tenuous under Babur's son Humayun. An Afghan challenge from eastern India led by Sher Shah Suri forced Humayun to flee the country in 1540 and take refuge in the court of Safavid Iran. Sher Shah (1540–45) brought about an imperial unification of much of northern India and set up an administrative framework, which was to be further developed by Akbar later in the century. The weakening of the Suri dynasty (1540–55) after Sher Shah's death enabled Humayun to return in 1555 to reclaim his Indian patrimony, but he had not been back in Delhi for more than a few months before he took a fatal tumble down his library stairs.

On the assumption of the imperial mantle, his son Akbar (1556–1605) faced an immediate challenge from an Afghan and Rajput Hindu military coalition, which he defeated at the second battle of Panipat. Akbar, undoubtedly the greatest of the Mughal emperors, was an able leader of military campaigns, an astute administrator and a patron of culture. In 1572 he launched a major campaign against Gujarat, and the following year made a triumphant entry into the Gujarati port city of Surat. In 1574 Akbar's army began its conquest of Bengal, which had more often than not been independent of Delhi during the period of the Sultanate, and finally subdued resistance by the 1580s. The conquests of Gujarat and Bengal gave the Mughals control over the agriculturally and commercially richest parts of the subcontinent. Among Akbar's other notable military successes were the conquests of Kabul in 1581, Kashmir in 1586, Orissa in 1592 and Baluchistan in 1595. The territorial expanse of the Mughal empire grew during the reigns of Akbar's successors, Jahangir (1605–27) and Shah Jahan (1627–58), and Aurangzeb (1658–1707). Although Jahangir managed to lose Kandahar and Shah Jahan sent an abortive expedition to Balkh and Badakshan in Central Asia, all three of Akbar's successors made territorial gains in the Deccan and further south, eventually defeating the powerful Adilshahi kingdom of Bijapur and the Qutbshahi kingdom of Golconda. The Mughal empire reached its territorial apogee under Aurangzeb in the 1690s. But Aurangzeb's Deccan adventures were fiercely resisted by the redoubtable Maratha leader, Shivaji, who refused to be co-opted into the Mughal system. The economic costs of the Deccan wars made sure that Aurangzeb's final successes would turn out to be pyrrhic victories.

The expansion and consolidation of the Mughal empire was roughly coterminous with that of two other great Muslim empires – the Safavid empire in Iran and the Ottoman empire based in Turkey but controlling much of west

Asia and north Africa. While there was much in common with these three formidable land-based empires, the Mughal empire was different in one important respect. In India the Mughals established an empire in which a majority of the subjects were non-Muslims. Akbar, who gave initial shape and form to the Mughal state, was acutely aware of this demographic fact and devised his policies accordingly. Although most of the nobility in Akbar's court consisted of Turks, Afghans and Persians, Akbar set about building a network of alliances with Hindus, especially through the regional Rajput rulers. The Mughals under Akbar drew the nobility into the tasks of defending and administering the empire through the *mansabdari* system. *Mansab* literally means 'rank', and a *mansabdar* was the holder of a rank of anything from ten to five thousand, and occasionally ten thousand. Theoretically, mansabdars of various ranks were supposed to supply the specified number of cavalry to the imperial army when needed. A mansabdar of ten was, therefore, expected to have ten men under his command, and so on. In practice, not all mansabdars were expected to perform military duties. Civilian administrators were also given ranks or mansabs by the Mughal emperor, and were paid salaries in cash equivalent to the amount that would be needed for the upkeep of a certain number of cavalry. Cash income from *jagirs*, literally 'land grants', was designated for various mansabdars. Mansabs were open to talent and the jagirs from which mansabdars were paid were not meant to be heritable. It was only in a later period of crisis that some mansabdars could not be paid in cash and tended to hold on to hereditary jagirs. Although the mansabdari system was the main framework of the Mughal administration, the imperial domains had territorial divisions known as *subahs* or provinces ruled by *subadars* or governors, who usually held high mansabs or ranks. Below the level of the subadars there would be *jagirdars* below the mansabdari, rank as well as *zamindars*, literally 'landlords', whose main task was to collect revenue from the locality.

Akbar included several Hindus in the ranks of the highest mansabdars. For instance, his top-ranking military general was Raja Mansingh of Amber, a Rajput, and his revenue minister was Raja Todar Mal, a Khatri, who supervised a detailed cadastral survey of the far-flung Mughal territories. Akbar displayed impartiality towards his subjects, regardless of religious affiliation, by abolishing the *jizya* – a tax imposed on non-believers in Muslim states. He also showed a pragmatic streak and a determination to adapt to the Indian environment by replacing the Muslim lunar calendar with the solar calendar, which he thought made more sense in an agricultural country like India. Akbar's public tolerance and efforts to build a truly Indo-Islamic empire were matched by his flexibility in private beliefs and practices. In 1582 he announced his adherence to a new set of beliefs, drawing on elements from the mystical strains in both Islam and Hinduism and deeply influenced by Zorastrianism, which he called Din-e-Ilahi or the Divine Faith. He did not, however, try to impose Din-e-Ilahi as a state religion. An amalgamation of diverse beliefs, it

Figure 7 The Rajput Arm of the Mughal Empire. Gateway to the palace of Raja Mansingh of Amber (Courtesy Sugata Bose)

was, in effect, a cult centred on the emperor's personality and even in its heyday had only eighteen followers at the royal court. The Ibadatkhana or place of worship in Akbar's red sandstone capital at Fatehpur Sikri became the venue for free and lively theological and philosophical debates attended by Muslims, Hindus, Zoroastrians, Jains, Jesuit Christians and Jews. His policies of public tolerance and private eclecticism were continued by his son and grandson, Jahangir and Shah Jahan. Akbar's favourite wife was a Hindu Rajput princess, Jodhabai.

The breadth of Akbar's outlook was looked upon with scepticism by some sections of the ulema. But during Akbar's reign the supremacy of temporal over religious authority was clearly maintained. Some ulema attempted to persecute Akbar's famous free-thinking friend and courtier, Abul Fazl, and found themselves behind prison bars. The most prominent orthodox critic of Mughal religious accommodations in the early seventeenth century was Shaikh Ahmad Sirhindi (1564–1624), who was the leading light of the Naqshbandi order and looked forward to a rejuvenation of the original purity of Islam at the turn of its second millennium. Sirhindi rejoiced at the death of Akbar, in whose reign 'the sun of guidance was hidden behind the veil of error', and was imprisoned by Akbar's son and successor, Jahangir.

The followers of Sirhindi were fiercely opposed to the innovative mystical blendings of Upanishadic philosophy and Sufism, of which Dara Shikoh, the eldest son of Shah Jahan, was a major proponent. Influenced initially by his eldest sister, Jahanara, who had a deep understanding of Islamic mysticism,

Figure 8 Mughal Memory. Jahangir's Tomb, Lahore (Courtesy Ayesha Jalal)

Dara was later drawn into the Qadiriyya Sufi order. Better versed in mysticism than in worldly matters, Dara Shikoh lost out in a bitter succession struggle to his younger brother, Aurangzeb, in 1658 and was killed after being defeated in the battle of Samugarh. Aurangzeb's reign saw a partial reversal of the politics of alliance building and religious flexibility under a mounting set of economic and political pressures. The jizya was reimposed, not necessarily for religious reasons but as a means of taxing the commercial wealth of Hindus and Jains within the empire. The switch back from the solar to the lunar calendar owed perhaps more to Aurangzeb's ideological rigidity, even though he did not make this change until some twenty years into his reign. Yet even at the end of Aurangzeb's supposedly puritanical reign nearly a quarter of the mansabdars were Hindus. Aurangzeb's doctrinal rigidity does not appear to have pervaded the female quarters of the royal palace. One of his daughters thought better of the mystical dimensions of Islam and became a patron of Sufic activities, gifting an entire complex of buildings in Delhi to the famous eighteenth-century mystical poet Mir Dard.

The early views of Mughal despotism emphasized material factors as much as ideological ones. The Mughal state was said to extract huge amounts of revenue from the agrarian sector. The proportion most commonly mentioned by generations of economic historians until very recently was 40 per cent, or the entire movable surplus. There can be little doubt that, as in other

Figure 9 Mughal Piety. The Badshabi Mosque, Lahore, built under the patronage of Aurangzeb (Courtesy Ayesha Jalal)

contemporary agrarian empires, the revenue demand on the peasantry was high, perhaps as much as a third of the product. But recent research suggests that the Mughals did not deploy a centralized bureaucratic administration as an engine to pump out revenues from the villages. The Mughal state typically entered into accommodations with the clan power of zamindars in the countryside, not only in the peripheral regions but also the environs of the capital. The agrarian surplus was distributed among various layers of appropriators, with the imperial household and the mansabdari nobility receiving only the final, albeit substantial, cut. Despite the elaborate details about revenue administration laid out in Abu Fazl's manual, *Ain-i-Akbari* (compiled in *c.* 1590s), many prosperous parts of the empire were never rigorously surveyed. There is a palpable lack of statistical data at the all-India level between the late sixteenth and nineteenth century, but recent studies of particular regions have shown that the seventeenth century was a period of vibrant agricultural growth, which would hardly have been possible if a centralized state had been draining away most of the local resources. The picture of an emaciated and oppressed peasantry, mercilessly exploited by the emperor and his nobility, is being seriously altered in the light of new interpretations of the evidence. The agrarian revolts that began to undermine the power of the Mughal empire from the later years of Aurangzeb's reign were not typically prompted by absolute poverty, but, paradoxically, occurred in regions which had enjoyed relative prosperity under Mughal auspices and were now minded to preserve their gains.

Primarily an agrarian empire, the Mughal state was also linked to long-distance overland and oceanic trade. From the mid-seventeenth century onwards the empire became more heavily engaged with the international economy and may have turned more mercantilist in character, relying for its economic viability as much on textile exports as on land revenues. Akbar may have viewed the sea for the first time upon his conquest of Gujarat, but his son Jahangir and grandson Shah Jahan ruled an empire heavily reliant for its economic prosperity on oceanic connections. The Mughals, however, unlike the Ottomans, did not possess a strong navy, despite exercising control over a significant number of pilgrim and merchant ships. This enabled European powers to gradually command the sea-lanes of the Indian Ocean.

Even before the establishment of the Mughal empire the Portuguese, led by Vasco da Gama, had landed on the south-western coast of India in 1498 and by 1510 had set up a major settlement in Goa. But the Portuguese never came close to achieving their professed aim of establishing a monopoly over sea trade in the Indian Ocean. Arab and Gujarati merchants in particular were resourceful enough to meet the Portuguese economic challenge. In the latter half of the sixteenth century, hailed by some Western writers as the Portuguese century, the trading outpost of Goa was economically less important than the Mughal port city of Surat. The Ottoman navy made certain that the Portuguese, even at the height of their power, were never able to close the Red Sea to Turkish, Persian, Arab and Indian trade. The Portuguese presence and influence remained limited to a few Indian coastal enclaves. As Ashin Dasgupta argued, 'after the first violent overture' the Portuguese in the sixteenth century 'settled within the structure and were, in a way, swallowed by it'.

The English, who succeeded the Portuguese as the leading European traders in India in the seventeenth century, were also supplicants of the Mughals and simply sought permission from the emperor to carry on quiet trade. The English East India Company, founded in 1600, first obtained permission to trade in India from Jahangir in 1619. But their political and military power was confined to a few factory forts in coastal areas. The English and also the Dutch in the seventeenth century worked, according to Dasgupta, 'within the indigenous structure' and were 'one more strand in the weave of the [Indian] ocean's trade'. The sixteenth and seventeenth centuries have been characterized by Blair B. Kling and M.N. Pearson as 'an age of partnership' between Europeans and Asians, while Sanjay Subrahmanyam in his work on southern India has dubbed it 'an age of contained conflict'.

To Indian merchants the Mughal state allowed a certain measure of autonomy in important trading towns and cities. At the same time, the Mughals were not directly dependent for their state finances on the services of these merchant groups. The empire could simply accrue benefits from the credit and insurance facilities provided by bankers and traders linking processes of inland trade and urbanization to wider networks of the Indian Ocean economy. Bankers and merchants helped achieve a degree of economic integration which matched the political integration sought by the Mughal empire. Since European traders were primarily interested in Asian goods, especially Indian textiles, to sell in European markets, the Mughal domains received large inflows of precious metals, particularly silver. Mughal India was, therefore, a great metropolitan magnet of wealth in the context of sixteenth- and seventeenth-century international trade. Mughal power, far from having despotic roots, rested on arrangements based on a large measure of political and economic flexibility.

In their administration of justice, the Mughals followed the pattern established by the Delhi sultans. Given the limited scope of the sharia, especially in providing for effective and speedy public justice, Muslim sovereigns everywhere had set up mechanisms to strengthen the judicial administration. Anxious to preserve law and order, the Mughals created a parallel system of courts alongside the specifically Islamic ones. Imperial edicts, or *qanun-e-shahi*, supplementing the Islamic sharia, allowed Mughal rulers and officials considerable room for administrative innovations. Muslim law officers like the *qazis* and *muftis* enforced the Islamic sharia less as a rigid legal code and more as a set of moral injunctions to be invoked in the light of circumstances. The goal was to assure the result of equity and justice rather than strictly apply the letter of the law. While brought under the purview of the Mughal system of criminal law in certain parts of India, non-Muslims had recourse to their own customary and religious law in matters to do with marriage and inheritance.

Although the Mughal empire on the whole made no distinctive contribution to improving the status of women, it is important to note the very considerable influence which the women of the *zenana* could exercise upon the royal throne. The close interplay between the private and the public domain became particularly pronounced once Akbar began contracting marriages with Hindu Rajput princesses. Eclectic and open-minded in his religious outlook, Jahangir celebrated Hindu cultural festivals with great enthusiasm. His highly refined artistic tastes are at least partly attributable to his wife, Nur Jahan, who established herself as a formidable member of the royal household, enjoying strong political influence over the emperor. Mumtaz Mahal, sadly, was not a historical agent in Nur Jahan's league. She had to die trying to bear Shah Jahan's fifteenth child, and her death became the inspiration behind the emperor's patronage of the Taj Mahal, one of the finest architectural forms ever constructed in the world. Shah Jahan's eldest daughter, Jahanara, established herself as a scholar of Islamic mysticism, winning accolades from her Sufi mentor, Mullah Shah. The women of the Mughal household were, of course, hardly representative of the typical Indian woman, Hindu or Muslim. But there can be no denying their role in the making of the majesty that was the Mughal empire.

Both the grandeur and the syncretism of the Mughal empire were reflected in the very considerable cultural achievements over which they presided. Persian was the court language of this Turkish dynasty. But at a more popular level Urdu became the language of Indo-Islamic culture in northern India, especially in the seventeenth century. Regional vernaculars continued to flourish in the provinces outside the Mughal heartland. Some of the finest literary and artistic achievements of the Mughals were their illuminated manuscripts. The autobiographies and chronicles of the Mughal emperors were written in flowing Persian, and were brilliant examples of calligraphy and visual illustration. Among the more famous of these manuscripts is Abul Fazl's history of Akbar's reign, the *Akbarnama*, and Abdul Hamid Lodhi's *Padshahnama*. Mughal scribes and artists not only chose Islamic subjects but also illustrated the famous Hindu epics, the *Ramayana* and the *Mahabharata*. Humayun had brought back with him from Persia two leading painters of the Safavid court, Mir Sayyid Ali and Abdus Samad. Talented Hindus joined them in Akbar's royal studio. Together they created a new Indo-Persian style of painting, lighter and more colourful than the formal ornamentation of the pure Persian. Mughal art reached its zenith of artistic expression in the reign of Jahangir. The Mughal miniature was much more than a single genre, exhibiting much variation as great painters such as Govardhan and Abul Hasan gave full play to their individual styles. In music the basic grammar of north Indian classical music with its thirty-six *raga* and *ragini* was composed under Mughal patronage. The most famous of music composers of this era was Tan Sen, one of the 'nine gems' at Akbar's court. Legend has it that Tan Sen could bring on torrential monsoon rains by his rendition of the raga *meghamalhar*. A distinctive style of vocal music, *dhrupad*, was developed during Shah Jahan's reign. The most famous treatise on the ragas, the *Raga Darpana*, was written in 1666 by Faqir Allah during the reign of Aurangzeb – the emperor being, ironically, a man not particularly fond of music.

Yet the greatest and the most lasting cultural achievements of the Mughals were made in the field of architecture. The buildings in Akbar's capital, Fatehpur Sikri, were based on a fusion of classical Islamic and Rajput styles. The *buland darwaza*, or great gateway, with its imposing arch, had a strong west Asian influence, while the balconies were adorned with Rajput decorative arts. The greatest of the Mughal builders, of course, was Shah Jahan, justly famous for having built the exquisite marble monument in memory of his wife, Mumtaz Mahal, in Agra. But he would have been remembered as a great builder even if he had not built the Taj Mahal. In Delhi, Shah Jahan constructed a magnificent capital. The towering mosque called the Jama Masjid in old Delhi commanded the inhabitants of the capital and continues to be a focal point of Muslim religion and culture in India. The centrepiece of the new capital, Shah Jahanabad, was the famous Lal Qila or the Red Fort, which came to be recognized as the most important symbol of sovereignty in India.

Mughal sovereignty was not wholly undermined until the British tried the last of the Mughal emperors, Bahadur Shah Zafar, in the Red Fort after the 1857 mutiny–rebellion. Bahadur Shah was sentenced to deportation for life and died in exile in Burma, while a British military officer exterminated the Mughal imperial line. It would be clear to the populace that British sovereignty in India had been undermined when, after another trial at the Red Fort in 1945, the British were unable to carry out their life sentence on three Hindu, Muslim and Sikh anti-colonial rebels in the face of intense public pressure. To this day Indian prime ministers make a ritual of addressing the nation on independence day from the ramparts of the Red Fort, even if by now they are no more than mere shadows of even the lesser Mughals. An early twentieth-century historical assessment of the Mughal empire by Aurobindo Ghose, a key nationalist and Hindu religious figure, was right on the mark. The Mughal empire was, in Aurobindo's view:

a great and magnificent construction and an immense amount of political genius and talent was employed in its creation and main-tenance. It was as splendid, powerful and beneficent and, it may be added, in spite of Aurangzeb's fanatical zeal, infinitely more liberal and tolerant in religion than any medieval or contemporary European kingdom or empire and India under its rule stood high in military and political strength, economic opulence and the brilliance of its art and culture.

INDIA BETWEEN EMPIRES
Decline or decentralization?

In the introduction to his *History of the Punjab* published in 1891, Syad Muhammad Latif contrasted the 'corruption, degradation and treachery' that 'stalked openly through the land' prior to the British conquest with the peace and tranquillity which followed in its wake. Under the 'fostering care of the English', he gloated, 'the same bands of fanatics, marauders and highway robbers who were once a terror to the people' had been 'turned into peaceful cultivators and useful citizens'.

This predominant nineteenth-century view of the eighteenth century as a period of anarchy between the age of Mughal hegemony and the imposition of Pax Britannica persisted until recently. Research during the past few decades has broken new ground and signalled fresh departures in late Mughal and early colonial historiography. From a balanced angle of vision the eighteenth century does not appear any more as a dark valley in the shadow of towering empires. What emerges is a mixed scenario of shadow and light, with high points and low points. It is important in any study of India between empires not to confuse the erosion of power of the Mughal court and army with a more general political, economic and societal decline.

The death of Aurangzeb in 1707 is generally seen to separate the era of the great Mughals from that of the lesser Mughals. Even as Aurangzeb projected Mughal power to its farthest territorial extent, the costs of military campaigns sorely undermined the financial basis of his empire. Agrarian-based revolts by Marathas, Sikhs, Jats and others, as well as the assertion of autonomy if not independence by provincial governors, did not bode well for the Mughal centre. While a process of fission, separation and renegotiation of the terms of suzerainty may have been built into the logic of the empire, dissent, from the turn of the eighteenth century, reached unprecedented levels of intensity. Influential historians of the early twentieth century, notably Jadunath Sarkar, had read into Maratha, Sikh and Jat resistance a strong element of 'Hindu reaction' against Aurangzeb's religious bigotry. But resistance to the later Mughals was not primarily Hindu in composition. The rulers and subjects, chroniclers and poets of Bijapur, Golconda and the Pashtun borderlands deplored Aurangzeb's wars of aggression quite as much as the Marathas.

Irfan Habib in his classic *The Agrarian System of Mughal India* depicted many of the anti-Mughal revolts as peasant uprisings owing primarily to economic oppression. According to this view, to the high Mughal revenue demand had been added the rapacity of the proliferating mansabdars bent on squeezing the resources of their fast-diminishing jagirs. But revolts against the Mughals appear to have occurred in the relatively prosperous regions and were usually led by locally wealthy zamindars, which casts some doubt on the validity

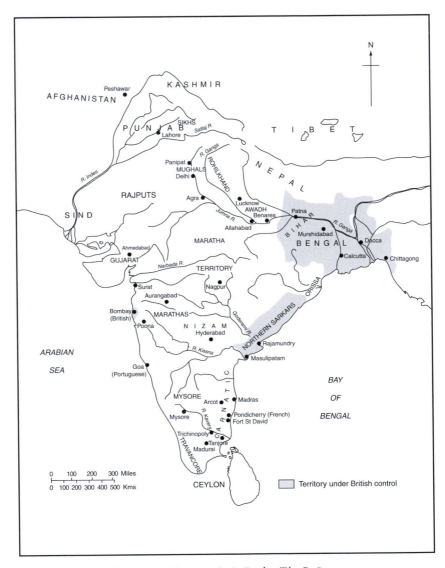

Figure 10 Map of India in 1765 (Source: C. A. Bayly, *The Raj*)

of the exploitation–poverty–resistance causal chain. Other historians have stressed factional conflict among the nobility at the Mughal court, a process related to the mansabdari crisis, and offered more nuanced explanations of the problem of jagirs. Another view pointed to the withdrawal of financial support to the empire in crisis by the great banking firms.

Research conducted since the 1980s has emphasized the regional aspect in the motivation and articulation of eighteenth-century revolts. Regionally based powers sought to replace the Mughal centre's control over the peripheries by manipulating central authority. In this process the later Mughals may well have been the victims of the stability and prosperity over which their predecessors had presided. Regions and local elites who dominated at that level were minded to protect their wealth and resist paying for the empire's expensive wars. Inter-regional imbalances of wealth and intra-regional disparities between classes combined in complex ways to weaken the leverage of the Mughal centre *vis-à-vis* the regions in the early eighteenth century. In addition to internal contradictions, a couple of major trends outside the subcontinent exerted serious pressures on the Mughal empire. First, a general South and West Asian crisis found expression in the eighteenth century in the form of tribal incursions from Central Asia, Eurasia and Afghanistan into the heartlands of the great Muslim empires – the Ottoman, Safavid and Mughal. The raids of Suvorov and Potemkin into the Ottoman domains were matched by those of Nadir Shah and Ahmad Shah Abdali into Iran and India. In addition to the more dramatic invasions that left cities devastated, there was a more steady flow of Afghan cavalrymen into many regions of the subcontinent. These incursions were initially sparked off as a reaction against imperial attempts to extract additional revenues from previously lightly taxed frontier zones lying athwart lucrative overland routes of trade. Second, in addition to the inter-regional crisis, disruptions to bullion flows from Europe, which the Mughal financial system had come to rely on, became more frequent in the early eighteenth century even as a surge in European production and trade began to alter the framework of Europe–Asia economic relations.

These multiple internal and external forces resulted in the steady attenuation of Mughal imperial power during the eighteenth century. In the 1730s vast tracts of central India passed from Mughal into Maratha hands. In 1739 Nadir Shah, who had earlier conquered Iran from his Afghan base, razed Delhi in a devastating looting raid and took back enough wealth to resolve for a generation Iran's balance of payments problem stemming from a decline in the silk economy. He also took with him the peacock throne from the Red Fort. The throne of the great Mughals was later carried away from Iran to England. The emperor Muhammad Shah was more devoted to music than statecraft and, on being warned of Nadir Shah's impending invasion, had reportedly commented '*Dehli door ast*' ('Delhi is far away'). By the 1740s the *subadars* (provincial governors) of Bengal, Awadh and the Deccan turned themselves into nawabs or independent kings. The Mughal emperor was not even a direct participant at the third battle of Panipat in 1761, in which the Afghan leader, Ahmad Shah Abdali, inflicted a crushing defeat on a Maratha army led by Sadasiv Rao Bhao. The defeat in 1761 was a major setback for the Marathas, potential inheritors of India's imperial mantle, just at a time when the English were beginning to shift from trade to political dominion. In 1757, after defeating Nawab Siraj-ud-daula at the battle of Plassey, the English East India Company took effective political control of Bengal. The Mughal emperor, a refugee at the Lucknow court of the nawab of Awadh, put up an army alongside the nawabs of Awadh and Bengal in the battle of Buxar in Bihar in 1764, a battle in which the company's army prevailed. The emperor was forced to concede the *diwani* (the right to the revenues) of Bengal to the company in 1765. Maratha power had a brief revival under their great leader Mahadaji Sindhia in the 1770s and 1780s. In 1784 Sindhia won acknowledegment as the protector of the Mughal emperor. It was only after overcoming fierce Maratha resistance that the British occupied Delhi in 1803.

The weakening of the Mughal emperor and nobility enabled the strengthening of other groups who were the products of dynamic processes of social mobility and change. Among the more important social groups rising to prominence were Hindu and Muslim revenue farmers, mainly Hindu and Jain merchants and bankers, and mostly Muslim service gentry. The merchants and bankers in particular provided critical financial sustenance to the regional states of the eighteenth century. This paved the way for a process of commercialization of political power and social relations. The layered dispersion of commercialized power occurred within the context of the authority if not the actual strength of the Mughal empire. The Mughal *shah-en-shah* or king of kings continued to be, as C.A. Bayly puts it, 'the highest manifestation of sovereignty'. Below the imperial level were regional rulers, small potentates and even *rajas* or little kings of villages. The eighteenth century saw an increasing devolution of real power to the lower levels of sovereignty. Mughal legitimacy proved to be longer lasting than Mughal power. Not only Muslim nawabs but also Maratha and Sikh leaders took part in ceremonial acknowledgements of the Mughal emperor as the ultimate repository of sovereignty. The eighteenth-century regionally based state system retained important elements of Mughal administrative practice in addition to respecting Mughal authority. Muslim service gentry and Hindu scribes well-versed in Persian continued to be the mainstay of eighteenth-century administrative structures.

A typology of Mughal successor states reveals at least three distinctive forms. First, there were the independent kingdoms where *subadars* or provincial governors had amalgamated offices kept separate by the Mughals and then asserted independence. Nawab Alivardi Khan of Bengal, Nawab Saadat Khan of Awadh, Nizam Asaf Jah of Hyderabad and the nawabs of the Carnatic (Arcot) enjoyed *de facto* independence by the 1740s. These regional states were dependent on merchant bankers such as the Jagat Seths of Bengal. The transition from prebendal to patrimonial land holdings, already set in motion in the late seventeenth century, was further expedited during the eighteenth century under the nawabs. Punjab represents the most striking example of a subadar's failure to accommodate regional aspirations by asserting autonomy and the consequent claims of a warrior aristocracy to independent statehood. Warrior states established by Sikhs, Jats and, most important, the Marathas were the second major form of the eighteenth-century state system. Although Sikh and Maratha rulers used non-Muslim religious symbolism and claimed to protect sacred places and cattle, their distinctiveness did not owe primarily to religion but to policies of military fiscalism that they adopted. Mahadaji Sindhia's army, for instance, contained as many Muslims as Hindus in the 1780s. The Marathas had resisted Mughal power, but they achieved the Mughal aim of a profitable symbiosis of military power and revenue resources better than the Mughals themselves. The third major form of Mughal successor states were compact local kingdoms whose sovereignty acquired more substance in the eighteenth century. Such were the Rajput petty states of the north and the polities of Telegu-speaking warrior clans in the south. Besides, free-riding Afghan cavalry led a process of state formation, which included the Rohilla sultanates nestling against the Jat states in the environs of Delhi and also small kingdoms in central India, the Deccan and even the deep south. These states resorted to military fiscalism within their compact domains, achieving varying degrees of success in extracting revenues from trade and production. Mysore under Haidar Ali and Tipu Sultan combined elements of a warrior state and a territorially compact kingdom and was probably most successful in gathering resources and maintaining the viability of the state without being utterly dependent on merchant bankers.

If the politics of the eighteenth century was marked more by decentralization than decline, except from a Delhi-centred perspective, economy and society were characterized by general buoyancy and creativity, despite some key weaknesses and contradictions. The economy did well in the spheres of agriculture, inland trade and urbanization. Pockets of agricultural decline – often because of inter-state warfare, as in Punjab and parts of north India – were more than counter-balanced by wider expanses of growth. The Maratha territories under Poona were noted for their low revenue rates and agricultural prosperity in the latter half of the eighteenth century. Mysore under Haidar Ali was described as a garden from end to end. The dynamism characterizing many agrarian regions since 1600 had not abated in the eighteenth century. States exacted tribute from systems of agricultural commodity production that tied villages to expansive networks of commercial mobility and exchange. It was this vibrant 'tributary commercialism', as David Ludden calls it, which made India look attractive to European companies.

It is noteworthy that except for a major subsistence crisis in south India between 1702 and 1704, the first seven decades of the eighteenth century in India were remarkably free of famine. The great Bengal famine of 1770, in which an estimated one-third of the population may have perished, occurred soon after the colonial conquest. This was followed by another disastrous

famine in northern India in 1783. It is difficult in the period immediately preceding colonial conquest to generalize about the condition of rural elites and
subaltern classes and the relations between them. Overall, a favourable land–
labour ratio had enabled highly mobile peasant and tribal labour to negotiate
reasonable terms with controllers of land. While some village notables managed to transform revenue farms into hereditary estates, others felt the squeeze
from powerful regional states such as Tipu's Mysore. Population, production,
prices and wages tended, generally speaking, to be on a gentle upward incline
during the eighteenth century.

Fragmented polities did not of themselves hamper the development of a
thriving inland trade in grain, cloth and cattle. Corporate merchant institutions transcended political boundaries in overseeing the transportation of
goods and the provision of credit and insurance services. This is not to say
that inter-territorial discord posed no threats of dislocation. The concentration
in the best recent research on intermediate social groups rather than on labour
makes any comment on the status of artisans tentative. It would seem,
however, that in the immediate pre-colonial era artisanal labour, especially
weavers, had ample scope for successfully resisting extravagant demands by
intermediate social groups and the state. Even an intrusive state like late
eighteenth-century Mysore appeared to attack intermediaries rather than
labour. Evidence from Bengal and Madras suggests that urban labour was
worse off in relation to the state and the market in the early colonial than in
the immediate pre-colonial period. While inland trade did well, there is little
question that Indian shippers and merchants involved in export trade declined
in the face of European advances. The great Gujarati port city of Surat lost its
importance around 1720. There was a resurgence of demand for Indian goods in
both West and South-East Asia late in the eighteenth century in addition to
European demand, but by now British merchants and shippers had achieved
dominance at the expense of Indians and took the bulk of the profits.

As the old commercial centres of Surat, Maslipatnam and Dacca degenerated,
colonial port-cities like Bombay, Madras and Calcutta took their pride of place.
The decline of the Mughal capitals Delhi and Agra, however, was offset by the
rise of regional capitals, including Lucknow, Hyderabad, the various Maratha
cities and Seringapatam. The level of urbanization was clearly higher in 1800
than a century before. What had changed in the urban centres was the relative
balance of power between rulers and merchants. In some instances, commercial
and financial magnates were arrogating to themselves the powers of the state.
But merchants faced a political backlash in some states, notably Tipu Sultan's
Mysore.

Even with the passing of Mughal grandeur, India in the eighteenth century
retained its cultural vitality. The tendency, according to C.A. Bayly, was
'towards greater complexity and richness of religious and cultural tradition
rather than towards homogeneity'. Devotional cults remained popular among
Hindus and Muslims and were patronized by regional rulers. The Marathas,

for instance, supported the old shrine of the Sufi saint Sheikh Muinuddin Chishti at Ajmer. Vaishnavite *bhakti* flourished in Nadia under the nawabs of Bengal. Important innovations took place within the high traditions of Islam and Hinduism as well. The *usuli* or rationalistic branch of Shia jurisprudence achieved a high level of sophistication in Awadh. The mobility characteristic of the eighteenth century brought even more southern Brahmins than before to Benares, infusing new life into the Hindu philosophy of the north. South Indian classical music took shape in the courts of the Carnatic in the eighteenth century. Devotional themes were depicted with great skill and passion in the Kangra, Bundi and various Rajasthani schools of painting, representing a fresh departure from Mughal miniature painting. The scramble for resources during the coming apart of a great empire did lead to some sectarian, communal and ideological conflicts between Shia and Sunni, Sikh and Muslim, and Hindu and Muslim. Shah Waliullah (1703–62) of Delhi and his son Shah Abdul Aziz (1746–1824) articulated a stern rationalist ideology of Sunni orthodoxy aimed at purging Islam of polytheistic accretions. Their teachings provided impetus for Sayyid Ahmad of Rai Bareilly's jihad against the Sikh kingdom of Punjab between 1826 and 1831. Hailed as the only real attempt to uphold the supremacy of Islamic faith in the subcontinent, the jihad had degenerated into an internecine conflict among Muslims by the time Sayyid Ahmad and Shah Ismail were martyred in the battle of Balakot in 1831. This is why the existence of a discourse on religious or sectarian differences and episodic religious or sectarian strife must not be confused with the twentieth-century notion of 'communalism'. If the eighteenth century was not an era of perfect amity, it was far less characterized by ingrained or overarching communitarian animosity.

Overall, India in the eighteenth century held out many attractions to Europeans, particularly the British, who set about to appropriate a relatively buoyant economy by harnessing the dynamic social and political changes taking place to their own advantage. In an early revisionist piece written in 1918, the same Aurobindo Ghose who had written in glowing terms about the Mughal empire argued that 'a new life' which 'seemed about to rise in the regional peoples' in the eighteenth century was 'cut short by the intrusion of European nations'. The next chapter will analyse the logic behind the early phase of British colonialism and the ways in which it was moulded by Indian collaboration and resistance.

6

THE TRANSITION TO COLONIALISM

Resistance and collaboration

The mid-eighteenth century saw the onset of a process of steady dismantling of the Mughal successor state system and its replacement by British domination. Beginning with the British conquest of Bengal in the 1750s and the 1760s, it was a long and arduous process that was not completed until the conquest of Punjab and the final annexation of Awadh in the 1840s and 1850s. The strongest organized resistance to British expansion came from the great warrior states of Mysore, the Marathas and the Sikhs. But there was also a strong strand of collaboration by Indian social groups, especially merchant capitalists, who helped undermine the regional states they had bankrolled in the past. Any interpretation of the transition to colonialism in India must address a set of related issues: the impetus behind European expansion; the reasons for colonial conquest in an era of decolonization and informal empire in other parts of the world; the basis of collaboration between the English East India Company and Indian intermediate social groups; and, finally, the critical factors which brought the British success.

The great spurt in European production and trade from the beginning of the eighteenth century provides the very general backdrop to the British move from trade to political dominion in India. Indian textiles were the most profitable item in the company's trade at this time. The goods had to be paid for in large quantities of silver imported from Europe. During the early eighteenth century the mercantilist critique of the drain of silver from Europe to Asia grew increasingly strident. Access to, if not control over, Indian revenues would be one way in which this problem could be solved. Yet the European desire to stop the flow of precious metals alone cannot explain the transition to colonialism. The opportunities for political intervention by the company were provided by internal contradictions in the economy and polities of India in the late eighteenth century. The withdrawal of support by commercial and financial magnates to the successor states was of critical importance. No less important was the growing involvement of the company's servants in India's internal trade. Some regional states were determined in the late eighteenth century to reduce their dependence on merchants and bankers by extracting additional resources from them, and to delimit the spheres within which Europeans could trade. It was the attempt by relatively powerful regional states to vigorously pursue the policy of military fiscalism which brought about a congruence of interests between the English East India Company and Indian merchant capitalists. To facilitate the transition to colonial rule, foreign capital promised initially to shore up indigenous merchant capitalists against the common threat posed by the so-called 'neo-Sultanist' states. European dominance over external trade and shipping, and hence over long-distance cash flows, as well as their slight edge in military technology, contributed to the wrecking of the eighteenth-century Indian regional state system.

In the course of subduing independent Indian states, the English disposed of a challenge presented by the French East India Company. European traders had been attracted by the buoyancy and profitability of Indian internal trade and politics. Paradoxically, the ultimate losers – the French – took an early lead in intervening in the affairs of Indian states. François Dupleix, the flamboyant governor of the French East India Company, was the original grandmaster of the game of nabobism. In return for offering military services in succession disputes and inter-territorial strifes, the French received substantial economic benefits. Lack of effective support from the metropolis and the superiority of the English at sea ensured that the French were eventually checkmated. The game had been fought with furious intensity in southern India during the War of the Austrian Succession between 1740 and 1748, and erupted again during the Seven Years' War between 1756 and 1763. During the 1740s, for instance, the English based in Madras and the French in Pondicherry supported rival nawabs of Arcot. In the end it was the English client, Mohammad Ali, who prevailed, albeit less as a true king than a pawn.

The decisive breakthrough for the English came in Bengal in 1757. The young nawab Siraj-ud-daula had succeeded his grandfather, the experienced and circumspect ruler Alivardi Khan, who had presided over a delicate balance of interests between the English and French companies in Calcutta and Chandernagore respectively, the great merchant bankers, including the Jagat Seths and Omichand, and agrarian notables (zamindars) in the districts. Determined to consolidate state power, Siraj-ud-daula called for an end to the building of English fortifications in Calcutta, demanded more money from the merchant bankers to finance his armed forces and levied higher taxes on the rural elite. Siraj may have opened up too many fronts at the same time, but there can be little question that all these forces had been undermining the effective exercise of state power by the nawab of Bengal. When the English continued with their fortifications – intended to ward off the French – the nawab led his army down from his capital in Murshidabad to Calcutta and inflicted a decisive defeat on the English company's forces in 1756. The death by suffocation of a number of English prisoners held overnight in a prison cell gave rise to the gory legend of the black hole of Calcutta. More level-headed research in recent decades has suggested that the black hole story was hugely exaggerated and that it was more an accident than a deliberate act of cruelty.

The English resolved to avenge their humiliation in Calcutta and a military force set sail from Madras under the command of Colonel Robert Clive, who had already won his spurs in battles against the French. On his arrival Clive entered into a conspiracy with the merchant bankers, Jagat Seth and Omichand, who in turn intrigued with Siraj's disaffected general, Mir Jaffar. At the battle of Plassey, an expansive mango grove in the district of Murshidabad, the bulk of the nawab's army under Mir Jaffar's command looked the other way while the English defeated the small detachment led by Mohan Lal and Mir Madan which did fight. The name Mir Jaffar in time came to mean 'traitor' and even today remains one of the worst terms of political abuse in modern South Asia. Siraj-ud-daula was killed and Mir Jaffar installed as the puppet nawab. Clive collected Rs 28 million or £3 million sterling as payment for the company's service and as personal presents. Jagat Seth paid half of the amount immediately, while the rest was to be paid off in instalments by the nawab. Mir Jaffar ceded the revenues of the 24-Parganas, south of Calcutta, to the company. Clive had told his superiors that Bengal, an 'inexhaustible fund of riches', would provide all the money needed for the company's trade and army. But in order to do so the company would progressively demand more territories and ever larger shares of Bengal's revenues.

Another Bengal nawab, Mir Kassim, tried in the early 1760s to cut the state's losses by confining the English East India Company's activities to western Bengal and building a base for himself in Bihar. Here he attempted to build a tightly knit administration capable of extracting revenues from the zamindars and keeping the merchant bankers in their place. The Jagat Seths met their nemesis when they were forced to pay up what they owed to the English and then to move, bag and baggage, from their mansion in Murshidabad, to be kept in virtual detention in Monghyr, Bihar. The English viewed the consolidation of Mir Kassim's power as a potential threat to their possessions around Calcutta. In 1764 the battle lines were drawn between the nawabs of Bengal and Awadh and the Mughal emperor on the one side, and the English East India Company on the other. The battle at Buxar saw the company breaking the back of the last organized armed resistance to their control over eastern India. In 1765 the British obtained from the Mughal emperor the diwani, or the right to collect all the revenues from Bengal. It was an apt conclusion to the colonial transition in Bengal, since it was the streamlined flow of revenues from the great zamindars, organized in the days of the Mughal subadar Murshid Quli Khan, which had made Bengal such an attractive proposition for the English in the first place. The availability of land revenue conveniently obviated the need to bring in silver from Europe.

Bengal's revenues were not only used to purchase Bengal's goods, which were sold at a profit in markets abroad, but also to finance the colonial conquest of other parts of India. As was rapidly becoming the norm, the company used their military force only after securing the collaboration of certain Indian intermediate social groups. The company's assumption of political dominion on the Coromandal coast in the south-east and the Malabar coast in the south-west was built on configurations of alliance between English traders and Indian men of commerce and finance. In the river basin of the Krishna and Godavari, north of Madras, a region later known as the northern Circars, the company's officials worked hand in glove with Hindu entrepreneurs in revenue and Gujarati banking houses to prise away territories from the control of the Nizam of Hyderabad. Further south, the company's servants operated in their private capacity as creditors alongside Indian revenue farmers and Hindu businessmen known as *dubash* (literally 'those who speak two languages') to hold the nawab of Arcot in a hopeless debt trap.

At first the company sought to control a state such as Arcot through a mechanism known as a subsidiary alliance, by which, in return for a subsidy or a tribute, the English would 'protect' the nawab from outside threats. The subsidiary alliance system was, however, inherently unstable, since the search for revenues to fund the subsidy alienated the puppet nawabs from key groups in society. The arrangement was also inadequate in warding off the more powerful independent regional states of the late eighteenth century. The Maratha threat to the northern Circars and Mysore's poaching on Arcot's territory led the company to dispense with the façade of subsidiary alliances and to directly take over the administration in these regions by the end of the eighteenth century. Resurgent Mysore challenged the company's intrusions from the 1760s, both on the south-east and the south-west coasts. At one point Haidar Ali's army threatened the gates of Madras. A combination of the company's alliance with Hindu merchants and the imperative to keep Mysore at bay prompted the English take-over of the Malabar region. Further north on the west coast, the collaboration of Hindu and Parsi financiers of cotton production and trade and the need for security from the Maratha threat led to the assumption of political dominion by the English in Gujarat by 1803.

Nineteenth-century historiography had distinguished periods of intervention and non-intervention in the story of British expansion in India. The periods of intervention were often simplistically related to the aggressive personalities of governors and governor-generals like Clive, Wellesley (1798–1805) and Dalhousie (1848–56). There can be little doubt that the pressures on the subsidiary alliance system and military campaigns against the great warrior states of Mysore and the Marathas came to a head during the governor-generalship of Wellesley at the turn of the nineteenth century and that Dalhousie hammered the last nail into the coffin of subsidiary alliances. The work of C.A. Bayly has shown that in the period of the revolutionary and Napoleonic wars in Europe the Wellesley generation was imbued with a new sense of British nationalism. It was a generation that believed in the projection of the power and dignity of the British state overseas and the morality of conquest by the racially superior British. Robert Travers suggests that the shift came earlier, in the late 1780s and 1790s, with Cornwallis, who showed none of the regard for the 'ancient' Mughal constitution displayed by his predecessor Warren Hastings, the first governor-general, in the 1770s. Even though Edmund Burke excoriated Hastings in parliament, the first governor-general had a healthier respect for Indian institutions and culture than those who came after him. There was no real contradiction between the ideology of free trade, as propounded by the critics of the company's monopoly of trade with Asia from the turn of the nineteenth century, and the ideology of nationalistic imperialism, since it was the deployment of state power that could open up vast colonial markets. It is not surprising, therefore, that in the Wellesley era the company state engaged in a squeeze play on its subsidiary allies and adopted a bellicose posture towards India's remaining independent states.

The best example of the erosion of the subsidiary alliance system was Awadh. The nawab of Awadh had agreed in 1765 to pay large annual tributes for the 'protection' given by the company's troops. The pressure to produce this subsidy led the nawab to alienate zamindars, peasants and also his own soldiers who could not be paid on time. It also led him into the debt trap that was usually the fate of subsidiary allies. In Awadh in the north and Arcot in the south, as Bayly has explained, 'the financial demands of the alliance merely served to erode the basis of the state, and ultimately to provide the conditions for British annexation'. Private English creditors of these nawabs had been quite prepared to keep their clients nominally independent and in perpetual debt. Wellesley's government, however, was determined to consolidate the corporate authority of the company state. Despite the divergence between the company and the private financial interests of its servants, the nawab of Awadh was forced to cede all his western territories in 1800. The migration of peasants and weavers from Arcot to Mysore and the military strength of the Mysore sultans produced a confluence of interest between the company and its servants working in their private capacity. The company also swallowed up the state of Arcot in 1800. Among the more important subsidiary allies, only Hyderabad escaped outright annexation, probably because the company did not wish to bear the costs of administering this large and sparsely populated territory. But the terms of the subsidiary alliance were made more stringent in 1798, and powerful British residents wielded enormous influence in alliance with the diwan's faction, consisting of Shia Muslims and north Indian Hindus, in the Nizam's court. In time a saying came to be coined that a whisper in the residency could cause a thunder in the palace.

The state of Mysore and the Maratha confederacy presented the most formidable obstacle to British colonial expansionism in India. Haidar Ali and his son Tipu Sultan constructed a powerful state characterized by efficient revenue management and the elimination of the special privileges of intermediate social groups. Haidar Ali is generally acknowledged to have ruled over a prosperous peasantry and a thriving but not overweening merchant community. Some historians have accused Tipu Sultan of resorting to coercion to extract revenues for the state.

Yet it is clear that Tipu's surplus was drawn more from *poligar* warrior overlords and intermediate revenue farmers than from the working peasantry. He increased taxes on mercantile wealth, but promoted trading facilities with Arabia and Iran. As late as the 1790s Mysore had a growing economy both in the rural and the urban sectors. Mysore was also closing the gap in military technology between Europeans and Indians. In addition to traditional light cavalry and white Deccan cattle, Mysore developed the capability to deploy infantry and artillery with telling effect. Tipu understood the gravity of the threat posed by the company and sent diplomatic missions to the Marathas, the Nizam of Hyderabad and the French. In the early 1780s he was in friendly correspondence with the Maratha leader Mahadaji Sindhia. In the war of 1781 to 1784 Mysore fought the English East India Company's army to a military stalemate. A setback in 1791 resulted in the cession of territories in the peripheries of the state. But it was not until 1799 that the faster-expanding economic resources of the British, who controlled the more productive coastal areas and had the use of fractions of indigenous capital, tilted the balance decisively against a defiant Mysore. Tipu Sultan died fighting gallantly at the gates of his capital, Seringapatam, preferring to live a day like a tiger than a lifetime as a lamb cowering before the British.

The Maratha confederacy did not rule over a state as compact as Mysore, but attempted some of the same methods of taxation and revenue management. Having arisen as a warrior state in western India out of a society marked by low social stratification and relative equality between genders (women flaunted their independence by riding on horseback in military camps), it had been transformed under the leadership of Mahadaji Sindhia in the 1780s into a far-flung empire which had begun to resemble the Mughal hegemony. Although Poona became the ceremonial capital, much in the manner of Delhi, the dissensions and divisions that were so characteristic of the later Mughals also plagued the expanded Maratha polity and society. The Maratha military consolidation, which included the setting up of ordnance factories in northern India, alarmed the British. Rivalries among the constituent units of the confederacy offered opportunities for British intrigue and intervention. Wellesley's armies forced the Marathas to submit to the status of subsidiary allies through the treaty of Vasai (Bassein) in 1802, which triggered a fierce Anglo-Maratha war. In 1803 the English East India Company's capture of Delhi marked the high point in British imperialist expansion. In 1817 the British carried out military campaigns against Pindari horsemen of Afghan and Rajput origin in central India. This made the Marathas suspicious of ultimate British designs and led them to take a desperate stand which ended in their final defeat in 1818.

Among the great eighteenth-century warrior states only the Sikh kingdom of Punjab, established by Ranjit Singh in 1790, still remained outside the British grasp. Punjab and also the neighbouring emirate of Sind were too distant from the British centres of power in the eighteenth century to be viewed as direct threats. Ranjit Singh built up a strong army and an economically powerful government deriving revenues from agriculture and commerce. The Talpur *mirs* of Sind also established state granaries and profited from taxes imposed on Indus valley trade. British concerns with the north-western frontier of their Indian empire eventually brought them into conflict with Sind and the Punjab from the late 1830s. Charles Napier, upon conquering Sind in 1842, proudly reported back in Latin: '*Peccavi*' ('I have sinned'). The Hotchands, who like the Jagat Seths of Bengal nearly a century earlier helped bankroll the British possession of Sind, paid for their sins by rapidly losing out in the area of shipping and seaborne trade, even though they managed to survive as landlords and bureaucrats. Between the taking of Sind and the conquest of Punjab, the British launched a catastrophic expedition to Afghanistan. The company's army lost nearly 16,000 men in the siege of Kabul and following a disastrous retreat from the Afghan capital in January 1842 only one man returned to tell the story of the débâcle.

The British were able to take advantage of splits in Punjabi society and polity following the death of Ranjit Singh in 1839. With the collaboration of some local Sikh magnates in eastern Punjab, the British, after two Anglo-Sikh wars, succeeded in subduing the Sikh state in 1849. One of the courtiers of the Lahore-based kingdom who aided the British was Gulab Singh, the Dogra ruler of Jammu. The British rewarded him through the Treaty of Amritsar of 1846, which handed over the valley of Kashmir 'for ever' to 'Maharaja Gulab Singh and the heirs male of his body' for a good sum of money. Gulab Singh acknowledged 'the supremacy of the British Government' and also agreed to remit annually a token tribute of 'one horse, twelve pairs of shawl goats of approved breed (six male and six female), and three pairs of Kashmir shawls'.

The wars against Punjab, Sind and Afghanistan had, naturally, drained the treasury. Dalhousie sought to recoup some of the costs of these expensive military adventures by annexing the more attractive subsidiary states. Utilizing the doctrine of lapse by which subsidiary states without a natural male heir conveniently fell into the hands of the company, Dalhousie took over Satara in 1848, Jhansi in 1853 and Nagpur in 1854, which brought in some five million pounds in revenue. Finally, it was the lure of another five million pounds that led to the formal annexation of Awadh in 1856. With the annexation of Awadh the roar of the British lion could be heard throughout the length and breadth of the Indian subcontinent. In a small corner of it could be heard the nawab of Awadh's plaintive song lamenting his departure from the magical city of Lucknow.

A close analysis of the transition to colonialism in India reveals the resistance offered by many of the regional successor states of the Mughal empire, as well as the interlocking relations between the English East India Company and indigenous merchant capitalists. But it also brings into focus the pressures exerted by British capital and the company state on Indian polities that, more than anything else, undermined the eighteenth century state system. The company state moved firmly to cut the cord between Indian commerce and political power, which had contributed to the undoing of the indigenous states and had the potential to threaten the colonialists. Once the British achieved state power, Indian intermediary capital was quickly reduced to inferior status in most parts of India, although it was to be allowed some opportunities in other regions of British supremacy in South-East and West Asia and later East and South Africa. Having risen to a position of dominance by riding the wave of a relatively vibrant eighteenth-century economy, the British resorted to a form of conquistador imperialism that contributed in no uncertain way to the economic stagnation of the early nineteenth century.

The following chapter explores the nature of the British colonial state and the colonial economy in the era of company raj.

7

THE FIRST CENTURY OF BRITISH RULE, 1757 TO 1857

State and economy

In the decades following 1757 the English East India Company, which had begun its career with a charter to trade in Asia, established an elaborate state apparatus to govern its Indian territories. An organization originally created to accumulate profits from oceanic trade now drew its basic sustenance from land revenues. The century of company raj in India has been a subject of lively historical debate. Revisionist interpretations of the eighteenth century tended to imply that the disjunction between the pre-colonial and early colonial era was not as great as had been assumed before. The bulk of the most recent research has emphasized the theme of continuity. The early colonial edifice was undoubtedly built on the foundation of existing indigenous arrangements, institutions and identities, which had not lost their vitality during the phase of political decentralization prior to the colonial advance. But it is important not to lose sight of the colonial state as a key actor in bringing about major changes in economy and society. While resilient indigenous entities moulded the colonial impact, fundamental alterations took place in the structures of the state and the character of the political economy. An overemphasis on the processes of adaptation to pre-existing networks and patterns must not obscure the crucial elements of qualitative change.

The essence of the company state as it developed in the late eighteenth century was military despotism. The European core of the company's army was supplemented by increasing numbers of Indian 'sepoys', a corruption of the Urdu word *sipahi* or soldier. After 1757 the company recruited soldiers into its Bengal army from among the upper-caste peasantry of northern India and Bihar. The number of sepoys rose from 25,000 in 1768 to 65,000 in 1814, divided into fifty-four infantry and eight cavalry regiments. By 1814 the jurisdiction of the Bengal army extended all over northern India. It was essentially a mercenary army whose loyalty would be strained if the soldiers were not paid properly and promptly. There were instances of disaffection, if not mutiny, among European officers and Indian ranks in 1764, 1766, 1791, 1795–96 and 1824. But on the whole the Bengal army proved to be an effective fighting force, not only in the subcontinent but also in Ceylon, Java and the Red Sea area in the early nineteenth century. In addition to the Bengal army, the company had a numerically weaker outfit known as the Madras army, drawn from Eurasians, Telugu warrior clans and Muslims who had been unable to find employment in the Mysore army, and also a detachment known as the Bombay marine. The total strength of the company's armed forces increased dramatically during the revolutionary and Napoleonic wars, from 115,000 in 1790 to 155,000 in 1805. This made it one of the largest European-style standing armies in the world. A standing army of this sort was a novelty in the history of institutions of state in India.

Alongside a mercenary standing army the company state fashioned a hitherto unknown centralized civilian bureaucracy between the 1760s and the 1780s. The court of directors in London exercised formal authority over the company's Indian affairs. Lord North's Regulating Act of 1773 and Pitt's India Act of 1784 attempted to bring the company's administration under the supervision of parliament through a board of control. Ideologues in parliament, such as Edmund Burke, could generate a good deal of controversy about the despotic and corrupt practices of the company's servants. The most dramatic manifestation of this was the impeachment of Warren Hastings, the first governor-general of the company, in the 1770s. But, India being six months' sailing distance away from the metropolis, the governor-general and his bureaucrats generally had substantial practical autonomy in the day-to-day running of the administration. After 1773 the governor-general and his council ruled with the assistance of a cadre of about 400 covenanted civil servants. The colonial bureaucracy became more racially exclusive and distant from lower levels of Indian clerks during the era of nationalistic imperialism represented by Wellesley at the turn of the nineteenth century. As Peter Marshall has noted, 'Indian agency at lower levels was still essential for the running of the government', but 'the ethos of the higher ranks of the service had become firmly British'. A clear chain of command descended from the governor-general based in Calcutta to the governors of the Bombay and Madras presidencies, and down to the administrators overseeing the collection of taxes and dispensation of justice in the districts. While a few naïve British district magistrates and collectors may well have been unsuspecting victims of crafty Indian manipulators, it is preposterous to suggest, as one or two historians have done, that the company's empire was more Indian than British. The structure and the logic of the bureaucracy assured the dominance of the higher-level British administrators.

Outside the directly administered territories the company entered into a series of treaty arrangements with a range of Indian rulers, big and small, who acknowledged British overlordship in return for a measure of autonomy in their respective domains. A system of British paramountcy was gradually elaborated from the second decade of the nineteenth century that brought nominally independent Indian rulers under tighter control. The subservience of these rulers was underlined by the restrictions on their defence and foreign policies and the refusal to allow them to enter into bilateral relations with one another. The British residents in these states – which came to be known as the Indian princely states in contradistinction to what eventually became the directly administered provinces of British India – managed to gain considerable leverage in the field of internal administration as well by influencing the diwans or finance ministers, who were generally under their thumb. The colonial construct of indirect rule was an ingenious device that complemented and did not contradict the efficacy of direct British colonial rule in other parts of the subcontinent. Power may have been exercised through indirect means, but it was not in any more than a formal sense limited in its potential to stamp out resistance.

The military and bureaucratic institutions of the company state in the directly ruled areas were designed to bolster selective but deep administrative interventions in Indian economy and society. The early colonial state's chief concern was the security and stability of land revenue – the principal source of its income. A variety of mechanisms were created in different parts of India to achieve this end. The earliest and most controversial arrangement was the permanent settlement of 1793, by which a private property right in revenue collection was assigned to the zamindars of Bengal. The revenue demand from these zamindars was settled in perpetuity; they were expected to collect rent from the *raiyats* and remit a part of it as revenue to the state. Cornwallis, the author of the permanent settlement with the zamindars, also hoped that they would become improving landlords modelled after the estate-holders of England. But the disjunction between property and production meant that these hopes were misplaced. The zamindars held some land as part of their personal demesne, but did not have actual possessory dominion over lands occupied and cultivated by various strata and categories of raiyats. Consequently, it was not always easy for the zamindars to collect rent and remit the assigned revenue to the colonial state. The revenue demand was, in any case, initially pitched very high. Many zamindars defaulted and their property rights were sold to other zamindars, their employees, service people and commercial groups in towns. In the early nineteenth century the colonial state armed the zamindars with formidable powers of extra-economic coercion, including physical distraint and eviction, to enable them to extract rent from the peasantry and regularly remit revenue to the government.

In parts of Madras presidency which were taken from Mysore, agrarian notables and little kings had already been squeezed out by Tipu Sultan's policies. This facilitated a revenue settlement between the colonial state and the raiyats, even though many of them were not actual tillers of the soil. Eventually about two-thirds of Madras presidency had a *ryotwari* arrangement, and the remaining one-third a settlement with large landlords or zamindars. Besides choosing varying strata or segments of rural society to invest with the property right in revenue collection, the colonial state desisted in later settlements from signing away its right to periodically enhance the revenue demand. This was usually done in the temporarily settled areas at thirty-year intervals. The entire period from the late eighteenth to the mid-nineteenth century was characterized by a revenue and rent offensive by the colonial state and its zamindari intermediaries.

Yet the broader economic context of the company state's operations changed about half way through the first century of colonial rule. The period from 1757 to the 1810s was one of straightforward plunder of India's revenues. These were 'invested' in the purchase of Indian manufactured products, especially textiles, for sale in world markets. In 1765 the grant of the diwani had given the company Bengal's revenues amounting to about £3 million. By the time the Marathas were finally defeated in 1818 the company's Indian revenues had soared to £22 million. But already from the turn of the century the company's monopoly in Asian trade had come under a barrage of criticism from the newly emergent industrial capitalist class in Britain, which espoused the doctrine of free trade in order to sell their products in eastern markets. During the 1810s India's artisanal economy lost its ability to compete with cheaply manufactured British textiles and to sell its products on world markets. The Charter Act of 1813 ended the East India Company's monopoly of trade with India. The sales of British cotton twist and yarn in India increased tenfold during the two decades following 1813, but the increase was not all that dramatic compared to the giant strides taken by British textiles in other markets. India, the homeland of cotton, was inundated with British cotton only from the 1850s onwards.

China tea had now replaced Indian textiles as the most profitable item of the company's trade. Without control over Indian territories the company would not have been able to survive for half a century after the loss of its Indian trading monopoly. The company met its requirement of remittances to the metropolis through the forced cultivation of indigo and financed the China tea trade by establishing a government monopoly over opium cultivation in India. Massive illegal sales of Indian opium in China made it unnecessary for the company to bring in silver to finance their purchase of tea. The opium monopoly provided about 15 per cent of the income of the company state, and accounted for nearly 30 per cent of the value of India's foreign trade until the mid-1850s.

The colonial state's role in consolidating indigo production for export was equally significant, though not as direct as in the case of opium. The indigo planters were predominantly private European entrepreneurs who initially received some advances from the government until 1802, but who later financed indigo production and trade with capital borrowed from trading and financial institutions known as agency houses. The early nineteenth century was a blue phase in dressing for European war and fashion. Demand was strong and about half a dozen giant European houses dominated the production and trade in indigo. Apart from outright coercion, the only reason why small peasants cultivated indigo prior to 1830 was the money advance that came with it. The indigo economy was acutely vulnerable to fluctuations in the capitalist world economy. The economic depression in Britain from the late 1820s was transmitted to India, and led to the collapse of all the leading agency houses between 1830 and 1833. There is no question that between 1830 and 1860 indigo cultivation by peasants was totally unremunerative, and the planters, like the zamindars, had to be assisted by the state with various coercive powers. Finances for indigo production and trade again became available between 1835 and 1840, but were adversely affected by the economic downturn in London markets in the 1840s and crashed during the depression of 1847–48. With the rising demand and prices for rice and jute from the mid-1850s, peasants came to resent the imposition of indigo as never before. The indigo system was overthrown in Bengal by the so-called 'Blue Mutiny' of 1859–60, but a less favourable configuration of class forces ensured its continued stranglehold over neighbouring Bihar until 1917.

An analysis of the structure and capacity of the early colonial state, particularly the ways in which it marshalled military force and extracted resources from peasants and weavers, suggests that it was qualitatively different from the pre-colonial states it had subdued. Having appropriated all that was vital and buoyant in India's pre-colonial economy, the company state did little to contribute to either economic growth or equity in the early nineteenth century. The weavers were squeezed by bringing production more directly under state control, even before they felt the full brunt of the impact of the industrial revolution in Britain. However, India's artisans proved resilient enough not to be wholly eliminated. The peasants found their earlier mobility restricted and were emaciated as a direct consequence of the state's revenue and rent policy. In southern India, where rights to resources had been expressed as shares in community institutions such as temples, the colonial state replaced this form of risk sharing by capital with the risks of the marketplace – which were now put squarely on the shoulders of the work force that produced. In other words, whereas earlier there were some restraints on the exploitation of labour by wealthier social groups such as landlords and merchants, the company's obsession with the doctrine of private property, together with more direct state control over production and distribution, removed the safeguards that had shielded the peasants and weavers. And in northern India, where proto-proprietary forms had a prior existence, smallholding peasant families and artisans came under relentless pressure from the newly empowered class of property owners, aided by the state's legal enactments. Intermediary capitalists may have prospered to begin with, so long as company state power was not firmly established. But the short-sightedness of these intermediate social groups, which had extended a helping hand to the company, became clear when they were in many instances reduced to the status of usurers (except in some pockets on the west coast, like Bombay, and other British colonies outside the subcontinent). As C.A. Bayly acknowledges in his major work *Rulers, Townsmen and Bazaars*, 'earlier despotisms were tempered by a political culture which insisted that rulers should offer service and great expenditures in return for high revenue demand' but 'the British acknowledged few such restraints'. The crisis of legitimacy of the early colonial state was, therefore, 'a moral as much as an economic one'.

It was to mask their essentially amoral political behaviour that the British retained some of the ceremonial trappings of pre-colonial state ideology. Even the racially arrogant Wellesley directed the company's servants to treat the person of the puppet Mughal emperor with reverence and respect, and struck coins bearing the emperor's profile. Persian was retained as the official language of government until 1835. This ensured a continued livelihood for the Muslim and Hindu service gentry, certainly in northern India. While steadily introducing English judicial procedures in the domains of civil and criminal law, substantive aspects of the Mughal legal system were retained. The company's officials not only consulted Mughal law officers – qazis, muftis and *pandits* – but also upheld their decisions as long as these conformed to the dictum of justice, equity and good conscience. A pragmatic policy for a newly colonizing power, it explicitly aimed at minimizing the threat of social reaction.

In keeping with this policy, special care was taken not to offend the sensibilities of colonial subjects by overtly tampering with Muslim and Hindu personal law. Here again the period of Bentinck in the 1820s and 1830s was something of an exception. The abolition of *sati* – the immolation of Hindu widows on the funeral pyres of their husbands – in 1829 was, on the face of it, a departure from the policy of non-interference in the religious practices of Indians. Yet, since the colonial state could establish a semblance of cultural legitimacy only by appropriating symbols and meanings that commanded authority in indigenous society, the distinction between public and private law was never an easy one to maintain. To galvanize Hindu commercial and clerical support in the south, the company state sponsored a somewhat spurious neo-Brahmanical ruling ideology based on the rigid *varna*-defined caste system. Similarly, the company's orientalist scholars gave far greater importance to doctrinal Islam or the sharia as propagated by the ulema than to the eclectic religion shot through with local customary practices which was followed by the vast majority of Indian Muslims.

But even cultural bribery had its limitations in winning legitimacy for the early colonial state. The influential south Indian mystical singer and poet Tyagaraja by and large ignored the company and its Indian clients. He sang:

> They chatter and blabber
>> pretending they're topnotch experts
>>> in melody and cadence, but
> They don't have a clue in their brains
>> about the distinctions
>>> of *raga* notes and *murchhana* trills.

Figure 11 The Church of England in India. St Mary's Church, Madras, the oldest
seventeenth-century British building in India (Courtesy Sugata Bose)

And the leader of the Chishti sufi shrine in Delhi simply turned his back on
Charles Metcalfe, the chief commissioner of the city, deriding him as 'an infidel
stinking of alcohol'.

During the last decade of company raj tentative attempts were made to
reform the state and soften the harsher edges of the political economy. But
nothing could bring about the company's moral regeneration. In the newly
conquered territories of Punjab and Sind relatively low revenue rates were

introduced and public investments were made in agriculture. Revenue rates were also sought to be moderated during revisional settlements in Bombay, Gujarat and parts of Madras. Even in Bengal, officials of the company toyed with the idea of introducing legislation providing raiyats with security of tenure and moderation of rent, even though the Rent Act was not actually passed until 1859. With the beginnings of European capital investments in railways from 1854, a gentle upward trend in prices and wages began. This was the prologue to the period of classical colonialism of the late nineteenth century, characterized by Indian exports of agricultural raw materials and imports of British manufactured products. Yet even a modernizing governor-general like Dalhousie, who introduced railways, telegraphs and a postal system, and rationalized the revenue administration, could not resist the temptation of looting the revenues of states that had hitherto been quasi-independent. This was adding insult to the already grievous injury inflicted on the Mughal successor state system. Reforms in the domain of political economy were too inadequate and uneven, particularly in the north Indian heartland, to stem the gathering tide of resentment against colonial rule. Detachments of the Bengal army were being dispatched to fight for Britain in China and South-East Asia in the 1840s and 1850s, even as tension and disaffection intensified in their home villages in northern India. Sporadic zamindari, peasant and tribal insurrection in different parts of India had dotted the entire history of colonial expansion and consolidation. These movements of resistance and their merging with a military mutiny in 1857, which brought the company raj to an end, will command our attention in the next chapters.

8

COMPANY RAJ AND INDIAN SOCIETY, 1757 TO 1857

Re-invention and reform of tradition

Indian society's negotiation of Western influences and pressures under company raj is a matter of wide disagreement between nineteenth-century writers and contemporary scholars, and also among modern historians of the subcontinent. The old model of studying European impact and Indian response is gradually being replaced by approaches more attentive to Indian initiative and agency. The nineteenth-century expectation that powerful forces of westernization would remould Indian social institutions and thought permeated earlier historical writing on the subject. From the early nineteenth century in particular, three potent forces of change were thought to have been unleashed on Indian society. First, the heady doctrine of free trade was supposed to jerk Indian society and economy out of their insularity and immobility. Second, the ideology of utilitarianism through the enactment of good laws was expected to do away with backward, if not evil, Indian social customs. Third, the impulse of evangelism was to have struck a powerful blow to established Indian religions, Hinduism and Islam alike, and Christianized and uplifted hapless colonial subjects.

Revisionist historians have recently pointed out that these expectations not only remained largely unfulfilled and misplaced, but also dramatic social changes such as these may never have been attempted in the first place. In other words, there was a gulf between ideological currents in the West and colonial social policy in India during the first half of the nineteenth century. The brief governor-generalship of the utilitarian Bentinck between 1828 and 1835 may have been the only exception to this trend. On the revisionist view, far from westernizing or modernizing India, the British in the nineteenth century invented and consolidated the traditional India of peasant and Brahman. Uncomfortable with, and threatened by, the mobility of eighteenth-century rural society, Pax Britannica and the British revenue-collecting machine sought to sedentarize and peasantize Indian society. The settled Indian village community was largely fashioned under colonialism during the nineteenth century in an attempt to tie it more closely to the wider world economy. As part of their search for social stability, the British gave substance to caste hierarchy and rigidity, dominated by the Brahmans, which had been available in theory but had been often ignored in social practice in the immediate pre-colonial era. Similarly, by injecting English procedural practices such as precedence into their rulings based on the sharia, the company's judicial officials transformed what Muslim law officers generally treated as a flexible set of moral injunctions into a strictly laid down legal code.

The debate between the old and the new historiographies is generally portrayed as one between the votaries of arguments emphasizing change or continuity under colonial rule. It would be more accurate to say that the disagreements are really about the *kind* of social change under the aegis of company raj in the nineteenth century. If indeed the Indian caste system, as we know it today, was largely a nineteenth-century colonial invention, then it must be regarded as one of the more important changes brought about by colonial social engineering. But there is already a sense of unease about the possible excesses of the revisionist school. One line of qualification suggests that, in consolidating the Indian peasantry and the status of the Brahman, the colonial state was re-inventing rather than inventing tradition and speeding up processes already in motion since the eighteenth century. Yet even the argument about the minimal impact of Western ideas and institutions, as well as the Christianizing mission, is probably overdrawn. A regime presiding over qualitative changes in state and economy was not entirely non-interventionist when it came to importing social and religious initiatives from abroad. A finely tuned historical perspective is needed to account for the multiple and occasionally contradictory social currents and cross currents and take a balanced view of the nature and direction of social change.

The injection of an element of periodization is essential in order to be clear about temporal trends. The late eighteenth century must, in important ways, be distinguished from the nineteenth. The early phase may have been a period of military aggression and economic plunder but it was not one of heavy-handed social intervention by conquerors imbued with a sense of racial superiority. Early British orientalist scholarship, of the sort being carried out, for instance, by the Royal Asiatic Society under William Jones, did not regard Indian culture and civilization to be inferior. There was, however, a bias towards studying the more exclusivist high traditions of both Hinduism and Islam rather than the more flexible and pervasive religious and cultural practices of the majority of the people. This may have been partly dictated by the need to formulate a neo-Brahmanical and, to a lesser extent, a pseudo-Mughal ruling ideology for the colonial state. But the bookish nature of early orientalist learning also made certain that the influence of Brahmans and ulema would be much greater on the colonial mind than uncodified cultural traditions.

The waves of free trade, utilitarianism and evangelism reached the shores of India only in the early nineteenth century. Of these three currents evangelical Christianity was the least successful, even if it was perceived as a potent threat. The 1813 Charter Act, which ended the company's monopoly of trade in India, also provided freer access to Christian missionaries. One Scottish preacher, Alexander Duff, arrived in 1820 with high hopes of converting the entire city of Calcutta to Christianity. He was sorely disappointed. Yet even a Thomas Babington Macaulay was not averse to the spread of Christianity as a secondary end of government, so long as it did not undermine the primary end of maintaining order. The utilitarian stream was a more direct product of the Western confidence in the superiority of the forces of science and reason. Colonial legal initiatives inspired by utilitarianism had a deeper social impact than is acknowledged by revisionist historiography. Changes in the prevailing system of civil and criminal law, intended to bolster the administration of public justice, could hardly fail to have far-reaching affects. Non-interference in personal law also proved to be more of a convenience than a moral stance on the part of conquerors anxious to avoid imposing their norms on a subject people. The efficacy of colonial social legislation, in any case, depended on the nature of the interaction with various strands of Indian reform and reaction. The economic changes being shaped by the tussle between free traders and monopolists also had important knock-on effects on Indian society. This is not to argue a case of economic determinism, but to note the complex inter-connectedness of developments in economy and society.

It is useful, for the convenience of exposition, to distinguish between social change in the rural interior and the urban centres. During the first half of the nineteenth century the physical environment of India's rural areas experienced devastating alteration. Pre-colonial states had been less interested in extracting resources from forest and pastoral land than from agriculture, nor did they demarcate a clear conceptual frontier between the two domains. Company raj redefined Indian forests as separate from the agricultural plains before launching a major onslaught on forests and forest peoples. Large-scale deforestation not only produced climatic change but also led to the disruption of tribal lands and the rude intrusion of money into tribal economies. With the assistance of Indian moneylenders and traders the company subdued India's newly redefined, internal tribal frontiers. For instance, the Bhils of western India were 'pacified' during military expeditions in the 1820s. The attack on forests was accompanied by an invasion of the nomadic and pastoral economy. In northern and central India groups engaged in cattle raising and horse breeding, such as Gujars, Bhattis, Rangar Rajputs and Mewatis, were subjected to the stern discipline and immobility of agricultural commodity production.

The biggest villains in the colonial demonology of wandering groups were the so-called 'Thugs' of central India, who were brought to heel by a British military officer, William Sleeman, at great cost. 'Thuggee', it is now emerging from historical research, was a colonial stereotype which afforded great scope for self-congratulation on the part of those claiming to have established Pax Britannica by crushing a supposedly organized cult of Kali-worshipping highway robbers who were alleged to have taken a million lives in the early

Figure 12 Colonial Conquest. A tiger hunt by colonial officials mounted on elephants (Source: print from drawing by William Daniell in the private collection of Sugata Bose and Ayesha Jalal)

decades of the nineteenth century. It is a story that is increasingly being viewed with searing scepticism in history books, but has now found its rightful place in Hollywood films such as *Indiana Jones*. The subjugation of tribes and nomads generally paved the way for the consolidation of commodity production in agriculture, where the settled peasant family was the most common work unit. But there were some enclaves, especially in the hills, where the British established plantations – for example, the coffee plantations in the Nilgiris in south India and the tea plantations in Darjeeling and Assam in the 1830s.

The settling of the countryside was sought to be buttressed by lending support to principles of hierarchy and ritual distinction. British scholars and officials, aided by Brahmanical interpretations of Indian society, set about the task of rank ordering Indian social groups in various localities. One of the better-known products of this enterprise is James Tod's *Annals and Antiquities of Rajasthan*, compiled between 1829 and 1832. From about 1830 onwards the empire's information apparatus began to privilege large-scale statistical enquiries over the embodied knowledge of earlier decades supplied by Indian informants. The quantitative leap in information gathering entailed a significant qualitative loss in colonial attempts to know the country. It is probable that Indian social practice was more hierarchically defined in the first half of the nineteenth century in response to colonial initiatives than it had been during the eighteenth century. However, some popular devotional cults continued to retain their vitality. Social movements, such as that of the Satya Narayanis of Gujarat, coexisted and competed with priestly hierarchies and even developed a coherent ideological rejection of Brahmanism. Reform movements within Islam, as well, called for a purification of the faith in order to effectively survive the colonial impact, but stopped short of overwhelming popular social practices in much of the countryside.

If colonial social engineering was largely limited to providing selective support to aspects of Indian tradition in the countryside, it allowed more scope for rationalism to have an impact and provoke a response in the urban centres. The ideological currents of science and reason reached the city of Calcutta at least a decade or so before the arrival of the socially interventionary governor-general Bentinck. It was largely at Indian initiative that the Hindu College, the first English-language higher educational institution, was established in 1818.

Figure 13 The First Steps of Western Education. The main staircase of Presidency College, formerly Hindu College, Calcutta (Courtesy Sugata Bose)

At least three strands are identifiable in Calcutta society's response to Western education and culture. The Young Bengal group, based in Hindu College and led by a dynamic teacher, Henry Derozio, was most enthusiastic about the new ideas from the West. They flaunted their Westernization even in their dress and eating habits and derided 'irrational' Indian social customs. The Dharma Sabha orchestrated the conservative reaction against the Young Bengal group. This society even petitioned against Bentinck's abolition of sati. Its leaders did not defend sati as such but stoutly opposed colonial legal interference in Indian social customs. Interestingly, the most prominent spokesman of the Dharma Sabha, Radha Kanta Deb, supported Western education and was a patron of Hindu College. The most creative strand, however, was led by Rammohun Roy, who attempted to adapt elements from all that he considered best in Indian and Western learning. Well-versed in Sanskrit, Bengali, Arabic, Persian and English, Rammohun Roy aimed at a regeneration of Indian society and culture through a process of thoroughgoing reform that would weed out the evils and anachronisms. He set up a society called the Brahmo Samaj, which rejected caste and idolatry and sought a return to the original monotheistic purity of the *Upanishad*s. He derided the evangelists but generally supported the utilitarians. His campaign against sati after 1818 and defence of Bentinck's 1829 abolition of sati, which he called a 'barbarous and inhuman practice', helped ensure that the measure was not overturned by the privy council, the ultimate court of appeal in London.

Ironically enough, Rammohun's spirited attacks against sati relied less on rational arguments than on his interpretations of the same scriptural sources, especially the Vedas, on which the conservative opposition also rested its case. In his earlier writings on the subject, Rammohun had argued that the ritual was more often than not a ploy by male family members to circumvent the provision allowing widows to inherit the property of their deceased husbands. His subsequent celebration of ascetic widowhood instead of sati was to seriously embarrass latter-day social reformers angling for legislation permitting widow remarriage. Despite his enlightened views on women, Rammohun at the time saw better sense in facilitating the colonial state's centralizing project of controlling the lives of its subjects by imposing restrictions on their right to suicide in the name of protecting Hindu 'tradition' from offensive customary practices like sati.

Bentinck's administration also borrowed heavily from Rammohun Roy's proposals to use public funds to promote Western education. Rammohun had written to Bentinck's predecessor, Amherst, in 1823:

> Neither can much improvement arise from such speculations as the following, which are the themes suggested by the Vedant: In what manner is the soul absorbed in the Deity? ... Nor will youths be fitted to be better members of society by the Vedantic doctrines which teach them to believe that all visible things have no real existence ... Again,

no essential benefit can be derived by the student of the Mimamsa from knowing what it is that makes the killer of a goat sinless by pronouncing certain passages of the Veds and what is the real nature and operative influence of passages of the Ved, etc.

He called upon the British nation, which had abandoned the system of schoolmen and embraced Baconian philosophy, to promote in India 'a more liberal and enlightened system of instruction, embracing mathematics, natural philosophy, chemistry and anatomy, with other useful sciences'. The 1820s and 1830s have been often referred to as the period of the Bengal renaissance, albeit hampered by colonial constraints, which saw major achievements in the fields of literature, the arts as well as social and religious reform. Social stirrings similar to those in Calcutta but not yet of the same intensity were also discernible in Bombay and Madras. Later in the century key intellectual figures such as Mahadev Govind Ranade in western India, Veereselingam in the south and Sayyid Ahmed Khan in the north played a similar role in the fields of education and social reform to that pioneered by Rammohun Roy in Bengal.

The promotion of Western education through the medium of the English language by Indian urban elites and British colonial officials stemmed from very different motives. For educated Indians it was seen as part of a process of self-strengthening and became almost proto-nationalist in character. Thomas Babington Macaulay, law member in Bentinck's council, made the colonial attitude explicit in his famous minute on education in 1835. All learning in Indian languages, according to Macaulay (who did not read or understand any), was useless. The aim of Western education was to 'form a class who may be interpreters between us and the millions whom we govern; a class of persons Indian in blood and colour but English in taste, in opinions, in morals and in intellect'. Urged on by Macaulay, Bentinck replaced Persian with English as the official language of the government and the higher courts in 1835. Later generations of English-educated Indians would refuse to allow the educational institutions to simply be a production line for Indian clerks. In any event, Bengali and Urdu continued to be important at the lower levels of the administrative and judicial structures in eastern and northern India. It was in Punjab that British officials, wary of adapting to yet another regional language, imported English and Urdu as languages of government. Despite colonial neglect and hostility, Punjabi continued to flourish in the informal social arenas of that province.

The immediate response to the change in official language by Hindu literate castes was to switch from Persian to English in order to find continued service in government. Although a few Muslims educated at the Delhi College and the Calcutta Madrasa also took to English and entered the colonial service, the vast majority of Muslims remained aloof from the new Western educational institutions. Smarting from the loss of sovereignty and state power, Muslims, especially in urban centres, resented the imposition of English and responded

Figure 14 Colonial Calcutta. Sculpture in front of the Marble Palace, a nineteenth-century Calcutta mansion (Courtesy Ayesha Jalal)

with much greater enthusiasm to reformist movements seeking an internal regeneration of Islam. Some of the more important Muslim reformist movements of the eighteenth century gathered further momentum and a more activist profile in the early decades of the nineteenth. These were directed by the Naqshbandiya Sufi order in Delhi, followers of Shah Waliullah, his son Shah Abdul Aziz and his disciple Sayyid Ahmed of Rai Bareilly; the Faranghi Mahal seminary in Lucknow; and the Chishti Sufi order in Punjab. The Naqshbandiya order had some links with the Wahabis of the Arabian peninsula and was quite influential among Muslim artisans in the major towns of northern India. Sayyid Ahmed of Rai Bareilly returned from *haj* and fought a jihad in Punjab and the north-west frontier region between 1826 and 1831. The Chishti order in Punjab was able to penetrate the countryside by making necessary compromises with the mediational and saintly forms of regionally variegated Islam. Movements to purify Islam were hardly ever frontal assaults on popular religion, which stressed the importance of saints, vernacular languages and time-honoured rituals. The Faraizi movement of Haji Shariatullah and his son Dudu Mian in Bengal called for a return to the Quran but did no more than replace the pir-murid (saint-follower) model, which smacked of servitude, with an ustad-shagird (teacher-student) relationship. The spectre of Wahabi conspiracies haunting the colonial mind was largely a function of British insecurity.

Though by no means reconciled to colonial rule, Muslim reformist movements laid more emphasis on internal strengthening for the effective reassertion of Islamic power.

Yet social resistance was a key feature throughout the first century of colonial rule. The company's attempt to draw revenues and commodities from settled agriculture was resisted by zamindars and peasants alike. The project to colonize the forests provoked elemental uprisings by tribal peoples. And the intrusion of the free-trader industrialists caused unease and unrest among artisans in the towns. For long, historians treated the early revolts against colonial rule as irrational and pre-political. The primary and early secondary sources were loaded in their characterization of insurgency as deviant, if not criminal, behaviour. In the prose of counter-insurgency, as Ranajit Guha has shown, peasants were equated with insurgents, Muslims with fanatics, and entire social groups were branded criminal tribes. Generations of historians relying heavily on colonial official sources tended to ignore rebel consciousness, even if they lauded rebel heroism. More recently a concerted attempt is being made to restore to peasants, tribals and artisans their subjecthood in the making of their own history. Resistance carried too many risks to be resorted to in a fit of absent-mindedness and was carefully planned and executed only after all alternatives had been exhausted. Underlying the violent outbreaks of major revolts there was also a more continuous process of everyday resistance to oppression and injustice.

It would be a mistake to concentrate exclusively on either the landed magnates or the subaltern classes in any study of resistance in the first half of the nineteenth century. Rural magnates opposed not only the higher land revenue demand of the colonial state, but also the erosion of their kingly authority. In south India, the poligars (warrior lords), believed that they were the inheritors of the shares of sovereignty of the erstwhile Vijayanagara rulers and put up ferocious resistance against the company during the Sivaganga revolt at the turn of the nineteenth century. Zamindari revolts flared up in other regions and at various times, but were most widespread during the economic downturn of the 1830s. Peasants resisted the demands both of the colonial state and its zamindari intermediaries. Some of the movements of peasant resistance articulated a religious ideology. The Faraizis of east Bengal, led by Dudu Mian, refused to pay rent and revenue, acknowledging only Allah's sovereignty over land. They also attacked Hindu traders and moneylenders and burnt down the houses and factories of the notorious indigo planters during the 1830s and 1840s. The Mapilla rebellions on the Malabar coast in 1802, the late 1830s and 1849 to 1852 similarly combined religious reform of their society and social protest against Hindu landlords and British officials. Most of the resistance movements in agrarian society before 1860 were communitarian struggles, which must not be confused with the 'communalism' of the twentieth century. The first major exception to the communitarian character of resistance was the indigo revolt in Bengal in the late 1850s, which displayed a strong class dimension, not only in composition but also in ideology.

Some of the most stubborn resistance to company raj came from the tribal peoples. An overemphasis in some of the historical literature on the paternalistic colonial discourse about tribes runs the risk of glossing over the political practice of repression and resistance. The Bhils in western India fought against the company's army in the 1820s and the Kols rose up in rebellion in Bihar between 1829 and 1833. The most famous instance of tribal revolt was the famous Santhal *hool* or uprising of 1855–56 on the Bengal–Bihar border. The Santhals, led by Sido and Kanhu, violently resisted the incursion of the *diku* (foreigners), among whom they included both the British who were tearing down their forests and the Indian moneylenders who were grabbing their best lands. The tribal uprisings were severely repressed. But in their aftermath legislation was passed restricting the alienation of tribal lands to non-tribals.

Urban resistance centred on dispossessed artisanal groups. Weavers rioted in north Indian towns in the 1810s and the 1830s. Occasionally the protest of Muslim artisans would target centres of Hindu wealth and prestige, especially of the merchant groups. But more often the uprisings took the form of grain riots, as in Delhi and north Indian towns between 1833 and 1838, and in Madras in 1806, 1833 and 1854. The newly introduced colonial systems of civil and criminal law had little legitimacy among urban groups who often called for the restitution of the Mughal law officers such as the *kotwals*, qazis and muftis.

So Indian society was astir throughout the period of colonial consolidation under the company state. Resistance was widespread, affecting all regions of the subcontinent and a variety of social groups, including rural magnates, peasants, tribals and urban artisans. The logic of the company state and political economy was quite as important as overt colonial social policy in creating turmoil among the subject peoples. What the movements of resistance lacked were, first, supra-local organization and second, convergence in time even though the 1830s must be regarded as a decade of more than usual unrest. The great civilian uprisings that accompanied the military mutiny of 1857 aimed at supplying these missing ingredients. Vastly expanded in scale and focused in time, the 1857 mutiny–revolt would turn out to be a watershed in India's colonial history.

9

1857

Rebellion, collaboration and the transition to crown raj

However one interprets the events of the fateful year of 1857, it is a date to conjure with in modern South Asian history. The year witnessed a serious military mutiny and very large-scale civilian uprisings which, for a fleeting moment, threatened to bring British rule to an end exactly one hundred years after the first colonial conquest in Bengal. Colonial officials-turned-historians usually referred to the uprising of 1857 as the sepoy mutiny. Early twentieth-century nationalist commentators proudly described it as the first war of Indian independence. There is no agreement among historians whether the revolt was a forward-looking freedom movement or a backward-looking restorationist struggle, a feudal reaction led by landed magnates or a peasant rebellion of the wretched of the earth; a 'secular' movement cutting across communitarian affiliations or a religiously inspired jihad; an anti-colonial revolt or a civil war pitting resisters against collaborators. There was probably a bit of all of these in the complex events of 1857, which has made its historiography somewhat confusing and confused. Yet this watershed year has also been the subject of some fine scholarship. Our aim is to assess the importance of the various strands and identify some points of emphasis.

Neither military mutiny nor civil revolt was uncommon in early colonial India. But in the past they had been rather disparate and uncoordinated. What gave the 1857 revolt its unique character was the convergence of multiple strands of resistance, the expansion of scale and a new level of intensity. The company's army was mercenary in nature and its different branches had shown signs of disaffection at various points in the first half of the nineteenth century. The Madras army had mutinied in Vellore in 1806 and the Bengal army in Java in 1815, Gwalior in 1834, Afghanistan during 1839 to 1842 and Burma in 1824 and 1852. During the 1850s the British carelessly added a number of new provocations. The refusal of units to fight in Burma led to the passage of the General Service Enlistment Act of 1856, which required recruits to undertake to serve abroad or, as the soldiers saw it, across the *kala pani* (dark waters). The Afghan débâcle had also led the British to widen the circle of caste and regional groups from which they recruited into the Bengal army. The Rajputs and Bhumihar Brahmans of Benares and Awadh, who had so far formed the

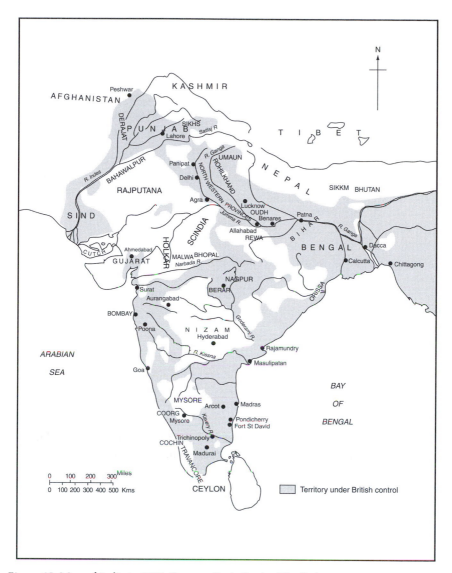

Figure 15 Map of India in 1857 (Source: C. A. Bayly, *The Raj*)

backbone of the Bengal army, thoroughly disliked the new recruitment policy. After the conquest of Punjab and Sind these soldiers lost their *bhatta* (pay bonuses) for service 'abroad', and with the annexation of Awadh in 1856 they lost prestige. At the same time their families were being subjected to a high land revenue demand.

The sepoys in the company's army were already suffering from a deep sense of social and economic unease when the greased cartridges for the new

Lee Enfield rifle supplied the fuel to spark the revolt. The cartridges were rumoured to have been smeared with cow and pig fat, repugnant to Hindus and Muslims alike, and this was widely seen as an insidious plot by the infidels to pollute Indians before forcing their conversion to Christianity. As soldiers refused to load the new rifle in the early summer of 1857, they were sentenced to imprisonment and sent off to jail in fetters. It was the sight of their compatriots humiliated in this fashion that led the XI Native Cavalry, based in Meerut, to mutiny on the night of 10–11 May 1857. The mutineers then marched to Delhi, where the reluctant and aging Mughal emperor, Bahadur Shah Zafar, was installed as the symbolic head of the revolt. Discontented landed magnates and peasants in the environs of Delhi lent support to the mutinous soldiers, as did artisans, labourers and rebellious policemen in the city of Delhi. The revolt spread to the north and the west of Delhi, enveloping garrison towns as well as the countryside. During June and July of 1857 the British military forces in the east were cut off from those located in the Punjab. Yet the rebels' concentration on Delhi, while providing a great boost to morale, proved to be a grave tactical error. Not only were they not quick enough to attack British forces coming from the Punjab, but also they failed to consolidate their grip over a liberated zone in which to establish their own legitimate administration.

The second, almost autonomous, focus of revolt lay to the east, in Awadh. Political and economic resentments ran deep in this region, only lately annexed by the British. The revolt here soon acquired a broad popular base in both rural and urban areas. *Taluqdars*, peasants and artisans joined the revolt in large numbers, bringing about the collapse of the newly installed British administration, and imprisoning a British garrison in the same residency in Lucknow from where the British had manipulated the downfall of the nawab. There was panic in the British camp that their rule would come to a catastrophic end on the hundredth anniversary of Plassey. British troops had to win back control of Awadh, fighting village by village and meeting fierce resistance spearheaded by local leaders, until the summer of 1858. The collaboration of the Bhumihar magnates of Benares, rivals of the Rajput brotherhoods up in revolt, was a critical element in the success of the British counter-attack.

A third focus of revolt was in central India, where the rulers and peasants of the Maratha territories seized the opportunity to be rid of the British. The Rani of Jhansi, whose kingdom was annexed by Dalhousie in 1853 utilizing the doctrine of lapse, led her people from the front in a fierce struggle and died fighting against the British on horseback. Another Maratha leader, Nana Sahib, led his troops up to Kanpur and inflicted a severe defeat on the British garrison stationed there.

The 1857 revolt was by and large confined to the northern Indian Gangetic plain and central India. In July of 1857 Rohilla Afghan soldiers joined urban groups in a revolt in Hyderabad, but the Nizam and some of his chiefs kept this southern kingdom away from a movement which was perceived by them to be led by their erstwhile rivals, the Marathas. Mutinies broke out in garrison towns of the Punjab, and Muslim pastoralist groups revolted in the western part of the province. But the loyalty of Sikh magnates in the east of the province, which the British had assiduously cultivated of late, enabled them to contain trouble in Punjab. The strong British military presence in Bengal, boosted by reinforcements from an expeditionary force diverted on its way to China in November 1857, was a deterrent to potential rebels. The uneven spread of colonial rule ensured that the new Bengali intelligentsia was not particularly enamoured of what they regarded as a movement of feudal oligarchs. So the British were really threatened in the north and central Indian heartland. June and July of 1857 were the most dangerous months for them, though sporadic guerrilla warfare raged even after Governor-General Canning formally declared the war to be over in July of 1858.

It is simpler, certainly far less controversial, to catalogue the course and the extent of the rebellion than to analyse its character. The 1857 revolt was infused with an inchoate sense of patriotism, if not nationalism, and had a shared objective of putting an end to colonial rule. To be more precise, it was fired by a series of regional patriotisms that since the eighteenth century were based on an emotional affinity with the homeland and a rational commitment to principles of good governance. The aspiration for freedom from colonial rule was expressed in the context of a legitimist reaction among the rulers and aristocrats at the indigenous courts. These kings and nobles were deeply aggrieved by British perfidy in tearing up established treaties whenever they proved inconvenient. This was like changing the rules in an unfair bid to win a chess game. The queen mother of Awadh gave voice to this sense of grievance when she referred to British deception in the cases of Awadh, Jhansi, Satara, Nagpur and even tiny Bharatpur, whose ruler 'on the one hand they salaamed and by the other hand they hanged'. These aristocratic leaders were offering those who were prepared to follow them into rebellion the legitimacy of a resurrected eighteenth-century state system under the highest sovereignty of the Mughal emperor. A powerful legitimizing ideology, it was nevertheless a source of weakness. The inter-state rivalries of the eighteenth century were mirrored in 1857 when, for instance, Hyderabad refused to throw its full weight behind a revolt that could re-establish Maratha power in their neighbourhood. The Mughal sovereign himself may have been a fading glory, as he himself acknowledged:

Na kisi ki ankh ka noor hoon
Na kisi ka dil ka karar hoon
Jo kisi ke kam na aa sake
Mein wo ek mooshtai gobar hoon
(I am neither the light of anyone's eye
Nor the solace of anyone's heart
Unable to serve anyone's needs
I am no more than a mere speck of dust)

Religious millenarianism was doubtless a theme that informed the revolt of 1857. In the immediate aftermath of the revolt, British officials exaggerated the religious factor when they singled out the Muslims as the main rebels and explained the rebellion as an insidious plot by Muslim fanatics. So it is important to be clear about the precise role played by religion. Prior to the outbreak many in Delhi interpreted the confrontation between Persian forces and the company in 1856 as a prelude to a general Muslim mobilization against the British. In Lucknow, Muslim millenarian preachers had been fore-telling the end of the company raj. During the height of the revolt thousands of *ghazis* (warriors of the faith), drawn from among the Pindaris and the Naqshbandi Sufi order, fought fearlessly against the British. In certain districts like Muzaffarnagar and Saharanpur, where declining Muslim service gentry had congregated, the revolt took on a distinctly millenarian flavour. In some of the towns and *qasbahs* (small country towns) of northern India, Muslim weavers were inspired by local calls for jihad or holy war given by men like Maulvi Ahmedullah Shah of Faizabad, Maulvi Liaquat Ali of Allahabad and possibly Maulvi Fazl Huq Khairabadi of Delhi, even though the role of the last-named remains mired in some controversy. The invocation of religion produced some complications. Some Sunni religious leaders were not particu-larly excited by the prospect of a resurgence of Shia power in Awadh, others made pragmatism a virtue and refused to proclaim a jihad, since success was hardly assured.

Some foreign fighters in Delhi may have thought they were fighting a jihad during the brutal summer of 1857, but Muslim intellectuals both for and against the 1857 revolt were engaged in a lively debate on the appropriateness of issuing a call to jihad. In keeping with Shah Abdul Aziz's *fatwa* in the early nineteenth century, ulema of the dominant Hanafi school of Sunni juris-prudence maintained that even if India had become a Dar-ul-Harb (an abode of war), jihad would become mandatory only if the British suppressed Muslim religious practices. Sayyid Ahmed Khan, who sided with the British in Bijnore, was decidedly against dignifying the rebellion with the appellation of a jihad. Even those who supported the uprising had doubts about interpreting this temporal war as a jihad. Care had to be taken to build and preserve Hindu–Muslim unity that, according to some historians, blunted the millenarian edge of the movement. Even the Maulvi of Faizabad's proclamation of jihad stressed the common threat posed by the *farangis* (foreigners) to Hindus and Muslims:

> These accursed English had written to the impure Victoria ... 'if your Majesty will permit us to kill fifteen maulvis out of every hundred in India and the same number out of every hundred pandits as well as five hundred thousand of Hindu and Mahomedan sepoys and ryots we will in a short time make all the people of India Christian.' Then that ill-stared polluted bitch gave her consent to the spilling of this innocent blood.

Other proclamations were more polite but displayed a similar concern about Hindu–Muslim unity. The famous proclamation of Azimgarh of 25 August 1857 pointed out that 'both Hindus and Muslims [were] being ruined under the tyranny and oppression of the infidel and treacherous English'. The 'loss of country' sentiment was shared by Hindus and Muslims alike. Hindu religious millenarianism did not figure in the revolt, but rebel leaders like Rani Lakshmibai of Jhansi and Tantia Topi became part of the folklore and festivals of more recent times.

Agrarian protest was the other important strand of the revolt. Peasant recruits supplied the link between the military mutiny and the rural uprising. As with other aspects of the events of 1857, there is a lively debate among historians about the motivation, composition and leadership of the agrarian dimensions of the revolt. The standard works on 1857 prior to the 1970s had argued that the loss of landed rights to urban traders and moneylenders was the main cause of discontent in the countryside. While the inroads of the *bania* (trader-moneylender) into the countryside undeniably took place, transfers of landed rights to them did not generally form the lion's share of such transfers. Careful district-level research in the 1970s also showed that revolt was often most intense in those regions where the moneylenders had been least successful in taking over landed rights. Eric Stokes pointed out that in some instances the moneylender was no more than 'the fly on the wheel'. Another round of research in the 1980s tended to resurrect the hated bania as one of the main culprits in the north Indian countryside. The chief villain, it is now agreed, was the British tax collector. The British revenue demand was arbitrary and high, and was especially insensitive to the subsistence needs of the drier districts. Yet economic factors on their own, in terms of either the moneylenders' or the revenue collectors' depredations, are not sufficient in explaining the motivation to revolt. Equally important was a sense of relative political deprivation. It was the decline of political clout and honour in relation to other neighbouring clans and communities that ferreted out the rebels from the collaborators of 1857. For instance, the Jat farmers of the south-west part of Saharanpur district were aggrieved because a high land-revenue demand was lowering their status relative to their social peers and marriage partners in other parts of the district.

It is more or less clear that the agrarian revolts were multi-class in character. Taluqdar magnates, village zamindars, tenant farmers, peasant proprietors and tribal communities, all participated in one region or another. In some regions agrarian dependants followed the lead of their landed chiefs, elsewhere they took the initiative and persuaded the elites to revolt. In other instances village brotherhoods displaying the *bhaiachara* (literally 'brotherhood') tenure collectively decided to take up arms against the forces of the colonial state. What emerges from the myriad complexities of a countryside in revolt is that 1857 witnessed much more than simply a feudal reaction. The participation and initiative of the subordinate classes reveals a collage of multifaceted revolt.

The leadership at the local levels was drawn not only from the 'traditional elites' but also from rather ordinary people from lower social classes and castes who came to the forefront during the throes of rebellion. Nawab Walidad Khan, a landed magnate, directed the agrarian revolt in Bulandshahr district until he vanished mysteriously in 1858. Shah Mal, a Jat farmer, emerged from relative oblivion to lead the rebellion in Baraut locality in north-western India until he was killed in combat. Devi Singh, a village-level raja in Tappa Raya in Mathura, set up a parallel government until he was caught and hanged. Gonoo, an ordinary Kol tribesman, led the rebellion in the Chhotanagpur region. There were clearly many other such local rebel leaders who galvanized their communities to resist the British and their collaborators.

The revolt of 1857, in its aristocratic, religious and agrarian aspects, was underpinned by feelings of patriotism. It was also a reaction against British racial arrogance – a key feature of the mid-Victorian era. The rebellion itself only served to harden the lines of racial animosity. There was brutality on both sides. Once the tide of the war turned in favour of the British, even many of the relatively temperate officers, outraged by stories of rebel atrocities against English women and children, found the punishment of death by hanging too lenient. Although most were hanged, thousands of captured rebels were strapped to cannons and blown to shreds. Hundreds of villages were torched simply because of their proximity to rebel centres. Long after the war had ended the mental and psychological wounds continued to fester.

It had cost an astronomical sum of £50 million (Rs 500 million) to quell the mutiny–revolt of 1857. The abolition of the company meant that this sum was included as part of the India debt which the newly created crown raj had to pay back to London. In order to restore the finances of the Indian administration, the taxation system was revamped. Land revenues were moderated but an income tax was imposed for the first time on wealthier urban groups. The most important restructuring under the crown was undertaken, however, in the domain of the armed forces. Upper-caste recruits from northern India were no longer deemed trustworthy. By 1875 nearly half of the British Indian army was drawn from Punjab, a fitting reward for loyalty during the crisis, and Gurkhas from Nepal now became the new shock troops of the infantry brigades. When the mutiny broke out a mere 40,000 British soldiers had counterbalanced nearly 240,000 Indian sepoys. After 1857 it was decided that the ratio of Indian to European troops was never to be more than 2:1. British officers were placed in exclusive charge of the artillery. Communication networks, particularly railways, were streamlined to defend the strategically important parts of the Indian empire.

Queen Victoria, in her proclamation of August 1858 taking India under the crown, made a few conciliatory gestures. Treaties with Indian princes, she assured, would be duly respected in the future. Colonial subjects in general were promised a relatively benevolent government. Yet even by the time Victoria was proclaimed Empress of India at a glittering durbar in Delhi in 1877, the

mood in northern and central India remained sullen and somber. Mirza Asadullah Khan Ghalib, one of the greatest-ever Urdu poets, who lived through
the cataclysm of 1857, captured the spirit of his times when he wrote in his
couplets:

Agehe ati thi hal-e-dil pe hansi
Ab kisi baat pe nahin ati
(Previously one laughed at the state of one's heart
now nothing at all elicits joy or laughter)

Or, in another wry reflection on the atmosphere of pessimistic gloom following
the passing away of sovereignty:

Kahte hain jeetay hain umeed pai log
Hum ko jeenay ki bhi umeed nahin
(It's said that people live on hope
I have no hope even of living)

10

HIGH NOON OF COLONIALISM, 1858 TO 1914

State and political economy

In the aftermath of the great mutiny–rebellion of 1857 the British crown decided to put an end to the company's by now well-advertised mismanagement of Indian affairs and extended its direct sway over the conquered territories. It is in the period from 1858 to 1914 that Britain is generally seen to have been able to extract solid strategic and economic advantages from its prize colonial possession. India was being fashioned into a colony not only to play a critical role in the international system of payments of the capitalist world economy for the sustenance of its hegemonic core, but was also indispensable in the strategic defence of that hegemony. The strategic imperative of using Indian troops for the defence of Britain's worldwide empire was achieved by amending the structure and composition of the army that had erupted in such serious revolt in 1857. India's economy was twisted to fit a classical colonial pattern of importing manufactured goods from the metropolis and exporting a variety of agricultural raw materials. Britain enjoyed a trade surplus with India. But it had a growing deficit in its overall international trade which was offset in this period by India's substantial export surplus with the rest of the world.

The switch from company to crown raj meant that instead of a governor-general India would now be ruled by the crown's viceroy. Instead of the company's court of directors in London, a secretary of state for India who was a member of Britain's cabinet now exercised control over Indian affairs. The most urgent task faced by the secretary of state and viceroy was the reorganization of the British Indian army and the civil bureaucracy so that the colony might once again play its crucial role in substantiating Britain's imperial dominance. So the state in India during the high noon of colonialism developed some novel institutional features.

The British Indian army was organized on the principles of maintaining a high European ratio which was never to fall short of 1:2 until the outbreak of the World War I. Next to what was seen as a grand counterpoise of a sufficient British force, there was to be the more insidious 'counterpoise of natives against natives'. The British now not only recruited from among new social groups, especially Sikhs, Gurkhas, Punjabi Muslims and Pathans, but they also mixed the regiments in such a way that, as the secretary of state put

Figure 16 British Majesty. The Victoria Memorial in Calcutta, started under the patronage of Lord Curzon (Courtesy Sugata Bose)

it in 1862, 'Sikh might fire into Hindu, Gurkha into either, without any scruple in case of need'. As justification for the new recruitment patterns the colonial masters concocted a new-fangled, anthropological theory of martial races and castes. Punjabis and Gurkhas, for instance, in the British view possessed martial characteristics, but Bengalis and Tamils did not. The need to favour the chief recruiting grounds in economic policy contributed to disparities in wealth and the uneven pattern of colonial economic development. The Punjab, for example, was favoured when decisions were made regarding public investment in irrigation. The discrepancies and distortions stemming from late nineteenth-century alterations in the structure and the composition of the army have constituted one of the more lasting legacies of colonial rule in the subcontinent.

A domestic rod of order and an international fire brigade, the British Indian army protected Britain's far-flung imperial interests from North Africa to East Asia. It helped put out the burning fires lit by the Mahdi uprisings of 1885–86 and 1896 in Sudan, the Boxer rebellion of 1900 in China and the Boer war in South Africa during 1899–1902. Britain used Indian troops in its intervention in Egypt in 1882, which set the ball rolling for the partition of Africa. Closer to the subcontinent, the British Indian army was deployed in Afghanistan in the late 1870s and the early 1880s, for the final conquest of Burma in the late

1880s, to impose British dominance in Tibet in 1902–3 and to bolster British influence in the Persian Gulf, especially southern Iran, Bahrain, Kuwait, Muscat and Aden in the first decade of the twentieth century. During World War I Indian troops were to play a critical role in the British campaigns in what was then called Mesopotamia, present-day Iraq. As many as 60,000 Indian soldiers died fighting for Britain during 1914–18. The costs of all these military adventures were, needless to say, borne principally by Indian taxpayers.

As for the colonial bureaucracy – the 'steel frame' holding up the raj – Indians within it were discriminated against along racial lines. The upper echelons of the bureaucracy were exclusively British in composition. These senior British officials were recruited into the Indian civil service through competitive examinations held in London. Indian nationalists demanded that simultaneous civil service examinations be held in Britain and India. Despite the passage of a resolution supporting simultaneous examinations by the House of Commons in 1893, this administrative reform was not implemented until after the end of World War I. Indians were needed at the lower levels of the administration, but even here many educated Indians faced racial discrimination. Some of them, notably Surendranath Banerji, turned to the nationalist cause in the wake of their disenchantment with the British colonial service.

Reordering of the political economy of colonial India was as important as restructuring the institutions of the state. From the early decades of the nineteenth century the free traders' lobby in Britain had been gradually prising open the Indian market for their manufactured goods, especially cotton textiles. But it was only from the 1850s that India was systematically cast into the role of exporter of agricultural raw materials, such as cotton, jute, tea, coffee, wheat and oil seeds. The colonial system required the annual transfer of funds from the colony to the metropolis to meet an array of home charges. These were funnelled through India's rising export surplus. Home charges included the cost of the secretary of state's India office in London, costs of wars at home and abroad, purchase of military stores, pensions for British military officers and civilian officials and a guaranteed 6 per cent annual interest on railways. At the turn of the century visible home charges annually amounted to between seventeen and eighteen million pounds sterling. The chief items on the bill in order of magnitude were the guaranteed railway interest, military expenses, interest on the India debt, purchases of government stores and pensions. In addition to all this, British officials serving in India made private remittances, and there were further transfers of profits by British merchants and 'invisible' charges for services, including shipping, banking and insurance. The silver-based Indian rupee, worth 2 shillings in 1872, had depreciated against the pound sterling by 1893, when it was shifted onto a gold-exchange standard, by nearly half – to 1 shilling and 2 pence. The depreciating value of India's currency during the two decades from the early 1870s to the early 1890s increased the real burden of India's payments to Britain.

This 'drain', estimated at 5 per cent to 6 per cent of the total resources of India, took place through the notorious council bill system. British buyers of Indian exports paid sterling for council bills obtained from the secretary of state in London. The council bills were then presented by British trading firms in India to exchange banks where they were exchanged for rupees from the government of India's revenues. The rupees were then advanced to finance the production and trade in export commodities, for example, jute. The rupee profits could subsequently be used to buy sterling bills at local branches of British-owned exchange banks and London paid sterling against these bills. The sterling could then once again be used to buy council bills, and so the annual cycle repeated itself.

Between 1870 and 1914 India's export surplus was critical for Britain's balance of payments. Growing protectionism in continental Europe and America made it difficult for Britain to sell its manufactured goods while being dependent on importing a broad range of their agricultural commodities. It was in this context that Indian raw material exports to America and continental Europe proved vital for financing Britain's deficits with the USA and Europe. This was possible because Britain had a surplus with India and a huge deficit with the rest of the world, while India had a deficit with Britain and a huge surplus with the rest of the world.

The drain of wealth theory, first articulated by early Indian nationalists like Dadabhai Naoroji and Romesh Chunder Dutt, has been a topic of lively debate ever since the late nineteenth century. The British denied that the unilateral transfers of funds from India to Britain constituted anything more than returns on capital and payments for services rendered. While it is hard to construe military campaigns abroad as services rendered to India's colonial subjects, it is true that finance capital could be raised and certain stores purchased more cheaply in London than in India of the late nineteenth century. However, the crux of the nationalist critique was that the wealth drained away represented a potential investible surplus which would have contributed to economic development if it had remained within the country. This is what lent credence to charges of exploitation during the era of high colonialism.

Such charges of exploitation called for tempering the rules of governance in India. The colonial state's law of property served as an instrument of compromise, mainly through tenancy legislation, albeit one that was now more orientated than before to free-trader capitalism, or more aptly to a one-sided free trader capitalism. In regions of zamindari revenue settlements, such as Bengal, the British legislated through the Rent Act of 1859 and the Bengal Tenancy Act of 1885 to give occupancy tenants moderation of rent and security of tenure. Elsewhere, as in Punjab, peasant proprietors were bolstered by passing laws such as the Punjab Land Alienation Act of 1900, which limited the possibility of land transferring from agriculturist to non-agriculturist hands. These measures were taken because the development of colonial India as a vast market for British goods could only rest on the expansion of broadly based purchasing power of India's predominantly agrarian populace. The cultivation of new cash crops, such as cotton and jute, could also be promoted by lightening the revenue and rent burden. Colonial capitalists now preferred the credit mechanism rather than the revenue and rent structure of the state as the main channel of appropriating the agrarian surplus. The same merchants who bought council bills in London advanced money through a network of traders and moneylenders to the peasants who were actually engaged in primary production. Many peasants in time fell into an annual cycle of debt, while the purchasing companies and their intermediaries obtained their products cheaply and siphoned off sizeable interest payments.

The growing commercialization of Indian agriculture based on commodity production for the world market did create some brief periods of boom, for example in the cotton tracts during the years of the American civil war. But peasants were now exposed to the vagaries of the world market as never before. The downward fluctuations of the 1870s and the 1890s hit primary producers hard, particularly since many small peasants had turned to high-value and labour-intensive cash crops to ensure their subsistence. Fits of optimism in the third quarter of the nineteenth century were followed by disappointments and, finally, in the late 1890s, were swept away in a spate of devastating famines in which millions perished, especially in the cotton-growing regions of India. Between 1906 and 1913 the jute-growing regions in eastern India enjoyed a boom which eventually collapsed during World War I.

If new ways were being devised to extract resources from the agrarian economy, the colonial state was coming under increasing pressure from the metropolis to institute fiscal policies designed to maintain India as the most important outlet for British manufactured goods. Despite facing a financial crisis during the Afghan war of the later 1870s, the government of India was prevented from raising customs duties by the Lancashire lobby in Britain. These duties were altogether abolished in 1882. When dire financial need compelled the colonial state to reintroduce customs duties on British textiles in the 1890s, London made sure that a countervailing excise duty was slapped on Indian manufactured textiles. This meant that the infant textile industry centring round Bombay and Ahmedabad, the only region where indigenous capital had moved from petty commerce to industry, was deprived of any protective tariffs. This stunted the industrialization process in India and prevented the rise of a factory-based textile industry at a time when the artisanal industry had suffered serious setbacks.

The theme of deindustrialization in late nineteenth-century India has been a matter of some disagreement. Nationalist critics generally pointed to the dwindling proportion of artisanal goods on India's export list. A few historians have tried to suggest that this is not sufficient evidence to sustain the argument of deindustrialization, and that India's domestic market may have been large enough to absorb both imported manufactures and domestic artisanal products. The poverty of the colony – the most optimistic estimate

Figure 17 Royal Railways. Victoria Terminus, Bombay, inaugurated on the occasion of Queen Victoria's Golden Jubilee, 1887 (Courtesy Ayesha Jalal)

of per capita national income suggested a figure of under Rs 40 or about £2 10 shillings compared to Britain's £52 at the turn of the century – casts some doubt over the buoyancy of Indian demand. It has also been suggested that Indian weavers benefitted from the supply of cheaper imported yarn. But this knocked out Indian spinners and also did not enable the Indian weaving industry to compete in costs with the factory-based manufacturing industry in Britain. Even if the older arguments about deindustrialization need some refinement, the disadvantaged status of the Indian colonial economy can hardly be in question.

Metropolitan imperatives invariably took precedence over the financial and political needs of the colonial state. The famous Indian railways, often cited as a great modernizing achievement of colonialism, were planned and constructed to serve the strategic and economic needs of the metropolis. Nearly five thousand miles of railway lines were laid by the close of the nineteenth century. But they generally facilitated the movement of troops, the dispersal of British manufactured goods and the extraction of raw materials from the hinterlands to the port cities. Since most of the equipment was imported from Britain, the building of the railways did not stimulate the growth of other ancillary industries. The deployment of British capital in this sector was a striking example of private investment at public risk, with investors receiving guaranteed interest payments whether the railways made profits or not. In the 1870s the outflow of interest actually exceeded the inflow of fresh capital into India.

British monopoly over the upper echelons of state institutions and over the reordering of the political economy to their advantage did not mean that they attempted to sustain their rule without the support of Indian collaborators. The search for reliable collaborators began soon after the end of the mutiny–revolt of 1857. The rebellion had been the last gasp of resistance by disaffected Indian princes. The crown raj took calculated steps to make sure that the preservation of ceremonial trappings and a measure of internal autonomy transformed the princely states into solid bulwarks of empire. The colonial state juxtaposed to its own conception of monolithic, unitary sovereignty at the centre a shallow, if not fake, version of sovereignty reposed in the persons of 'traditional' rulers. This kind of sovereignty, which was merely the other side of the coin on which the supremacy of British sovereign power was clearly engraved, was later extended from the subcontinent to the coastal polities of the Persian Gulf and the Arabian Sea.

The colonial re-invention of 'traditional' authority as part of its ideology of state had large consequences, helping to transform princely India into a reliable base of support for the empire and freeing rulers legitimized by colonial 'tradition' from the trouble of seeking popular sanction. The crown that adorned the princely head was by no means a 'hollow' one, as Mridu Rai has shown, when it came to the pact of dominance between ruler and subject. While the princes may have been weakened in relation to the paramount power, the British guarantee of personalized sovereignty, for instance of the Dogras of Jammu and Kashmir *vis-à-vis* their subjects, obviated the need for rulers to seek legitimacy through the time-honoured practices of material munificence and cultural patronage. The buttressing of princely autocracy was then one of the key changes brought about by colonialism in the latter half of the nineteenth century, involving a very dramatic shift in ideas about sovereignty and legitimacy. Having imported the notion of unitary sovereignty from post-enlightenment Europe into colonial India to replace pre-colonial India's view of layered and shared sovereignty, the crown raj made certain it stymied any move towards the acquisition of substantive citizenship rights. In colonial India there were to be no citizens, only subjects of the empire and of 'traditional' princes.

The British search for collaborators did not stop with the princes. Those taluqdars of north India who had remained loyal in 1857 were extended economic protection. Elsewhere, the nurturing of the landlord class as potential friends of the raj was balanced by an effort to promote export-oriented agriculture and preserve peace in the countryside by affording a measure of protection to peasants. The deepening financial troubles of the government of India and the increasing pressures brought to bear upon it by the metropolis led the colonial state to make institutional innovations that might widen the network of collaborators. One way to try to soften the blows dealt by the metropolis on Indian society was to push for the introduction of local self-government. This brand of representative government was not quite substantive democracy, but rather its obverse.

Beginning with the Indian Councils Act of 1861, provincial councils were created in Bengal, Madras and Bombay. In these councils British officials had a majority, but a few nominated non-official Indians were consulted on legislative matters. In 1882 the viceroy, Ripon, extended the principle of granting Indians a measured say in local affairs; municipal and local boards were formed in most of the provinces. The costs of running these local government bodies and financing local development works were met by raising new taxes in the localities and provinces. This, it was hoped, would insulate the central state from the charge of imposing new taxes. It was also a convenient way of lowering administrative costs. And while most of the members of the boards were to be nominated, the British partly accepted the notion of elected representatives by agreeing to seriously consider the recommendations of certain Indian organizations. The proportion of non-official Indians in the councils was increased by another Indian Councils Act of 1892. But it was only in 1909 that the Morley–Minto reforms extended the links between the higher and lower councils, thus building bridges which local men with power and pelf could hope to cross, to reach the provincial and, in exceptional cases, even the governor-general's legislative council at the centre.

More importantly, British social engineering through censuses helped create supra-local caste and religious categories to which the colonial state could distribute differential patronage. The 'depressed classes' and the 'Indian Muslims' were such constructs. They were respectively accorded reservation of seats and separate electorates for election to local and other representative bodies set up by the Morley–Minto reforms of 1909. This principle not only survived but also was extended under the 1919 Montagu–Chelmsford reforms and later incorporated into the Government of India Act of 1935. While dividing and categorizing their subjects according to new principles of social enumeration, the raj also had, in the words of Rajat Kanta Ray, 'the overriding character of an imperial power which set apart its subjects in a block with interests fundamentally antagonistic to those of the rulers'.

If at the turn of the nineteenth century the Wellesley generation had brought to bear a new British national pride on their attitudes towards Indian society, the Curzon generation at the turn of the twentieth century exhibited a fully developed form of the racial superiority and arrogance that had gathered momentum in the middle and late Victorian era. The British had hoped that the diamond jubilee of Victoria's reign in 1897 would be an occasion for the display of imperial pomp based on a sense of quiet confidence. But there were too many strands of insecurity flowing from the intense competition with European rivals for supremacy in relatively new and semi-colonies in Africa as well as South-East and East Asia. Adding to the feelings of insecurity was the new assertiveness of nationalist opponents, some of whom were talking back to the colonial masters in their own language. The general condition of the colonial subjects was dismal in 1897. 'The shadows darkened and deepened in their horrors as the year advanced,' Mahadev Govind Ranade recorded grimly,

Figure 18 Royal Welcome. Gateway of India, Bombay, erected on the occasion of the
visit of King George V in 1911 (Courtesy Ayesha Jalal)

'and it almost seemed as if the seven plagues which afflicted the land of
the Pharoahs in old time were let loose upon us, for there is not a single province
which had not its ghastly record of death and ruin to mark this period as the
most calamitous year of the century within the memory of many generations
past.' As famine and pestilence stalked the land, the radical critique of moderate nationalism grew more strident. By the time Curzon was building a
marble monument in Victoria's memory on the sprawling green of Calcutta,
Indian nationalists were already discussing *swaraj* (self-rule) and planning to
turn the raj itself into a bad memory.

11

A NATION IN MAKING?

'Rational' reform, 'religious' revival and *swadeshi* nationalism, 1858 to 1914

Historians who focused on the politics of Western-educated elites had little hesitation in identifying the beginnings of modern nationalism, narrowly defined, as the most important historical theme of late nineteenth-century India. The foundation of the Indian National Congress in 1885 provided a convenient starting point for those with a penchant for chronological precision. The recent reorientation of modern Indian historiography towards the subordinate social groups has dramatically altered perspectives and added confusion, complexity, subtlety and sophistication to the understanding of Indian society at the high noon of colonialism. Anti-colonialism can be seen now to have been a much more variegated phenomenon than simply the articulate dissent of educated urban groups imbued with Western concepts of liberalism and nationalism. The currents and cross-currents of social reform informed by 'reason' and its apparent rejection in movements of religious revival are being weighed and analysed more carefully. The overlapping nature of the periodization of resistance is being recognized. The *ulgulan* (great tumult) of 1899–1900 of the Munda tribe on the Bengal–Bihar border was, after all, roughly coterminous with the first major attempt by the educated urban elite to mobilize mass support for the *swadeshi* movement of 1905–8.

What was novel, however, about the late nineteenth century was the interconnectedness, though not necessarily convergence, of social and political developments across regions on an unprecedented scale. In that general sense it was during this period that the idioms, and even the irascible idiosyncrasies, of communitarian identities and national ideologies were given a semblance of coherence and structure. There were multiple and competing narratives informed by religious and linguistic cultural identities seeking to contribute to the emerging discourse on the Indian nation. If Indian nationalist thought can at all be construed as a derivative discourse, it was derived from many different sources – not just the rationalism of post-enlightenment Europe, but also the rational patriotisms laced with regional affinities and religious sensibilities that were a major feature of late pre-colonial India.

Some of the impetus to the redefinition of social identities and the quest for social mobility was provided by the initiatives of the colonial state. The decennial censuses began a process of enumeration and rank ordering of castes that spurred a great competition among many sub-castes by jati for high varna status. Upwardly mobile social groups rewrote their caste histories and changed their caste names as they climbed the ladder of respectability. For example, in north Tamil Nadu the Pallis claimed high varna status in 1872 and started calling themselves Vanniyas; in south Tamil Nadu the Shanans did the same in 1901 and referred to themselves as Nadars. Between 1872 and 1911, the Kaibartas of west Bengal became Mahishyas, the Chandals of east Bengal Namasudras and the Koches of north Bengal Rajbanshi Kshatriyas. The desire for higher social status through census manipulation was discernible among Muslims as well: butchers started calling themselves Quraishi and weavers Mumin. Many Muslims claimed foreign descent in order to gain recognition as members of the ashraf classes in northern India and Bengal.

Although in 1858 the colonial power had announced its intention not to interfere in the private realm of 'religion' and 'custom', its policies in the late nineteenth century ensured that precisely these concerns had to be bandied about in the 'public' arenas of the press and politics. A plethora of communitarian narratives written in 'modernized' vernacular languages, therefore, filled the pages churned out by a burgeoning press and publications market. In order to gain the attention of a colonial state minded to disburse differential patronage, publicists needed to dip their pens in the ink of community. A direct public statement of anti-colonial politics ran the risk of running foul of the laws of sedition enshrined in a battery of vernacular press acts. The fictive separation of religion and politics in the colonial stance was breached the moment the British took the momentous decision to deploy religious enumeration to define 'majority' and 'minority' communities. Colonial constitutional initiatives lent religiously based communitarian affiliations a greater supra-local significance than regional, linguistic, class and sectarian divergences might otherwise have warranted. The most important step in this regard was the construction of the political category of 'Indian Muslim'. Whatever the internal differences among India's Muslims, this encouraged them to lay emphasis on their religious identity in putting forward political claims. Not all of the social stirrings, of course, are reducible to colonial stimulus even if they occurred within a broad colonial context of British rule. Brahman social dominance, bolstered by a British-sponsored neo-Brahmanical ruling ideology, provoked a strong anti-Brahman or non-Brahman backlash in parts of western and southern India. A prominent example of such a lower-caste movement in Maharashtra is Jyotirao Phule's Satyashodhak Samaj (Society for the Quest of Truth), established in 1873. The debates between rival schools of Islam in Punjab and Bengal also had a measure of autonomy from colonial manipulations. The redefinition of a more religiously informed cultural identity among Muslims in the late nineteenth century should not be mistaken, however, for a kind of 'communalism' that has been read back into this period in retrospectively constructed 'nationalist' pasts.

Social reform and religious revival were once seen by historians of the nineteenth century as stark contradictory processes. Hindu revival in the late nineteenth century was reckoned to be gaining the upper hand over reformist activities set in motion in the 1820s and 1830s. Educated Muslim society was deemed to be experiencing a tussle between pro-West reformers and conservative revivalists. Social trends among Hindus and Muslims alike were much too nuanced to be captured by the reform–revival, modernity–tradition or indeed our (Indian) modernity–their (Western) modernity dichotomies. It is true that Brahmo reform was limited to a small circle and Ishwarchandra Vidyasagar's support for widow remarriage in the 1850s was the final episode in which reformers prevailed in the public debate in Bengal. The atmosphere was markedly more conservative during the controversy over the Age of Consent Act of 1891, which raised the legal age of marriage for girls from ten to twelve. The intrusiveness of the colonial state seeking to impose Western medicine during the plague epidemics of the late 1890s elicited an even more virulent protest all over India. This did not amount to a wholesale rejection of the potential benefits of Western science, but represented an attitude of resistance to an authoritarian colonial state. The conflation of the colonial state with Western/modern medicine has led some historians to view modern science primarily in terms of a grave assault on the body of the colonized and to greatly exaggerate the anti-modern, religious overtones of resistance against epidemic measures. A more powerful critique of the colonial state would concentrate on its inaction, if not complete dereliction of responsibility, in the arena of public health, and a more historically fine-tuned analysis of the attitudes of colonial subjects would reveal strands of resistance to as well as selective appropriation of new scientific knowledge.

Religious sensibility could in the late nineteenth century be perfectly compatible with a rational frame of mind, just as rational reform almost invariably sought divine sanction of some kind. Speaking at the eleventh Social Conference in Amraoti in 1897, Ranade scored a debating point against his 'revivalist' critics:

> When my revivalist friend presses his argument upon me, he has to seek recourse in some subterfuge which really furnishes no reply to the question – what shall we revive? Shall we revive the old habits of our people when the most sacred of our caste indulged in all the abominations as we now understand them of animal food and drink which exhausted every section of our country's Zoology and Botany? The men and the Gods of those old days ate and drank forbidden things to excess in a way no revivalist will now venture to recommend.

What lay at 'the root of our helplessness', Ranade declared, was

> the sense that we are always intended to remain children, to be subject to outside control, and never to rise to the dignity of self-control

by making our conscience and our reason the supreme, if not the sole, guide to our conduct … We are children, no doubt, but the children of God, and not of man, and the voice of God is the only voice [to] which we are bound to listen … With too many of us, a thing is true or false, righteous or sinful, simply because somebody in the past has said that it is so … Now the new idea which should take up the place of this helplessness and dependence is not the idea of a rebellious overthrow of all authority, but that of freedom responsible to the voice of God in us.

Seven years later, in a 1904 article entitled 'Reform or Revival', Lala Lajpat Rai sought to argue that, while the reformers wanted reform on 'rational' lines, the revivalists wanted reform on 'national' lines. Attempting to turn Ranade's argument on its head, Lajpat Rai wrote:

Cannot a revivalist, arguing in the same strain, ask the reformers into what they wish to reform us? Whether they want us to be reformed on the pattern of the English or the French? Whether they want us to accept the divorce laws of Christian society or the temporary marriages that are now so much in favour in France or America? Whether they want to make men of our women by putting them into those avocations for which nature never meant them? … Whether they want to reform us into Sunday drinkers of brandy and promiscuous eaters of beef? In short, whether they want to revolutionise our society by an outlandish imitation of European customs and manners and an undiminished adoption of European vice?

By this time Ranade was dead and he could not reply that there need be no necessary contradiction between the rational and the national.

In late nineteenth-century Maharashtra, Hindu 'revival' centred on Poona and it had a clear and strong Brahmanical content. Yet it was also from its Maharashtra base that Ranade's Social Conference sought to make a case for reform rather than revival. Lajpat Rai was a legator of the Arya Samaj (Aryan Society) led by Dayanand Saraswati which had, in late nineteenth-century Punjab and western U.P., sought to include reformist postures on issues such as child marriage, widow remarriage, idolatry, travel overseas and caste – within a framework of the assertion of Hindu supremacy over other religious faiths. If Hindu regeneration in Maharashtra had a Brahmanical flavour and the variant in Punjab had supremacist overtones, Hindu 'revival' in Bengal certainly had its ambiguities. Ramakrishna Paramhansa, a priest in a Kali temple north of Calcutta who cast an almost hypnotic spell over the Calcutta intelligentsia (including staunch 'rationalists'), clearly posed an antithesis to the Western concept of rationality. But his disciple Swami Vivekananda, who gained international fame, preached the twin messages of self-strengthening and social service. He told young men that it was more important to play football than to pray and predicted a millennium in which the poor, the downtrodden and the Shudra would come into their own. Vivekananda seemed to have little difficulty in combining reason with his vision of nation and religion. He derided the conservative opponents of the Age of Consent Bill and commented on northern Indian protectors of the sacred mother cow – 'like mother, like son'. Vivekananda was also generally respectful towards other religious faiths, including Islam, and took a clear stand against what he called religiously inspired 'fanaticism'. So there was in the late nineteenth century a great deal of interplay and overlap between the strands of reform and revival, whose meanings varied by region.

A sharply defined fault-line between tradition and modernity as well as Indian and European modernity makes it impossible to take full account of the contestations that animated the creative efforts to fashion a vibrant culture and politics of anti-colonial modernity. These efforts were not just staked on claims of cultural exclusivity or difference but also on imaginative cultural borrowings and intellectual adaptations that consciously transgressed the frontier between 'us' and 'them'. Even within the charmed circle of the Bengali Hindu middle-class intelligentsia there were many different responses to the challenge of Western modernity. Rationalism and humanism were drawn upon by men like Rabindranath Tagore from both India's pre-colonial and Europe's post-enlightenment intellectual traditions in projects of internal, social regeneration and reform which, on the whole, strengthened the ability to contest Western colonial power in the arenas of politics and the state. In its attitude to European modernity the first radical intellectual challenge to moderate nationalism was remarkably discriminating, judicious and balanced. Aurobindo Ghose's remarks on this point in his sixth essay, 'New Lamps for Old', published on 4 December 1893, bears quoting at some length:

No one will deny, – no one at least in that considerable class to whose address my present remarks are directed, – that for us, and even for those of us who have a strong affection for original oriental things and believe that there is in them a great deal that is beautiful, a great deal that is serviceable, a great deal that is worth keeping, the most important objective is and must inevitably be the admission into India of Occidental ideas, methods and culture: even if we are ambitious to conserve what is sound and beneficial in our indigenous civilization, we can only do so by assisting very largely the influx of Occidentalism. But at the same time we have a perfect right to insist, and every sagacious man will take pains to insist, that the process of introduction shall not be as hitherto rash and ignorant, that it shall be judicious, discriminating. We are to have what the West can give us, because what the West can give us is just the thing and the only thing that will rescue us from our present appalling condition of intellectual and moral decay, but we are not to take it haphazard and in a lump; rather we shall find it expedient to select the very best that is thought and known in Europe, and to import even that with the changes and reservations which our diverse conditions may be found to dictate. Otherwise instead of a simple ameliorating influence, we shall have chaos annexed to chaos, the vices and calamities of the West superimposed on the vices and calamities of the East.

To put it in another way, colonized intellectuals were clearly seeking alternative routes of escape from the oppressive present, not all of which lay through creating illusions about *our* past and denouncing *their* modernity.

An extension of the scope of enquiry to Muslim ashraf classes of northern India immediately reveals more intellectual variations on the theme of colonial and anti-colonial modernity. The variety of the Muslim elite's responses to British colonialism and Western modernity cannot be captured within the facile distinctions between 'liberals' and 'traditionalists' or 'modernists' or 'anti-modernists'. A reform-oriented current within Indian Islam was led by Sayyid Ahmed Khan, who sought to alter British conceptions about inherent Muslim disloyalty and urged his co-religionists to accept Western education, but not necessarily all its ideals. It was religious narrow-mindedness, according to him, that had prevented Muslims from taking advantage of the new education. In 1875 he established the Aligarh Anglo-Muhammadan Oriental College, which attracted the sons of Muslim landlords of northern India and drew British patronage. While making some compromises with the British, the Aligarh movement initiated by Sayyid Ahmed jealously guarded against intrusions into custom as well as personal law. Many affluent Muslims in north India and Bengal challenged the British attempt to draw a distinction between legal public *waqfs* (charitable institutions) and illegal private ones established for the benefit of family members. Since charity begins at home, they saw no reason why they should be debarred from preventing the fragmentation of property through recourse to the time-honoured loophole in Islamic inheritance laws. After all, in the Punjab it was customary law rather than the Islamic sharia that decided matters related to inheritance. Sayyid Ahmed's rational approach to Islamic theology and law nevertheless earned him the hostility of the ulema bunched in the theological seminaries at Deoband and, less vociferously, Faranghi Mahal in Lucknow.

The ulema were not alone in opposing Sayyid Ahmed's new-fangled views. His ardent promotion of Western knowledge and culture as well as loyalty to the raj drew acerbic comments from Muslims attached to their societal moorings and the ideal of a universal Muslim *ummah*. The anti-Aligarh school was given a fillip by the great preacher of Islamic universalism Jamaluddin al-Afghani, who lived in Hyderabad and Calcutta between 1879 and 1882. In India al-Afghani tempered his adherence to the political principles of Islamic universalism with calls for Hindu–Muslim unity against British colonialism. The poet

Akbar Allahabadi, in his satirical verses, mercilessly ridiculed Sayyid Ahmad Khan and his associates for their shallow imitation of Western culture:

> The venerable leaders of the nation had determined
> Not to keep scholars and worshipers at a disadvantage
> Religion will progress day by day
> Aligarh College is London's mosque

Akbar Allahabadi was equally derisive towards obscurantist maulvis. Maulana Shibli Numani, an associate of Sayyid Ahmed Khan, endorsed the Aligarh line that Indian Muslims were British subjects, and not bound by religion or Islamic history to submit to the dictates of the Ottoman Khilafat. Yet on matters closer to home, Shibli's Islamic sentiments led him to take political paths different from those charted by Sayyid Ahmed Khan. By 1895 he was publicly opposing Sayyid Ahmed's policy of Muslim non-participation in the Indian National Congress. So in the 1890s, although there were serious instances of Hindu–Muslim conflict – for instance, over the cow protection issue, the question of Hindi versus Urdu and the nature of electoral representation in much of northern India and beyond – intra-communitarian debates, tensions and contradictions were almost quite as important as inter-communitarian ones.

Deepening the historical perspective to include subalternity along lines of gender and class makes the cognitive map of colonial and anti-colonial modernity even richer and more complex. Rokeya Sakhawat Hossain's early twentieth-century tract *Sultana's Dream,* in which all the men were put in purdah, is perhaps an extreme but revealing example of male dominance without hegemony. In any case, an overemphasis on the discourses of elite men and the 'modern' political associations formed by them would provide a very incomplete picture of the multifaceted contestations of the hubris of colonial modernity. Anti-colonial resistance in the late nineteenth century certainly took many forms. Civilian insurrections of the sort noted in the early nineteenth century were less frequent but not uncommon. A multiclass rural revolt took place in Maharashtra in 1879. Tenants' protests against landlords took on a religious flavour among the Mappillas of Malabar. The new context of colonial tenancy law appeared to rob peasant resistance in Bengal of its communitarian character and injected a legalistic and quasi-class dimension, as in the anti-rent agrarian movements of the 1870s in Pabna district. The collapse of the cotton boom created the conditions for the Deccan riots of the mid-1870s, in which Marwari moneylenders from the north were prime targets. No-revenue campaigns were launched in Assam and Maharashtra in the 1890s. Where forests met the plains in Gujarat, Tamil Nadu, central India, Bengal and Bihar, tribes revolted against the incursions of foreigners, white and brown. The most serious millenarian tribal uprising occurred in eastern India, led by Birsa Munda in 1899–1900. Subaltern anti-colonialism predated the attempts by an urban elite to engage in the politics of 'mass mobilization' against British rule.

Figure 19 The Face of Subaltern Resistance. Birsa Munda, leader of the Munda 'ulgulan' of 1899–1900 (Courtesy of the archives of the Nehru Memorial Museum and Library, New Delhi)

In the cities at this time, sections of the intelligentsia were articulating their disaffection in organized fashion and the small class of industrial labour made their early protests in a combination of class and communitarian modes brought from the rural areas. Educated Indians had been forming political associations at the regional level since the 1870s. The more prominent among these were the Poona Sarvajanik Sabha (1870), the Indian Association (in Bengal, 1876), the Madras Mahajana Sabha (1884) and the Bombay Presidency Association (1885). After coming together at a couple of national conferences, these city-based professionals were able to set up a permanent organization – the Indian National Congress – in 1885. Seventy-three self-appointed delegates attended the first annual session of the Congress. The political character and role of the early spokesmen of Indian nationalism varied according to region. In Bengal the professionals who formed the Indian Association had broken ranks with rentier landlords, who had their own British Indian Association since 1851. The fact of European dominance of commerce and industry in eastern India also facilitated a certain autonomy and radical disposition of the Bengali intelligentsia. Elsewhere, the *vakils* (lawyers) who played such a dominant role in early nationalist organizations were no more than publicists tied to the interests of the *shetias* (commercial men) in Bombay or the *raises* (local notables) in Allahabad.

The early leadership of the Indian National Congress was moderate in its methods and aims. The preferred method was the constitutional way of prayers and petitions. The chief political aims were expansion of the elective principle in the legislative councils and greater Indianization of the administration. On the economic front, nationalist writers and spokesmen developed a powerful critique of the whole gamut of colonial policies – the high land-revenue demand contributing to famines, the drain of wealth leading to general impoverishment and the use of indentured labour on plantations in India and abroad resulting in degradation and oppression. There were persistent calls for cutbacks in military expenditure and greater opportunities for elected Indians to discuss the government budget. The successes of the moderate Congress in extracting concessions from the British were modest at best. From the mid-1890s a new generation of nationalists began to criticize the mendicancy of the moderate leaders and called for a bolder approach. The intellectual critique of moderation gathered momentum in Bengal from 1893, took concrete form in Tilak's Ganapati festivals from 1894, no-revenue campaigns and protest against the countervailing excise duty on Indian cotton in 1896, and then dramatically announced itself with the first terrorist assassination of two British officials – including Walter Rand, the hated plague commissioner in Poona – by the Chapekar brothers in 1897. But it was Curzon's aggressive imperialism between 1899 and 1905 that provided fuel to the 'extremist' strands of Indian resistance in the first decade of the twentieth century.

Curzon tried to roll back some of the concessions granted to educated Indians by his predecessors in the fields of education and local government. He passed laws restricting the autonomy of universities from officialdom and reducing non-official Indian representation on municipalities. By far his most controversial decision was to partition the province of Bengal in 1905. Although justified on grounds of administrative efficiency, the partition was clearly a political move. As Curzon's home secretary put it, 'Bengal united is a power; Bengal divided would pull in different ways ... one of our main objects is to split up and thereby weaken a solid body of opponents to our rule'. More insidious was the attempt to pit Muslim against Hindu by claiming that the creation of a separate Muslim-majority province in eastern Bengal with Dhaka as its capital would almost resurrect the lost glories of the Mughal empire. Curzon received support from some Muslim landlords, particularly Nawab Salimullah of Dacca, on whose estate the Muslim League was eventually born in December 1906. Two months before that, in October 1906, a deputation of Muslim landlords from northern India had called on Curzon's successor, Minto and, with some prompting, requested separate electorates for Muslims and representation in proportion to their social and political importance rather than numbers alone. The partition was an affront to most educated Bengali students and professionals, Hindu and Muslim alike, who were proud of their common language and culture. Even the moderate Surendranath Banerji vowed to 'unsettle' what Curzon claimed to be the 'settled fact' of partition. Rabindranath Tagore gave poetic expression to Bengali determination:

Bidhir bandhan katbe tumi?
Emni shaktiman, tumi emni shaktiman!
(You will cut the bond decreed by Providence?
you are so powerful, are you!)

Resistance to partition signalled the beginning of the swadeshi (own country) movement. Although Bengal was the main centre of agitation, the reverberations were felt in other parts of India. The Indian National Congress took up the cause and the sophisticated moderate leader from Bombay, Gopal Krishna Gokhale, stated in flattery of the Bengalis: 'What Bengal thinks today, India thinks tomorrow'. The swadeshi movement of 1905–8 has often been seen as the initial coming together and the subsequent parting of ways of the moderate and extremist nationalists. It would be more accurate to identify, as Sumit Sarkar has done, at least four strands within the nationalist movement in this period. First, there were the old moderates who believed in constitutional methods but were deeply offended by Curzon's aggressive measures (men such as Surendranath Banerji and Gopal Krishna Gokhale). Second, the

Figure 20 Lal, Bal and Pal, Lala Lajput Rai of the Punjab, Balawantrao Gangadhar Tilak of Maharashtra and Bipin Chandra Pal of Bengal (Courtesy of the archives of the Nehru Memorial Museum and Library, New Delhi)

leaders of society who until 1905 had called for a process of self-strengthening or *atmashakti* before engaging in a head-on collision with the British raj. Rabindranath Tagore is a good example of this legion. Third, a new generation of assertive leaders who propounded the doctrine of passive resistance, which was to include relentless boycott of British goods and institutions but also resort to violence if repression became intolerable. Among the main votaries of this form of political extremism were Aurobindo Ghose, Lala Lajpat Rai, Balwantrao Gangadhar Tilak and Bipin Chandra Pal, the last three forming a popular troika of Lal, Bal and Pal. Finally, there were small bands of angry and impatient young men, and some women too, who took to the cult of the bomb, believing revolutionary terror to be the only language that the colonial masters would understand.

In the early stages of the swadeshi movement, the political extremists and the believers in atmashakti came to the forefront with their programme of boycott and national education. Moderate constitutionalists were stampeded into accepting not only new methods of struggle but also a redefined goal of *swaraj* (self-rule), which the passive resisters interpreted as something close to full independence. During 1905–6 boycott of British cotton textiles and other consumer goods was quite effective. There was nearly a 25 per cent fall in the quantity of cotton piece-goods imported in the first year of the agitation. The bonfires of cotton cloth and the shunning of official courts and educational institutions foreshadowed some of the methods of mass agitation to be used more widely later, in the Gandhian era. The cry 'Bande Mataram' was used as the main nationalist slogan. As Aurobindo Ghose argued in 1907, it was only when 'the Mother had revealed herself' that 'the patriotism that work[ed] miracles and save[d] a doomed nation [wa]s born'. He credited Bankim Chandra Chattopadhyay with having caught the first modern glimpse of this grand spectacle: 'It was thirty-two years ago that Bankim wrote his great song and few listened; but in a sudden moment of awakening from long delusions the people of Bengal looked round for the truth and in a fated moment somebody sang *Bande Mataram*. The mantra had been given.'

Bankim's hymn to the Mother, originally written and printed in 1875 as a filler for a blank page in his journal *Bangadarshan* (Vision/Philosophy of Bengal), had a chequered and controversial career in the service of the nationalist movement:

> *Bande mataram,*
> *sujalaang suphalaang, malayaja sheetalang,*
> *shasya shyamalaang mataram …*
> *saptakotikantha-kalakala-ninada-karale,*
> *dwisaptakotibhujaidhritakharakarabale,*
> *abala keno ma eto bale!*
> *Bahubaladhaarineeng, namami taarineeng,*
> *ripudalabaarineeng mataram.*

(I bow to you, Mother,
well-watered, well-fruited,
breeze cool, crop green,
the Mother!
Seven crore voices in your clamorous chant,
twice seven crore hands holding aloft mighty scimitars,
Who says, Mother, you are weak?
Repository of many strengths,
scourge of the enemy's army, the Mother!)

The magic number of seven crore (seventy million) refers, of course, to Bengalis, and the Mother whom Bankim had in mind in 1875, even though there is no specific mention, is Bangamata or Mother Bengal. It might have been less controversial and more universally acceptable if the last verse had not gone on to equate the mother country with the mother goddess and, more importantly, the song had not been inserted in 1882 into Bankim Chattopadhyay's novel *Ananda Math*, which dripped with anti-Muslim prejudice.

In rendering their homage to the mother country, the political extremists decided in 1905 to avoid violence. The decision was tactical, not ideological. With the Indian populace totally disarmed, Aurobindo pointed out that the use of violence would be unwise because it carried the battle on to a ground where Indians were comparatively weak, from a ground where they were strong. Yet there were points of weakness even in the strategy of boycott. Educated professionals, students and small sections of the working class in Calcutta and Bombay were the main supporters of Swadeshi. Boycott of foreign goods also enabled something of a revival of artisanal crafts and industries, but indigenous mill owners in Bombay and Ahmedabad took the opportunity to hike up prices and make unconscionable profits. Swadeshi soon proved to be an expensive indulgence for the common Bengali peasant. There were some outbreaks of violence in east Bengal in which Muslim peasants attacked Hindu landlords, moneylenders and traders. Rabindranath Tagore captured the changing mood. In 1905 he had composed songs celebrating the unity of Bengalis responding to the mother's call. His novel *Ghare Baire* (Home and the World) reflected the sombre spirit of 1908 – by which time the coercive methods of swadeshi agitators had alienated the Muslim poor. When the masses refused to rise in rebellion the young swadeshi nationalists fell back on individual terror.

Outside Bengal political extremism took root in Punjab, Maharashtra and parts of Madras presidency. In Punjab, the British decision to put up canal-water rates provoked much peasant discontent in 1906–7. In Maharashtra, extremists under Tilak's leadership used religious symbolism and Maratha folklore to enthuse the richer peasantry in the interior and workers in the textile mills. In Madras, there was much sympathy for the Bengali cause and a spurt in swadeshi industry in the extreme south of the province. But by and large the rest of India remained quiescent. In 1907 the extremists found themselves on the defensive at the annual session of the Congress at Surat, and left the meeting after hurling shoes at the moderates. The latter had by now reneged on the resolutions on boycott and swaraj, declaring 'steady reform of the existing system of administration' to be their goal. They had correctly anticipated that constitutional concessions were on the anvil. In fact the Morley–Minto reforms had the avowed objective of rallying the moderates. As the extremist leadership was cast into prison, or sent into exile, the liberal secretary of state, Morley, could only ruefully confess that he was becoming 'an accomplice in Cossack rule'. Tilak was sent off to spend six years in a Burmese prison. Other Swadeshi leaders and activists who went into self-imposed exile in continental Europe, the United States and Japan fashioned a new internationalist strand of the nationalist movement. In this sense, the Swadeshi movement did not end in 1905, but continued on its international itinerary well into the period of World War I. At home the extremists won a pyrrhic victory. The British went back on the promises made to their Muslim allies and annulled the partition of Bengal in 1911. This embarrassed the loyalist Muslims and cleared the way for the capture of the Muslim League by nationalist professionals, including Wazir Hasan and Mohammad Ali Jinnah, in 1912–13. The British also decided to remove their capital from the troublesome province of Bengal. As viceroy Hardinge made a ceremonial entry on an elephant into Delhi in 1912, he was greeted with a Bengali revolutionary's bomb.

The swadeshi era was distinguished by a bold redefinition of nationalist aims and strategies as well as an accompanying cultural awakening. Despite a measure of derivation in nationalist thought at the founding moment of modernity in the so-called material domain of the state, there was a powerful critique as well of modular forms supplied by the West. The national or anti-colonial definitions of modernity aspired to be both different and universal. The claim to difference in the realm of the state was, for instance, articulated by Aurobindo Ghose when he wrote that political 'unification ... ought not to be secured at the expense of the free life of the regional peoples or of the communal liberties and not therefore by ... a rigidly unitarian imperial state'. The 'lifeless attempt' to 'reproduce with a servile fidelity the ideals and forms of the West' was, in his view, 'no true indication of the political mind and genius of the Indian people'. The claim to universality was perhaps most eloquently stated in the works of Rabindranath Tagore. Tagore's writings on nationalism and modernity disdainfully rejected European forms of the nation-state without surrendering an anti-colonial intellectual position, while at the same time advocating and accepting universalist ideals of reason and humanism. Bipin Chandra Pal had explicitly articulated a claim to difference and universality in the inaugural issue of the English weekly *New India* on 12 August 1901:

New India can, therefore, no more ignore the ancient spiritual treasures of the Hindus, than the higher elements of Muhammadan culture, or the intellectual and moral ideals of modern European civilization. Its standpoint is intensely national in spirit, breathing the deepest veneration for the spiritual, moral and intellectual achievements of *Indian civilisation*, and distinctly universal, in aspiration, reaching out to all that is noblest and loveliest in *Western culture*.

Steering a creative path between an unthinking eulogy of European 'enlightenment' and an undiscriminating assault on the 'modern', the more imaginative strands of anti-colonial modernity fashioned a cultural and political space where there was no necessary contradiction between nationality and human community.

On the key questions of relations between the overarching Indian nation on the one hand and religious communities and linguistic regions on the other, anti-colonial thought and politics of the late nineteenth and early twentieth centuries left contradictory legacies. The anti-colonialism of both Hindus and Muslims was influenced in this period by their religious sensibilities. But since the colonial state's scheme of enumeration had transformed one into the 'majority' and the other into the 'minority' community, it became easier for Hindu religious symbolisms and communitarian interests to be subsumed within the emerging discourse on the Indian nation. Even a Sayyid Ahmed Khan, his loyalism notwithstanding, was more opposed to majoritarianism of the Congress variety than the idea of an Indian nation. Class and regional affiliations shaped his political postures more than religion. Others more inclined to making common cause with the Congress and seeking location within the construct of the Indian nation found it increasingly difficult to be accepted as both Muslim communitarians and Indian nationalists. The granting of 'communal' electorates in 1909 compounded the problem even further. As Maulana Mohamed Ali complained to his Congress colleagues in 1912, the educated Hindu 'communal patriot' had turned Hinduism into an effective symbol of mass mobilization and Indian 'nationality', but 'refuse[d] to give quarter to the Muslim unless the latter quietly shuffles off his individuality and becomes completely Hinduized'.

If religiously based notions of majority and minority were already beginning to pose problems for a unified Indian nationalism, as yet there appeared to be little contradiction between Bengali or Tamil linguistic communities or 'nations' on the one hand and a broader diffuse Indian 'nation' on the other. The poetry of Rabindranath Tagore and Subrahmanian Bharati could be equally harnessed in the service of regional patriotisms and all-India nationalism, and indeed forged a connection between the two. Abanindranath Tagore's painting 'Bharatamata' was originally conceived as Mother Bengal and then ungrudgingly offered in the service of a wider Indian nation. Few, if any, of the nationalist ideologues were thinking at this stage of the acquisition of power in a centralized nation-state. The swadeshi nationalist Bipin Chandra Pal pointed out that the legendary king Bharata had been described in ancient texts as *rajchakravarti*. Pal took some pains to explain that the 'literal meaning of the term is not emperor, but only a king "established at the centre of a circle of kings". King Bharata was a great prince of this order'. His position was 'not that of the administrative head of any large and centralized government, but only that of the recognized and respected centre', which was the 'general character' of all great princes in ancient times. Under Muslim rule, according to Pal, Indian unity, 'always more or less of a federal type', became 'still more pronouncedly so'. He left his readers in little doubt about the type of state he would prefer once swaraj was won. India's two most celebrated poet-philosophers, Rabindranath Tagore and Muhammad Iqbal, writing in Bengali and Urdu respectively, had produced in 1904 and 1905 patriotic narrations of linguistic and territorial nations of effervescent literary quality. But what they saw of the swadeshi movement in Bengal – communitarian bigotry in Punjab as well as the European rivalries of a murderous sort – turned both into powerful critics of the Western model of the territorial nation-state. They were prepared to be patriots, not nationalists.

At the height of the swadeshi movement, a key leader had written warmly about national ego, but also saw nationalist India preserving itself in a kind of cosmopolitanism, somewhat as the individual preserves itself in the family, the family in the class, the class in the nation, not destroying itself needlessly but recognizing the larger interest. The relatively comfortable coexistence of a multiplicity of identities – linguistic, regional, religious, national and international – would not be left undisturbed in subsequent decades.

12

COLONIALISM UNDER SIEGE

State and political economy after World War I

The severe dislocations wrought by World War I in Indian economy and society set the stage for the mass nationalist movements of the early 1920s. Wartime exigencies led to the abandonment of some of the old axioms underlying the organization of the colonial state and political economy. It is important, therefore, to get a clear understanding of the impact of World War I on the structure of the colonial state and the economic relationship between metropolis and colony. Apart from addressing this theme, the present chapter also draws a broad analytical framework to take into account continuities and changes in the state and political economy, enabling us to contextualize the mass politics of the 1920s, the economic and political crises of the depression decade, and upheavals around and during World War II.

The first casualty of the outbreak of war in 1914 was the strict 1:2 ratio of British and Indian troops in the army. The British Indian army adopted a policy of large-scale recruitment. By the time war ended in 1918 the total strength of the Indian army stood at 1.2 million. Punjab alone provided as many as 355,000 of the new recruits. In August 1918 the governor of Punjab reported proudly that in one district, Gujranwala, the ratio of soldiers to the adult male population had risen from 1:150 to 1:44 over the course of just one year. Large quantities of food and fodder were exported to the war zones in the Middle East, while some regions in India faced famine conditions. In some military campaigns, such as in Mesopotamia in 1915, Indian troops were themselves used as cannon fodder. All told, nearly 60,000 Indian soldiers were killed fighting for Britain in the European and Middle Eastern theatres during World War I. 'I am very glad,' Hira Singh wrote home to Punjab from Kitchener's Indian Hospital in Brighton on 9 July 1915, 'that you are in India. For the people of India [*sic*] are very unlikely to see India again. The black pepper [Indian troops] has all been used up, and there is only a little of the red pepper [British troops] left. I have nothing more to say, for I cannot write more plainly.'

Back in India it was the financing of the British war effort that had the most detrimental effects on large sections of Indian society. India's defence expenditure increased by some 300 per cent during the war. The colonial government had to increase the income tax and customs duties, and aggressively raise subscriptions to war loans. The land revenue demand was not increased but continued to remain a heavy burden. The colonial government's rapid expansion of public expenditure fuelled inflationary pressures in the economy. In order to secure its war supplies, the colonial state resorted to the printing of money against some credit building up in the Bank of England. The currency circulation in India increased from Rs 660 million in 1914 to Rs 1530 million in 1919. The increased money supply was now chasing fewer goods available in the economy, since imports had fallen drastically. Shortages and high prices of essential commodities became the order of the day. The worst effects of the government's inflationary policy were seen in the countryside, where grain prices rocketed and articles of daily use, such as cloth, kerosene oil and medicines, were scarce and expensive. What was more, the prices of coarse grains – the staple food of the poor – rose higher and faster than prices of better quality rice or wheat. Prices of primary products like raw jute and raw cotton remained low. By contrast, European manufacturers of jute sandbags and Indian manufacturers of cotton textiles reaped a windfall.

Although large sections of India's rural populace suffered serious hardship during the war, Indian industrial capitalism – especially in the cotton sector of Bombay and Ahmedabad – achieved a major breakthrough. Dislocations in transport had resulted in a sharp decline in the import of cotton piece goods from Britain, and the raising of the import duty from 3.5 per cent to 7.5 per cent to meet the government's financial needs in 1917 gave the Indian textile industry its first taste of protection. During 1917 and 1918 Indian mill production of cotton cloth surpassed the volume of Lancashire imports. Indian gains, however, were limited to this one sector. After a short-lived post-war boom in 1919–20, India's trade was caught in the web of the worldwide slump of 1920–22. The value of the rupee had been held down until 1917. It was raised that year and reached a peak of 2 shillings and 4 pence in December 1919 and fell drastically during the slump, hitting a low of 1 shilling in early 1921. Given the violent fluctuations in the rupee exchange rate over this period, the Indian economy was not able to recover the wartime credits.

To what extent were the British able to use India's human and economic resources for the war without provoking serious nationalist resistance? Sporadic food riots, isolated armed insurrections and measured moderate demands never came close to unsettling British rule during the course of the war. In fact the British were able to reduce the number of British troops in India and send them across to places where they were more urgently needed. Even Gandhi, who returned to India from South Africa in 1915, saw no contradiction between his non-violent creed and his efforts to recruit soldiers for the British Indian army. There were, at the same time, some radical nationalist elements minded to take advantage of the international war crisis. Moderate Western-educated nationalists also wanted something in return for valuable services rendered during the war. By procuring small quantities of German and

Turkish arms, revolutionaries in India were able to raise their level of activities from assassination of individual British officials to small-scale armed insurrections in localities. Attempts were also made to instigate mutinies among Indian soldiers in 1915, but these met with very limited success. Quite a few Muslim theologians and religious leaders, including Maulana Abul Kalam Azad, carried on propaganda against the use of Indian men and materials in the prosecution of Britain's war, especially in the Middle East. Obaidullah Sindhi, a Deobandi scholar and a key modern protagonist of Shah Waliullah's ideas, used Afghanistan as a base to try to plot a transnational jihad against the British with German, Russian and Turkish assistance.

The mid-point of World War I saw the coming together of moderates and erstwhile extremists who had parted ways in 1907, as well as increasing cooperation between the Indian National Congress and the All-India Muslim League. Tilak, who returned to India after a long, six-year spell in Burmese prisons, was welcomed back by the Congress in 1915. The Muslim League had been captured by a younger generation of nationalists drawn from urban professional classes in 1913. Mohammad Ali Jinnah, a staunch Congressman since the turn of the century, had joined the Muslim League at the invitation of Wazir Hassan that year. Jinnah played an important role in coordinating the political programmes of the Congress and the League. The crowning achievement of their dialogue was the Lucknow Pact of 1916, by which Congress accepted the principle of separate electorates for Muslims in the larger interest of forging a united Hindu–Muslim front against colonial rule. Some British officials saw this unity as paving the way for *vakil raj* – rule by Indian lawyers. At about the same time, Tilak and Annie Besant, inspired by the Irish model, set up a number of Home Rule Leagues in different parts of the country.

All this persuaded the British that some initiative had to be taken to assuage Indian public opinion. While taking harsh repressive measures against groups wedded to revolutionary violence, the British wanted to offer something to moderate nationalists. In 1917 the secretary of state for India, Edwin Montagu, declared that 'the progressive realization of responsible government' would be the goal of British rule in India. A largely discredited Whiggish or liberal view interpreted this announcement as the starting point of a unilinear movement towards the grant of Indian independence. The expression of British good intentions, on this view, implied that the mass nationalist movements of the post-1920 period were somewhat redundant. But the path of British decolonization in India was not paved with good intentions. Even the moderates were disappointed with the measure of responsible government conceded by the Montagu–Chelmsford reforms of 1919. While broadening the basis of Indian political activity, the British retained the 1909 policy of balancing interests by creating separate categories for the Muslims, landlords and the Depressed Classes. The 1919 reforms did, however, go a step further than the 1909 reforms in granting the principle of 'dyarchy'. This placed responsibility for certain less sensitive subjects like local self-government in the hands of non-official Indian ministers. Not that this was a first step towards responsible government at the centre: all that the 1919 reforms intended was to divert Indian attention away from the centre and into the provincial arenas. The new franchise, based on property and educational qualifications, was tilted in favour of the raj's friends, not its critics.

Throughout the remaining years of the raj in India, the centre was kept firmly in British hands. The 1935 Act, which accepted the principle of an all-India federation, widened the franchise to thirty-five million and gave the provinces a large measure of autonomy. Dyarchy was scrapped and Indians were associated with decision-making in all departments of provincial government. But full responsibility at the centre was something for the future; the executive was not responsible to the legislature; Indians had no say over defence; the act gave the viceroy vast discretionary powers, and defence and foreign affairs – the vital aspects of sovereignty – were kept firmly within his grasp. Despite much song and dance about provincial autonomy, the centre was equipped with all the authority necessary to curb powers in the provinces. Moreover, there was a clear disjunction between provincial autonomy and the creation of an all-India federation. While the provinces were to become autonomous after the first general elections under the act, the initial steps towards federation were to be taken only after one-half of the Indian princely states had voluntarily agreed to accede. With both the viceroy and the provincial governors enjoying special powers in the executive and the legislative spheres, the 1935 Act aimed at preserving British rule in India by taking into account an altered political environment.

In the early twentieth century the colonial state was almost forced to devolve authority in certain parts of India – Bengal for example – while its constitutional reforms acted as a spur to political activity in others – Madras for instance – which had remained more quiescent during the first two decades of the twentieth century. What the institutional structures of the colonial state did was to bring relatively isolated localities into greater contact with one another, allowing for the creation of alliances transcending local boundaries in the formal political arenas. So the constitutional reforms were both concessionary and pre-emptive in nature. Their overall aim was to direct Indian political attention away from the all-India centre, which the British were determined to keep in their own hands in order to promote and perpetuate their imperial interests – both strategic and economic – and direct it towards safe local and provincial pastures where the policy of pitting Indian against Indian could ensure the stability of the colonial state. The challenge faced by Indian nationalism was not to be wholly limited to or co-opted by the inadequate representative institutions in the locality and the provinces set up by British constitutional reforms.

In addition to adaptations in the institutional structures of the colonial state in the changed circumstances of World War I and its aftermath, the political economy of late colonialism was different in many respects from the 'classical patterns' established during its high noon. After the end of World War I the colonial state in New Delhi was finding it increasingly difficult to service the needs of the metropolis while holding on to the vital attributes of Britain's political and economic dominance in India. Already the dislocations of the war had provided effective, though not formal, protection to India's cotton textile industry, an opportunity it was quick to seize, to the relative detriment of Lancashire. In 1922 London was forced to concede fiscal autonomy to the colonial government of India. This meant New Delhi could now impose taxes, including import duties, without having to seek the permission of the metropolis. But if the fiscal authority and industrial dominance of Britain was being sapped during the 1920s, the shock of the Great Depression of the late 1920s and early 1930s overturned most of the equations of the metropolis–colony relationship. Import-substitution gathered momentum in India, displacing many of the traditional privileges enjoyed by British manufactured products. Lancashire decisively lost out to Bombay and Ahmedabad, whose cotton production outstripped British imports. In 1929 nearly twelve hundred million yards of British cloth had been imported into India; ten years later less than a hundred and fifty million yards of cloth came in. It was not that the British did nothing to stem the rot. The Ottawa agreement of 1932 produced a system of imperial preference by which British imports enjoyed preferential tariffs compared to duties imposed on goods from non-empire countries. This staved off a serious invasion of the Indian market by Japanese and, to a lesser extent, German manufactured goods. While the British were able to use the colonial connection to withstand Japanese competition, they were forced to yield ground to indigenous Indian industry.

If the Depression damaged British industry's access to the Indian market, it completely wiped out India's export surplus with the rest of the world through which colonial India's payments to metropolitan Britain had been channelled. In 1929–30 the value of Indian commodity exports, which stood at Rs 3.1 billion, was well in excess of the value of imports, which was approximately Rs 2.4 billion. By 1932–33, the value of exports and imports had both fallen to about Rs 1.3 billion. How, then, did the colony manage to maintain its payments, including home charges to Britain, in the dramatically altered economic scenario? In September 1931 the British pound sterling was taken off the gold standard, and the rupee tied to it at a fixed exchange rate of 1 shilling and 6 pence. With the pound and the rupee effectively devalued against gold, and the rupee artificially pegged to the pound at a high exchange rate, a dramatic out-flow of gold – up to a conservative estimate of Rs 3.4 billion in value between 1931 and 1934 – took place from India. Short-term profits made on sales of gold masked a long-term disinvestment by India, especially its agrarian sector. Hoards of gold ornaments came out of the Indian countryside and much of it was eventually melted down in British warehouses. Distress sales of gold enabled Britain to continue the process of transferring wealth from colony to metropolis, even after India's export surplus had evaporated. Incidentally,

Britain was not able to keep all of the gold it acquired during the Depression era. Some of it flowed across the Atlantic into the hoards of the Federal Reserve of the United States of America.

The advanced industrialized countries of the West, including Britain, had responded to the crisis of the Depression with policies of deflation, erection of protective tariff barriers and huge cutbacks in foreign lending. The deflationary policies and the tariff walls accentuated the collapse of agrarian prices, which had already been on the downslide because of a slackening of demand in Western markets. The stoppage in the flow of foreign funds from Britain to India, once Indian export prospects looked bleak, resulted in a massive credit crunch. The annual inflow of these funds had been critical to the financing of agrarian production and trade, and the annual addition of a key portion of the money supply. From the perspective of India's regional economies, the dishoarding of gold from 1931 onwards represented a desperate attempt to maintain liquidity.

While Britain's commercial dominance of India was dented during the Depression, the metropolitan power managed to retain control of finance. It was British financial wizardry which deflected Indian attempts to win a real measure of autonomy in this sphere. Britain was forced to set up a central bank, known as the reserve bank of India, in 1934. But it was to be under London's and not New Delhi's ultimate jurisdiction. Although denied financial autonomy (relating to currency and credit), colonial India did of course have fiscal autonomy (relating to taxes), which it used to set up protective tariffs for certain kinds of Indian industry. The mid-1930s saw the establishment of subsidiaries of British multinational firms inside colonial India's tariff walls. Some of the more important firms were Dunlop, Unilever, Metal Box and Imperial Chemicals. So financial finesse and multinational manoeuvring enabled Britain to continue to derive economic benefits from its Indian possession.

Throughout the inter-war period India remained the linch-pin in the strategic defence of the British empire, especially the new lucrative oil-producing areas of South-West Asia. But the nature of India's economic importance to Britain had been undergoing fundamental change. It had required the most ingenious of financial manipulation and stolid rearguard action by the British to continue to derive economic benefits from India. Agrarian distress provided major impetus to the Gandhian mass movements of the 1920s and 1930s, but it also gave rise to other forms of communitarian and class conflicts in some regions. While making tactical concessions to a rising nationalist movement, the British were able to retain the vital attributes of sovereignty and centralized power in their own hands. A measure of Britain's success in fending off nationalist challenges can be detected in viceroy Linlithgow's lament in 1939: 'Hitler has rather overset our Indian plans'. Yet the outbreak of World War II also strengthened Britain's will to hold on to empire. Churchill grandly declared, on becoming prime minister in 1940, that he had not become the king's first minister to preside over the liquidation of the British empire.

In India the colonial government prepared contingency plans to ban the Congress organization as a whole in the event of another campaign of civil disobedience. The British were determined at the outset of World War II to put their professed aim of progressive realization of responsible government in India into cold storage for the duration of the war.

An analysis of the structures of the late colonial state and political economy simply provides us with a general picture of what Indian society and nationalist political organizations had to contend with. In the subsequent chapters we will shift our focus from structures – more static than changing – to the dynamics of Indian social change and political protest. These social and political processes included not only the high drama of Gandhian non-cooperation and civil disobedience movements but also the dissenting politics of the All-India Muslim League and Muslim-majority provinces. There were also radical left-wing challenges to Gandhian leadership of the Congress, and various popular upsurges working inexorably and decidedly outside the pale of Congress organization.

13

GANDHIAN NATIONALISM AND MASS POLITICS IN THE 1920s

In the late nineteenth and early twentieth centuries Indians had opposed the British raj through constitutional methods of prayers and petitions, extra-constitutional methods of individual revolutionary violence, and futile attempts at armed insurrection during World War I. By 1919 constitutionalism had proved ineffectual in winning major concessions and sporadic, isolated armed resistance had been crushed. It was at this juncture that Mohandas Karamchand Gandhi appeared on the all-India political stage with his strategy of non-violent non-cooperation. He was to stride the arena of Indian nationalist politics like a colossus until World War II.

Gandhi was born in 1869, into a Gujarati *bania* family. He studied law in England but was unable to establish a successful practice in either Bombay or Ahmedabad. From 1893 to 1914 he lived in Natal, South Africa. It was his successful organization of non-violent protest against the racist policies of South Africa's white government towards the large expatriate Indian community that brought him into political prominence. In 1908 Gandhi wrote a short book entitled *Hind Swaraj* (The Freedom of India), which provides some of the best insights into his early political beliefs and philosophy. *Hind Swaraj* contains a powerful critique not only of British rule in India but of modern industrial civilization and the Western concept of civil society as a whole. 'When I read Mr Dutt's economic history of India,' Gandhi wrote, 'I wept; and as I think of it again my heart sickens. It is machinery that has impoverished India.' Gandhi believed that it would not be sufficient simply to win political swaraj, which would result in 'English rule without the Englishmen'. 'India's salvation', he declared, 'consists in unlearning what she has learnt during the past fifty years or so. The railways, telegraphs, hospitals, lawyers, doctors and such like have all to go, and the so-called upper class have to learn to live consciously and religiously and deliberately the simple life of a peasant.' Endorsing Napoleon's pejorative description of the English as a nation of shopkeepers, Gandhi denounced Britain's greed for commercial profits achieved through economic imperialism. He opposed British political autocracy but saw no virtue in Western representative institutions. Gandhi likened parliament, for instance, to 'a sterile woman and a prostitute': the first because it could never enact a law according to its own

111

judgement and the second because it continuously shifted its allegiance from one set of ministers to another, depending on which happened to be more powerful. He called instead for a state of enlightened anarchy in which national life would be so self-controlled that representatives would become unnecessary. His utopia was *Ram Rajya* (the kingdom of Rama) of the great Hindu epic *Ramayana*. Ram Rajya was a patriarchy in which the ruler, the embodiment of moral virtue, always gave voice to the collective will. It is no coincidence that Gandhi's model for Indian women was Sita, the wife of Rama, whom he interpreted to be a chaste and submissive woman. Passive resistance and the nationalist ritual of spinning the *charkha*, he was to argue later, was especially suited to the 'nature' of women. Gandhi's musings in the *Hind Swaraj* may have sounded a trifle obscurantist to most urban educated groups, but his critical evaluation of Western industrialism and political institutions struck a chord among large sections of Indians ruined as much by factories as by law courts.

Upon returning to India Gandhi spent more than a year travelling across the subcontinent, surveying the social and political scene. During 1917–18 he felt confident enough to try out his political strategy of non-violent non-cooperation in three local agitations. Two of these were conducted in his home province of Gujarat: the first in Kheda district against the colonial state's high revenue demand at a time of economic distress; the second in Ahmedabad, where he successfully mediated a conflict between Indian workers and industrialists in the city's textile mills. The third agitation took place in Champaran district of Bihar, where Gandhi took up the cause of peasants being forced to grow indigo by European planters. These movements, albeit local and specific in character, had a much wider demonstration effect and established Gandhi's reputation as an effective leader of mass agitations.

The disappointments and fears of 1919 afforded Gandhi the opportunity to launch his first major all-India agitation. Not only had the Montagu–Chelmsford reforms not gone far enough, but the Rowlatt Act, which perpetuated wartime ordinances into peace-time legislations – enabling the British to hold Indians in detention without trial – contradicted the spirit of the reforms. Indian public opinion was outraged. Gandhi described the Rowlatt law as a 'black act' passed by a 'satanic' government. He seized the moment to call for an all-India mass protest movement, relying on political networks like the Home Rule Leagues, an array of groups inspired by Islamic universalism and anxious about the fate of the Khilafat in the aftermath of the defeat of Ottoman Turkey, as well as his own creature – the Satyagraha Sabha. The Congress was conspicuously absent; it had no organizational machinery for agitational politics of the sort Gandhi had in mind. This needs some emphasizing, since the 1919 agitation was the largest and most violent anti-imperialist movement India had witnessed since 1857.

The swadeshi movement against the partition of Bengal in 1905 had fore-shadowed some of the Gandhian techniques of non-cooperation, but it paled in comparison with the sheer ferocity of the 1919 agitation. Reeling under the social and economic consequences of World War I, the people of India were ready to storm the gates of the British raj. The Muslims of India had felt a deep sense of unease about British intentions ever since the Balkan wars of 1912–13, the Kanpur mosque incident of 1913 in which many Muslims were killed, and the implications of the outcome of the 1914–18 war for the Islamic ummah. It was these misgivings that persuaded pro-Khilafat Muslims, led by the charismatic Mohamed Ali and his elder brother Shaukat, to join forces with Gandhi at war's end in the hope of more effectively challenging the colonial state. As the anti-Rowlatt *satyagraha* merged with the Khilafat movement, attacks on the symbols of British authority – banks, post offices, the railway stations and town halls – as well as assaults on British civilians were followed by brutal repression.

The 1919 agitation had many remarkable features, among which was a courageous display of unity among Hindus, Muslims and Sikhs. The Punjab, generally considered to be the least nationalist-orientated of the British Indian provinces, had to be placed under martial law, and at least one of its towns was the target of aerial bombardment. It was also the Punjab which gave the satyagraha its best-known martyrs. On 13 April 1919, a peaceful and unarmed crowd of villagers who had come to Jallianwallah Bagh in Amritsar, looking for a fair, oblivious of the martial law regulation prohibiting meetings, were fired upon by General Dyer's men; 379 innocents were felled by British bullets and more than 1200 were injured. Initially Gandhi had called upon all those opposed to the Rowlatt legislation to respond to his programme of non-violent protest. Gandhi described the violence that erupted during the course of the movement as 'a rapier run through my body'. The tally of fatalities was hugely uneven on the British and Indian sides, but the killing of even a few British officials was an indication that Gandhi had not yet fine-tuned his agitational techniques and was not fully in control.

Gandhi's political genius fused love for a territorial homeland with the extra-territorial loyalty of religion in the mass nationalist movement of 1920. Without detracting from his distinctive qualities, the Mahatma's reason needs to be rescued by historians from the mystical haze created by latter-day cultural critics flying the banner of indigenous authenticity. It is sometimes too easily supposed, as Partha Chatterjee does, that Gandhi's thought did not accept 'the conceptual frameworks or the modes of reasoning and inference adopted by the nationalists of his day' and 'emphatically reject[ed] their rationalism, scientism and historicism'. An overemphasis on *Hind Swaraj* has led to a rather lop-sided view of Gandhi's political thought and practice, missing in the process the key location of India's Muslims in Gandhi's first mass movement. The classic 'moment of manoeuvre' in the history of Indian nationalism, if ever there was one, came with Gandhi's espousal of the cause of the Khilafat, which not only paved the way for his rise to power within Congress, but also enabled him to achieve a quite spectacular success in popular mobilization, cutting across lines of religious community.

Urged by C.F. Andrews to publicly clarify his position on the Khilafat, Gandhi wrote in *Young India* on 21 July 1920:

> I should clear the ground by stating that I reject any religious doctrine that does not appeal to reason and is in conflict with morality. I tolerate unreasonable religious sentiment when it is not immoral. I hold the Khilafat claim to be both just and reasonable and therefore it derives greater force because it has behind it the religious sentiment of the Musulman world.

Gandhi could 'conceive the possibility of a blind and fanatical religious sentiment existing in opposition to pure justice'. Under those circumstances he would 'resist the former and fight for the latter'. But since the Indian Muslims had an issue that was first of all reasonable and just and on top of that supported by scriptural authority, 'then for the Hindus not to support them to the utmost would be a cowardly breach of brotherhood and they would forfeit all claim to consideration from their Mahomedan countrymen'.

The crux of Gandhi's case was Lloyd George's 'broken pledge' to respect the immunity of the holy places in Arabia and Mesopotamia and of Jeddah and not deprive Turkey of its capital or lands in Asia Minor and Thrace. Instead Smyrna and Thrace had been taken away 'dishonestly', mandates established in Syria and Mesopotamia 'unscrupulously' and a British nominee set up in the Hejaz 'under the protection of British guns'. Gandhi believed 'the spirit of Islam' to be 'essentially republican in the truest sense of the term' which would not stand in the way of Arab and Armenian independence from Turkey if the Arabs and Armenians so wished. On this point he endorsed Mohamed Ali's call for a mixed, independent commission of Indian Muslims, Hindus and Europeans 'to investigate the real wish of the Armenians and the Arabs and then to come to a *modus vivendi* whereby the claims of the nationality and those of Islam may be adjusted and satisfied'. The 'most thorny part of the question', Gandhi recognized, was Palestine. The British had made certain promises to the Zionists. But Palestine was 'not a stake in the war' and so under 'no canon of ethics or war' could Palestine be given to the Jews 'as a result of the war'. If the Muslim claim had been unjust there may have been cause for hesitation, but an intrinsically just claim backed by scriptural authority was irresistible.

Gandhi could not have been more forthright in acknowledging the extra-territorial nature of Muslim sentiment:

> Let Hindus not be frightened by Pan-Islamism. It is not – it need not be – anti-Indian or anti-Hindu. Mussalmans must wish well to every Mussalman state, and even assist any such state, if it is undeservedly in peril. And Hindus, if they are true friends of Mussalmans, cannot but share the latter's feelings. We must, therefore, co-operate with our

Mussalman brethren in their attempt to save the Turkish empire in Europe from extinction.

Closer to home, Gandhi supported the proposal of 'Brother Shaukat Ali' that there should be three national cries – *Allaho Akbar*, *Bande Mataram* or *Bharat Mataki Jai* and *Hindu-Mussalmanki Jai*. Gandhi called upon all Hindus to join Muslims in the first cry 'in reverence and prayerfulness', since Hindus 'may not fight shy of Arabic words, when their meaning is not only totally inoffensive but even ennobling'. He preferred *Bande Mataram* to *Bharat Mataki Jai*, as 'it would be a graceful recognition of the intellectual and emotional superiority of Bengal'. And since India was nothing without 'the union of the Hindu and the Muslim heart', *Hindu-Mussalmanki Jai* was a cry never to be forgotten.

Gandhi appeared to have devised the perfect formula for harnessing the emotive power of nationalism in the linguistic regions and forging Hindu–Muslim unity based on a respectful attitude towards the fact of religiously informed cultural difference in an anti-colonial movement on an all-India scale. Gandhi was not using religious means for political ends; nation and religion were precious ends in themselves, religion perhaps even more so than nation. For both Maulana Mohamed Ali and himself, he asserted, the Khilafat was 'the central fact': with the Maulana because it was 'his religion' and 'with me because, in laying down my life for the Khilafat, I ensure the safety of the cow, that is my religion, from the Mussalman knife'. 'Both hold Swaraj equally dear,' he added, 'because only by Swaraj is the safety of our respective faiths possible.' The entire movement of non-cooperation was, in his view, 'a struggle between religion and irreligion' because the motive behind every crime perpetrated by a Europe nominally Christian but beset by Satan was 'not religious or spiritual, but grossly material', while the Hindus and Muslims had 'religion and honour as their motive'.

In 1920 Gandhi wove together more explicitly the negative value of *ahimsa* (non-violence) with the positive value of *satyagraha* (a quest for truth through mass political activity). He emphasized the importance of discipline and loyalty to the leader in campaigns of satyagraha by using a military metaphor: 'a soldier of an army does not know the whole of the military science, so also does a satyagrahi not know the whole science of satyagraha. It is enough if he trusts his commander and honestly follows his instructions and is ready to suffer unto death without bearing malice against the so-called enemy ... [the satyagrahis] must render heart discipline to their commander.' In order to enlarge his political base, however, Gandhi offered the method of non-violence to the Congress party and his country as a political weapon and not as a moral philosophy. He even told a group of revolutionaries in Bengal that if India had the sword he would have asked her to draw it. But since India did not, he asked the revolutionaries to try his programme at least for a year. 'I do believe,' Gandhi wrote, 'that where there is only a choice between cowardice and violence I would advise violence ... Hence also do I advocate training in arms for those who believe in the method of violence. I would rather have India resort to arms in order to defend her honour than that she should in a cowardly manner become or remain a helpless witness to her own dishonour.' However, he held non-violence to be 'infinitely superior' to violence. Gandhi made it amply clear in a later speech to the Congress in 1942: 'ahimsa with me is a creed. But it is never as a creed that I placed it before India ... I placed it before the Congress as a political weapon to be employed for the solution of practical problems.' The restraining value of non-violence, the leadership principle and the Congress party organization which Gandhi was able to fashion to his needs made it possible for him to launch powerful, yet controlled, mass movements.

Gandhi's techniques paved the way for his capture of the Congress at Nagpur in 1920. This he was only able to achieve with the help of pro-Khilafat Muslims. Gandhi succeeded in outmanoeuvring the moderate elements. A man like Mohammed Ali Jinnah, who had tried forging Hindu–Muslim unity on a different basis, deplored Gandhi's mixing of religion with politics. Jinnah was shouted down at the Nagpur Congress. But the Ali brothers and other Muslim leaders stuck to their programme of using the Khilafat agitation to bring their community firmly into the mainstream of Indian nationalism. Contrary to the fears of their detractors, the Khilafatists hoped that by juxtaposing Gandhi's chosen symbols – the *charkha* (the spinning wheel) and *khadi* (hand-woven cloth) – with the Islamic crescent and the Turkish *fez* they could reconcile, not aggravate, Hindu–Muslim differences.

There were other elements of the Gandhian programme that came in for some criticism. The great Bengali poet Rabindranath Tagore did not support the idea of boycotting educational institutions, remembering the inadequacies of national education in the Swadeshi period. Tagore wrote disapprovingly in 1921:

> To one and all he simply says: Spin and weave, spin and weave. Is this the call: 'Let all seekers after truth come from all sides'? Is this the call of the New Age to new creation. When nature called to the bee to take refuge in the narrow life of the hive, millions of bees responded to it for the sake of efficiency, and accepted the loss of sex in consequence. But this sacrifice by way of self-atrophy led to the opposite of freedom. Any country, the people of which can agree to become neuters for the sake of some temptation, or command, carries within itself its own prison-house.

But the All-India Congress Committee (the AICC), including sceptics like C.R. Das and Motilal Nehru, endorsed Gandhi's programme to boycott the reformed councils and launch a non-cooperation movement. Gandhi was in the driver's seat, albeit temporarily. The Congress constitution was modified; its goal was

116

to attain swaraj through all legitimate and peaceful means. Provincial Congresses were reorganized along linguistic lines, since Gandhi well knew that the emotive power of anti-colonial sentiment often sprang from linguistic nationalisms. At his insistence steps were taken to transform Congress into a truly mass political party. But the adoption of a mass programme by the Congress was more in the way of a symbolic gesture, an effort by Gandhi – a brilliant politician – to make political capital out of the populist ferment sweeping India at the time.

The years 1919 to 1922 were marked by widespread labour unrest and *kisan* (peasant) movements owing little or nothing to the Congress. So Gandhi's programme had an immediate psychological impact. His somewhat rash promise of swaraj within a year aroused millenarian hopes in the remotest villages of India, and his call for village reconstruction based on an economic revival through the charkha and khadi was greeted enthusiastically. But it would not be too far-fetched to assert that the national leadership was being pushed by the pressures which the colonial state's economic policies were generating below into taking positions they might otherwise have wanted to resist. Indeed, at each crucial twist of the non-cooperation movement of the early 1920a we find the Gandhian Congress ready to press the brakes, fearful of people running ahead of the leadership and redefining the organization's cherished goal of swaraj.

This is why Gandhi laid special emphasis on issues cutting across India's manifold class, caste and religious divisions. For example, the Congress under the Mahatma considered adopting the non-payment of rent and revenue as part of its official programme. Kisan movements in various parts of the country were already urging peasants not to pay rents and revenue. So, although the Congress did accept non-payment of revenue after much hesitation, it refused to extend the programme to the non-payment of rent. After agrarian conflicts in U.P., Gandhi 'deprecated all attempts to sow discord between landlords and tenants and advised the tenants to suffer rather than fight'; they had to 'join forces [with their landlords, however oppressive] for fighting against the most powerful zamindar, namely the [British] Government'. Gandhi adopted much the same line with labour, lest his business and industrialist supporters be put off by Congress radicalism.

Despite the Mahatma's willingness, even eagerness, to keep populist forces on a leash, his prestige among the populace was undeniable. Images of Gandhi as Mahatma were, as Shahid Amin has shown, crafted by the spread of popular rumour. Peasants who may have seen the leader once from a distance, or perhaps not seen him at all, could interpret in their own way the message of Gandhi *Maharaj* – the great king Gandhi. If local and regional variations bring out the contradictions in the non-cooperation movement, the perception of Gandhi as a veritable messiah explains why, in spite of the 'disparate aspirations and grievances', the main ingredients of Indian nationalism became, as Rajat Ray has claimed, 'somehow generalized into unities stronger than their own contradictions'.

The boycott of British goods and institutions was much more effective in 1921 than it had been in 1905. The sense of alienation from the raj also expressed itself in the successful boycott of the visit by the Prince of Wales in late 1921. In most towns and cities the prince only saw closed shutters. By early 1922 the phase of boycott appeared to have reached a peak. Although most leaders and activists other than Gandhi had been cast into prison, there were many more ready and eager to escalate the movement into a no-revenue campaign, which Gandhi had declared would begin in the Bardoli district of Gujarat in late February 1922. So it is hardly possible to exaggerate the feelings of disappointment when Gandhi abruptly called off the non-cooperation movement after receiving news that twenty-two policemen had been killed in a police station set alight by angry peasants at Chauri Chaura in Gorakhpur district of U.P. on 5 February 1922. Chauri Chaura, in time, came to signify an aberration in the official story of Indian nationalism.

Gandhi's compromise – and there were to be many more – brought the divisions in the Congress out into the open. Men like C.R. Das and Motilal Nehru, who had wanted to extract substantial political concessions from the British while the Congress movement had the upper hand in late 1921, now favoured entry into the Montagu–Chelmsford councils, on the grounds that since non-cooperation had been called off it made sense to try and wreck the structure of the raj from within. Unable to persuade Gandhi – so often given to obduracy – Das and Nehru with their followers broke with the Congress to form a Swaraj party. So the end of the non-cooperation movement of 1920–22 left the Congress split down the middle between no-changers and pro-changers on the question of the policy of boycott. But it was worse than that. The heyday of Hindu–Muslim unity during the Khilafat fervour was followed by tension, conflict and violence between these religious communities on an unprecedented scale. The worst-affected provinces were U.P. and Punjab, where the anti-imperialist struggle was replaced with Hindu social movements of *shuddhi* (purity) and *sangathan* (organization) and Muslim counterparts named *tabligh* (religious preaching) and *tanzeem* (organization).

As Congress president at Cocanada in December 1923 Mohamed Ali called for an accommodation of religious differences through the creation of a 'federation of faiths' rather than just a 'unity of opposition'. In Bengal the far-sighted Deshbandhu C.R. Das reached a generous agreement with Muslim leaders, known as the Bengal Pact, based on a 50:50 principle in the allocation of future government posts and jobs. But at the all-India level the Punjab line articulated by Lala Lajpat Rai had won out over the Bengal line advocated by C.R. Das. Lajpat Rai represented the Punjabi Hindu desire to make full capital of the colonial logic of a 'Hindu majority' at the all-India level, while refusing to accept its implications in a province where Muslims were in a majority. So while the formal arenas of politics in Punjab had been successfully provincialized by the British and were dominated by the loyalist Unionist party headed by Fazl-i-Husain, the informal arenas were coming to be influenced by a noxious brand of religious bigotry. The absence of generosity on the part of the Congress augured poorly for the future of a Hindu–Muslim compromise and, by extension, for the anti-colonial struggle. It may be tempting to see this as the logical conclusion to the dangerous blending of religion and politics by Gandhi and his Khilafat allies. But religion as faith within the limits of morality and of reason had not impeded the cause of anti-colonial unity and in fact assisted its realization at a key moment of struggle. The variegated symbols of religion as culture had enthused nationalists of many hues without embittering relations between religious communities until they became hostage to the bigoted politics of majoritarianism and minoritarianism. Religion had proven to be less of a barrier to forming a common front against the British than a politics of nationalism devoid of any spirit of accommodation of internal differences.

It was the British who inadvertently created the prospects of Indian unity with the announcement of an all-white commission led by John Simon in November 1927. The Simon Commission was to enquire into the future of constitutional reforms in India. This intensified pressure on the Congress to chalk out its future course of action. Having resolved to boycott the Simon Commission, the Congress set up its own committee under Motilal Nehru to formulate the elements of a future constitution. The Muslim League led by Mohammed Ali Jinnah offered to cooperate on the basis of a reasonable charter of safeguards for the Muslim minority, but was rebuffed by the Congress acting under pressure from a fringe group known as the Hindu Mahasabha. Interestingly, it was about this time that the term 'communal' acquired its pejorative connotation as the lesser 'other' of nationalism. Claims to speak for Muslim interests by any individual or organization outside the Congress fold now ran the risk of being labelled 'communalist'. This represented a departure from the acknowledgement and accommodation of religious differences that was seen until the early 1920s as the basis for forging Hindu–Muslim unity in the anti-colonial cause. In November 1930 Mohamed Ali made an impassioned plea for Indian freedom, while strongly advocating the 'Muslim case' for separate electorates, safeguards and majority provinces:

> I have a culture, a polity, an outlook on life – a complete synthesis which is Islam. Where God commands I am a Muslim first, a Muslim second, and a Muslim last, and nothing but a Muslim ... But where India is concerned, where India's freedom is concerned, where the welfare of India is concerned, I am an Indian first, an Indian second, an Indian last, and nothing but an Indian.

A perfectly legitimate 'nationalist' position in 1920, such an expression of the multiple identities of India's Muslims in 1930 by a former Congress president entailed being nailed a 'communalist'.

In the late 1920s the Congress continued to dither over the all-important question of complete independence. And this despite the efforts of its more radical wing, led by Subhas Chandra Bose and Jawaharlal Nehru, to force the Mahatma's hand on the matter. The Motilal Nehru report had recommended a demand for dominion status. A resolution moved by Subhas Chandra Bose at the Calcutta session of the Congress in December 1928, calling for complete independence, was narrowly defeated after Gandhi intervened in the debate. The reason for Gandhi's hesitation is not difficult to identify: he had always insisted on leading a controlled movement against the raj and was afraid of giving the forces of popular radicalism their head. But the forces of radicalism were not about to wait for Gandhi to switch on the green signal. The year 1928 saw India, and Bombay in particular, rocked by a spate of labour strikes and radical protest by urban youth and students. At the Maharashtra Provincial Conference of 1928 Subhas Chandra Bose called for 'a coalition between labour and nationalism' and the transformation of India into 'an independent Federal Republic'. He warned Indian nationalists not to become 'a queer mixture of political democrats and social conservatives', arguing:

> If we want to make India really great we must build up a political democracy on the pedestal of a democratic society. Privileges based on birth, caste or creed should go, and equal opportunities should be thrown open to all irrespective of caste, creed or religion. The status of women should also be raised and women should be trained to take larger and a more intelligent interest in public affairs.

Bengal meanwhile was once again in the grip of a systematic revolutionary campaign. By the time Gandhi came around to accepting *purna swaraj* (full independence) as the goal at the Lahore session of the Congress in December 1929, labour militancy and urban youth radicalism had been to a large extent repressed. The British had charged thirty-one labour leaders of allegedly Communist leanings for conspiring to overthrow the government. The trial came to be known as the Meerut Conspiracy Case of 1929. Significantly, it was only very reluctantly that Congress adopted the release of the Meerut prisoners as one of its demands during the civil disobedience movement of the early 1930s.

The British design of provincializing Indian politics was successfully circumvented, if not subverted, by the forces of Indian nationalism through the use of new techniques of struggle in the early 1920s. Congress was certainly altered from being a club of the educated elite to a more broad-based mass political party. Yet the Congress under Gandhi, espousing an ideology of class conciliation, more often than not represented the class interests of the middle to richer peasantry and industrial capitalists in the urban sector. Urban professionals not impressed by Gandhi's political ideology nevertheless accepted his leadership as a matter of expediency. For the poor suffering from economic oppression and social discrimination in rural and urban areas alike, Gandhi simply offered the palliative remedy of trusteeship. According to this concept, the wealthy and relatively powerful would hold not only property but also the interests of the subordinate classes in trust. Once the mass movement had been called off, Gandhi and the Gandhians fell back on constructive work in the villages. The Swaraj party's attempts to wreck the reforms from within were relatively successful in some provinces, such as Bengal and the Central Provinces, but a complete failure in others, notably Punjab. Gandhi's suspension of the mass campaign and the Congress's refusal to support C.R. Das's strategy to assure Hindu–Muslim unity opened the way for the politics of loyalism on the one hand and bigotry on the other.

By the late 1920s urban educated students and youth as well as industrial workers were showing an inclination to identify with more radical organizations and ideologies within and outside Congress. The British, for their part, sought to rest their regime on the support of princes, rural elites in regions where politics had been successfully provincialized, and sections of religious minorities which had never felt at home in the Gandhian Congress. With the passage of the purna swaraj resolution in December 1929, Gandhi and the Congress faced the challenge of undermining the colonial structures of domination and collaboration while harnessing the various and competing strands of opposition to the British raj without being overwhelmed by them. In the early 1920s Gandhi had been instrumental in transforming India's political landscape. Would the Mahatma's magic work a second time?

14

THE DEPRESSION DECADE
Society, economics and politics

The economically decisive decade of the 1930s witnessed significant changes in social relations and a quickening of the political pace. The huge impact of the Depression showed how closely the Indian economy was tied to the capitalist world economy, and how vulnerable Indian society was to its dramatic downturns. The acute economic crisis of the early 1930s provided the context for the revival of mass nationalist agitations held in suspended animation since 1922, but also unleashed a whole range of other types of conflicts along lines of class, caste and religious community. The colonial state responded to the political challenges initially with repressive measures, and by mid-decade with a new round of political engineering which made concessions at the provincial level but gave away little at the centre. In the late 1930s some part of the social discontent was channelled into the provincial electoral arenas defined by the 1935 Government of India Act. At the same time the Gandhian old guard of Congress came under fire from the radical and socialist elements within and outside the party. The Muslim League, which offered cooperation against the British until 1937, was rebuffed by the Congress after the elections and began its search for an alternative political strategy.

Indian economy and society experienced the Great Depression in two major ways – a collapse of prices and a rupture in the circuits of monetary credit. Prices had been weakening since 1926, with the slowing down in the rate of growth of demand in Western markets. A crash in prices of agricultural commodities was postponed by the efforts of various governments to withhold stocks from the market. In 1929 a glut was reached and prices tumbled. The crisis in agrarian production and prices coincided with a major disorder in the industrial economies of the West. The protective tariffs and deflationary policies resorted to by Western governments intensified the trade slump and accentuated the fall in prices. Between 1929 and 1932 the prices of India's major cash crops more than halved. Once India's export prospects looked bleak in 1930, the flow of foreign funds into India's agrarian sector was suddenly withdrawn. This resulted in a generalized liquidity crisis affecting prices of all commodities, a trend exacerbated by the government's manipulation of the financial instruments of currency and credit.

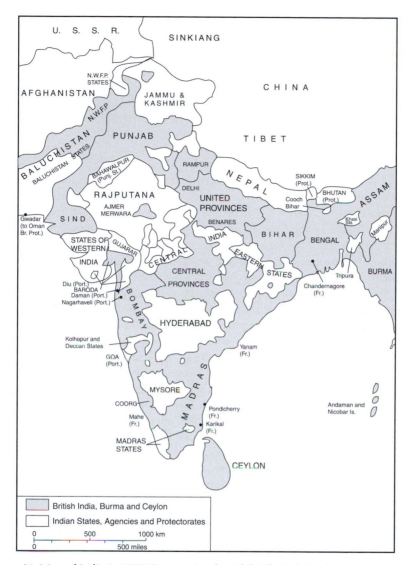

Figure 21 Map of India in 1937 (Source: Ayesha Jalal, *The Sole Spokesman*)

As the financial superstructure stopped pouring vast amounts of liquid capital down the trading and credit networks, small trader-moneylenders in the rural areas were left high and dry. Small landlord-usurers were unable to recover any interest from peasant debtors and had nothing to lend. The bigger creditors simply pulled out of the unprofitable business of rural moneylending. Peasants suddenly discovered that the trader would not appear at their doorsteps, and at the village mart no one was prepared to pay a remunerative price for their produce.

Unable to service their debts, peasants would be refused new loans in cash. Where landlord-moneylenders held large personal demesnes, grain loans were continued in return for labour and the ties of dependence were strengthened. But in many other instances the rupture in credit relations had the effect of snapping social bonds and undermining the unequal symbiosis that had characterized relations between peasant debtors and trader/landlord creditors. The slump brought economic hardship to peasants and rural labourers but also damaged the principal mode of social dominance available to sections of the rural elite. Since food prices fell almost as much as cash crop prices, the rural poor were able to struggle through the Depression decade, albeit at a much reduced standard of living and in greatly straitened circumstances. The long-term damage to credit relations meant, however, that when prices rose with the outbreak of the war, the prospect of starvation stared them in the face.

The experience of the Depression in the urban areas was much more mixed. Unemployment and low wages were the norm in many industrial sectors, for example, the European and Marwari-dominated jute mills in eastern India, and the indigenous cotton textile industry in western India. Industrial capitalists were generally able to shift losses to the workforce and the agrarian sector by resort to measures such as short-time working. The flow of capital from the rural to the urban sectors and a measure of protection for certain commodities gave a boost to some sectors of urban industry. The cement industry, for instance, did well as new residential areas grew up in the metropolitan cities of Calcutta, Bombay and Madras and the process of urbanization gathered pace in the smaller towns. Tariffs against imports of Javanese sugar provided an opening for the Indian sugar industry. Low prices brought comfort to the urban salaried classes and workers fortunate enough to retain employment. So the Great Depression affected the urban classes and the rural masses rather differently. But it is important to note that the 1930s were good times for urban consumption and not necessarily for urban industrial investment. Between 1930 and 1938 some 155 million rupees' worth of alcohol was imported into India, a figure close to the total amount invested in this period in cotton-textile machinery.

It was in the context of a dramatically altered economic scenario that the Gandhian civil disobedience campaigns of the early 1930s were launched. Gandhi's specific demands and programme, unveiled in early 1930, were something of a disappointment compared to the purna swaraj or complete independence resolution of December 1929. Five of Gandhi's eleven demands listed in an ultimatum to viceroy Irwin related to economic issues. The call for the abolition of the salt tax and the reduction of the land-revenue demand by half were designed for India's peasant masses. On behalf of India's industrial bourgeoisie Gandhi demanded protection for the indigenous textile industry, reservation of coastal shipping for Indians (since international shipping was almost entirely British owned), and a reduction of the rupee–pound exchange rate from 1 shilling and 6 pence to 1 shilling and 4 pence in order to stimulate Indian exports. The

British did not budge, other than in making a concession to the textile interest. So in March 1930 Gandhi chose the salt issue to kick off the civil disobedience movement. Even Jawaharlal Nehru was forced to admit that the Mahatma's choice of salt as the central issue was a trifle too eccentric for his liking. But, as ever, Gandhi had his way and, what was more, he had a point. His march to the coast in western India to make salt in violation of an unjust law had an electrifying effect across the subcontinent. The civil disobedience movement got off to a good start with no-tax and no-revenue campaigns and boycott of British goods and institutions. This was not altogether difficult, since all the Congress had to do was to rubber-stamp the multifarious discontents seething in the Indian countryside and, to a more limited extent, in the towns as well.

As the year drew on, however, the movement showed signs of flagging in some regions and tendencies towards increased radicalism in others. Peasant movements began to display a no-rent mentality, which directly affected Indian rentier landlords. In certain regions, such as east Bengal, mostly Muslim peasant debtors rose against mostly Hindu moneylenders, giving what was at this stage a primarily economic struggle a potentially communal complexion. Revolutionary violence, which had reared its head during the militant student, youth and workers' movements of 1928–29, showed few signs of abating. Bhagat Singh, who had assassinated a British police officer in Punjab in 1928 and hurled a bomb inside the central legislative assembly in 1929, was widely regarded as a folk-hero in 1930–31. Among the more daring revolutionary acts were the Chittagong armoury raid in April 1930 and the assault on Writers' Building, the seat of government in Calcutta, by three young men – Benoy, Badal and Dinesh – in December 1930. Gandhi's peasant followers often had to rely on these types of revolutionaries in the face of British repression. In Midnapur district of Bengal, where Gandhian civil disobedience was especially strong, the British district magistrate wrote in 1930: 'We have not got the force to deal with these mobs with lathis [wooden sticks] and the effect of lathis is insufficient. The best thing that could happen would be to have a few more shootings ... unless this is done collection of taxes will I am certain be extremely difficult.' A few more shootings did take place in this district. The district magistrate and two of his successors were among those who were killed. Sometimes individual terrorism impeded mass movements in India, but on other occasions the two were closely connected, and tended to complement and strengthen each other.

Unbridled revolutionary or radical fervour was not something the Mahatma was inclined to encourage. So he opened talks with viceroy Irwin. Winston Churchill, a diehard imperialist temporarily in the political wilderness, may have found it 'nauseating' to see 'a half-naked fakir' striding up the steps of the viceregal palace to 'parley on equal terms' with the representative of the king-emperor. But most nationalists, and the people who responded to the call of civil disobedience with alacrity, were dismayed that Gandhi was again abandoning the struggle at the wrong moment and giving away too much for too little. The Gandhi–Irwin Pact of March 1931 – based on three vague principles of federation, Indian responsibility and safeguards for minorities – signalled the suspension of civil disobedience. There was an emotional outcry at Gandhi's refusal to press for a commutation of the death sentence passed on Bhagat Singh and his associates. But Gandhi had won a ticket to attend the second round table conference (the Congress had boycotted the first) in London, where the future shape of India's constitution was under discussion. On his arrival in Britain, a reporter asked Gandhi what he thought of Western civilization. 'I think it would be a good idea,' the Mahatma replied. But for all his wit and charm, Gandhi returned politically empty handed from London at the end of the year and called for a resumption of civil disobedience in January 1932. The British had been steeling themselves to crush the second stage of the civil disobedience movement. The numbers arrested between January 1932 and March 1933 rose to 120,000, compared to 90,000 between March 1930 and March 1931. This was more an index of the success of British repression than of the strength of the civil disobedience movement. By 1934 both the non-violent resisters and the violent revolutionaries had been subdued.

The British resorted not simply to outright repression but also to a new round of political engineering to divide and deflect the nationalist challenge. The British prime minister, Ramsay MacDonald, announced the communal award in August 1932, specifying representation in elected bodies for various communities, which gave separate electorates to the 'depressed classes' (lower-caste Hindus). Gandhi, seeing this as a sinister British plot to divide Hindus after successfully creating a separate electoral arena for Muslims, threatened to fast to death in his prison cell. Talks with the 'depressed classes' leader, B.R. Ambedkar, who was sharply critical of Gandhi's patronizing attitude towards the lower castes, resulted in the Poona Pact of 1932 by which, in return for a larger number of reserved seats, the lower castes gave up the idea of separate electorates.

A new set of constitutional reforms was eventually passed collectively by the British parliament as the Government of India Act of 1935. The Act had two main parts – provincial and federal. At the provincial level dyarchy was abolished and all government departments were brought under the control of elected Indian ministers. But the British kept sufficient emergency and reserved powers to dismiss ministries and bring the provincial administration under the direct sway of the British governor and his civil servants whenever they deemed it necessary. In any case the British were going to hold on to all the vital attributes of sovereignty and key powers in the areas of finance and defence at the centre. The federal part of the 1935 Act projected a future 'federation' in which representatives of the princely states would be a counterpoise to the elected representatives of the British Indian provinces. The rules of representation were laid down in a way that negated the possibility of a nationalist majority in the projected federal legislature.

Jawaharlal Nehru denounced the 1935 Act as 'a new charter of slavery'. In the words of Subhas Chandra Bose, it was a scheme 'not for self-government, but for maintaining British rule in the new political conditions, through the help of the Indian princes and sectarian, reactionary and pro-British organizations'. M.A. Jinnah, leader of the recently revived Muslim League, who had kept open the lines of communication with the Congress, found the federal provisions of the 1935 Act 'most reactionary, retrograde, injurious and fatal to the vital interest of British India *vis-à-vis* the Indian states'. By directing Indian political attention towards the provinces and bringing in autocratic and subservient princes to redress the balance against the democratic and nationalist challenge in British India, the 1935 Act sought to safeguard British rule in India, not to weaken it.

After some soul searching and hard-headed calculating, Congress decided to take the pragmatic course of contesting the provincial elections scheduled for 1937. The franchise, still based on a property qualification, had been expanded to encompass nearly thirty-five million voters, including women. The restricted nature of the franchise ensured that the social base of the Gandhian Congress, limited to the middle and richer peasantry in the countryside, would be an asset, not a handicap. The civil disobedience campaigns of the early 1930s paid handsome dividends at the ballot boxes in 1937. The Congress won a major electoral triumph and, after some dithering over office acceptance, formed ministries in seven, and by 1938 in eight, provinces of British India.

The late 1930s witnessed a growing competition and conflict between the radical left-wing within and at the edges of the Congress on the one hand and the cautious, conservative and compromising Gandhian right-wing on the other. Jawaharlal Nehru and Subhas Chandra Bose represented the broad left-wing tendency within the Congress. A more closely organized pressure group within the organization, the Congress Socialist Party, had been active since 1934. Two smaller groups – the Communist Party of India, active since the early 1920s but using the National Front label in the late 1930s, and the Radical Humanists led by M.N. Roy – were also part of the leftist camp. Gandhi tried initially to co-opt the radical elements by conferring the presidency of the Indian National Congress on Jawaharlal Nehru and Subhas Chandra Bose in 1936–37 and 1938 respectively. Nehru believed that the solution to the problems of the world lay in 'socialism', both as a scientific economic doctrine and as a philosophy of life. He saw as Congress president in 1936 the 'great and fascinating unfolding of a new order and a new civilization' in the Soviet Union as 'the most promising feature of our dismal age'. But he added: 'Much as I wish for the advancement of socialism in this country, I have no desire to force the issue on the Congress and thereby create difficulties in the way of our struggle for independence.'

Subhas Chandra Bose not only stood for a more radical social and economic programme based on a form of socialism adapted to Indian conditions, but also a more militant nationalism which would brook no compromise on

Figure 22 The Nationalist Leadership. Mahatma Gandhi, Subhas Chandra Bose, Vallabhbhai Patel and Jawaharlal Nehru (standing) at the Haripura session of the Indian National Congress, February 1938 (Courtesy of the archives of the Netaji Research Bureau, Calcutta)

issues such as federation with the princely states. In 1938 Bose set up a national planning committee with Nehru as chairman to draw up a blueprint of the socialist reconstruction of India once freedom had been won. Bose managed to defeat Gandhi's candidate in a fiercely contested election for the Congress presidency in 1939. But the Gandhian old guard refused to accept the democratic verdict, intriguing and manoeuvring successfully to get Bose to resign. Bose then formed a Forward Bloc within Congress and tried to consolidate leftist forces on a radical, socialist and democratic platform. The Gandhian leadership saw this as indiscipline and barred him and his elder brother Sarat from holding elective office within the Congress organization for three years.

On the eve of World War II the Indian National Congress was split into conservative and radical segments. More ominously, concerted Muslim opposition under the leadership of Jinnah and the Muslim League was fracturing the nationalist movement's unifying appeal (a theme elucidated more fully in Chapter 16). Jinnah had long deplored the leadership style of the Gandhian

Congress and its compromises with the more bigoted representatives of Hindu interests in some of the provinces. He had nevertheless extended cooperation to the Congress against British collaborators until he was spurned, following Congress's strong showing in the 1937 provincial elections. Between 1937 and 1939 the League denounced the Congress provincial ministries as it searched for a new basis to safeguard Muslim interests.

With the outbreak of war the winds of inflation began blowing and the Indian economy emerged from a long Depression. But the stage was about to be set for the stark contradictions between the economic requirements of Britain's war and the subsistence needs of a subject people. Viceroy Linlithgow's declaration of India as a belligerent in the war against Germany, which he made without bothering to consult the Congress or the provincial ministries, left Congress leaders deeply embarrassed. Upon failing to extract a satisfactory definition of war aims from the British, Congress resigned office in the provinces. The Muslim League declared it a day of deliverance. As Gandhi inched his way towards the face-saving device of an individual satyagraha campaign, the more militant among Indian nationalists prepared to take full advantage of the international war crisis to strike for Indian independence.

15

NATIONALISM AND COLONIALISM DURING WORLD WAR II AND ITS AFTERMATH

Economic crisis and political confrontation

When war broke out in Europe in September 1939 the British political will to hold on to their Indian empire was as strong as it ever had been, despite the qualitative changes in the economic relations between the metropolis and the colony. The forces of Indian nationalism were more radicalized but were also more divided than they had been in the past. The Congress leadership, having just fended off a left-wing challenge, asked the British to define their war aims before they agreed to any support for the British cause. Congress leaders had been deeply offended and embarrassed by viceroy Linlithgow's decision to declare India a belligerent in the war against Germany without bothering to consult the Congress high command or the provincial ministries. Once it became clear that the British were not of a mind to make any immediate concessions to Indian nationalist aspirations, Congress had little choice but to resign from holding office in the provinces, as a mark of protest.

From the Indian nationalist point of view the world war was a conflict between old and new imperialist powers. That Britain was fighting for freedom and democracy was simply not credible to its colonial subjects unless they too were given a taste of these values. In 1940, Gandhi, not yet prepared to signal the beginning of a mass movement, called upon his followers to offer individual satyagraha. So satyagrahis made anti-war speeches and courted arrest in large numbers. While non-violent protestors were herded into detention camps, the British moved decisively to imprison radical leaders and workers, including Subhas Chandra Bose and his followers, in 1940. Japan's entry into the war in December 1941 and its military sweep across South-East Asia in early 1942 provided the occasion for one futile round of negotiations but ultimately served to strengthen Britain's resolve to use the coercive powers of the colonial state to the fullest extent, when necessary, to keep nationalists at bay.

Political denial was matched by economic interventions on an unprecedented scale. Indian resources were marshalled to finance Britain's war effort as never before. While the Depression decade had seen a steep decline in prices, the war economy came to be characterized by galloping inflation. The inflationary pressure emanated largely from the massive expansion in public expenditure. Between 1939 and 1945 nearly Rs 3.5 billion were spent for defence purposes in India. While Indian revenues were to be used for the defence of the colony, the metropolitan government agreed, in a major departure of policy, to foot the bill for the use of Indian forces in the defence of the empire. But the treasury in London was short of cash. So, in a typical example of British financial jugglery, a mechanism was devised by which India would pay here and now and be reimbursed after the end of the war. Part of the total war expenditure would be recoverable as sterling credits for India accumulated in the Bank of England. For now, the government of India would finance the war by making the mints work harder. The money supply in India rose from about Rs 3 billion in 1939 to Rs 22 billion in 1945. Since imports had dropped drastically, due to the dislocations of war, and government purchases of war-related material diverted some goods from Indian consumption, serious shortages developed and prices soared for essential commodities like cloth, kerosene oil and, most important of all, food.

The majority of India's rural poor, as well as workers and salaried groups in urban areas, were hit harder by the inflation of the war period than they had been by the Depression of the past decade. The phenomenon of daily necessities going beyond the purchasing reach of large sections of the populace caused privation in most parts of India. But the most dramatic manifestation

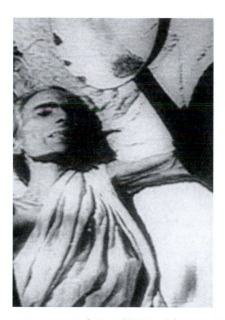

Figure 23 Famine. A starving woman during the Bengal famine of 1943 (Courtesy Sugata Bose from his film *Rebels against the Raj: India during World War II* – original footage in the archives of the Netaji Research Bureau, Calcutta)

of this was in Bengal, where a devastating famine in 1943–44 killed between 3.5 and 3.8 million people. Recent researches have made it clear that there had been no aggregate food-availability decline in the province of Bengal in 1943. Famine mortality stemmed from drastic declines in exchange entitlements of vulnerable social groups. To begin with, military construction works took place on a bigger scale in Bengal, which was on the front line against Japan. British colonial policy shielded its own troops and urban industrial classes deemed to be critical for war production against higher inflation. Agricultural labourers and smallholding peasants lost their entitlement to food in their millions. Rural wages and employment declined as prices rocketed. The relative price of jute, Bengal's premier cash crop, remained low in relation to rice, Bengal's staple food crop, and rural credit relations continued to be in a state of disrepair, forcing exclusive dependence on a volatile product market where food had to be paid for in cash. The colonial state's fabled famine code of the late nineteenth century was not even invoked. The deliberate absence of relief measures contributed to one of the more catastrophic, though least publicized, holocausts of World War II.

Wartime exigencies and the experience of the Bengal famine, however, brought about a reversal of the debt relationship between metropolis and colony, as well as the nature of the links between the colonial state and the economy. Throughout the colonial era India had owed a debt to Britain, but at the end of the war it was Britain that owed a large debt of £1.3 billion to the colonial government of India. In order to provision troops and key urban classes, the colonial state had intruded into the food market, procuring grains from the countryside and selling them through ration shops in the towns and cities. Social groups such as the rich farmers of the Punjab, who might have been expected to make large profits from rising grain prices, were prevented from doing so by the colonial state's procurement and price-control policies. The poor in one region of India, Bengal, perished on account of the state's lack of action; the better-off in another region, Punjab, complained bitterly about the state's heavy-handed interventions, which they deemed to be detrimental to their own interests.

It was in the context of a deepening economic crisis that the major political confrontations between nationalists and the British colonial state occurred. Radicals and socialists had always wanted to take advantage of the international war situation to advance the cause of Indian independence. It was in pursuit of this strategy that Subhas Bose had escaped from India in January 1941, having determined to subvert the loyalty of the Indian element within the British Indian army. The German invasion of the Soviet Union in June 1941 not only upset his plans of an armed invasion from the north-west, but led Indian communists to redefine what had been an 'imperialist war' to a 'people's war' – in which they went to the extent of lending support to the British against the nationalists. This decision of the Indian communists led to a serious rift between them and the socialists within the anti-colonial movement; the latter saw Britain's difficulty as India's opportunity. Communists, as well as the followers of M.N. Roy, were subsequently to find it extremely difficult to live down what came to be widely viewed as their betrayal of the anti-colonial nationalist movement at a critical moment during World War II.

Japan's defeat of Britain in South-East Asia during early 1942, especially the fall of Singapore in February that year, emboldened even the Gandhian Congress to make more strident demands. It was to prevent the Indian nationalists from allying with the enemies of Britain that Churchill reluctantly agreed to send an emissary to hold talks with Indian political leaders. It is now clear, from British documents of this period, that both Churchill and Linlithgow, acting under pressure from Labour party constituents of the National Government and President Roosevelt of the United States, wanted to see the Cripps mission fail. And it did fail because Stafford Cripps was unable to meet the minimum Congress demand for immediate control of the defence portfolio at the centre. Gandhi reportedly dubbed the Cripps offer a post-dated cheque on a crashing bank. The Cripps offer as it related to provinces and communities, particularly Muslims, is also of great interest (it is discussed in the following chapter). Gandhi drafted a resolution in April 1942 calling upon the British to quit India. He indicated in interviews that he would be 'prepared to take the risk of violence' to end 'the great calamity of slavery'. The 'ordered anarchy' that he saw around him, he felt, was 'worse than real anarchy'. Gandhi believed in his own ability to negotiate with the Japanese, who would have no reason to invade India if the British left. In any event, he was prepared to tell the British to leave India to anarchy or to God. A somewhat watered-down version of Gandhi's 'quit India' resolution was eventually moved by Jawaharlal Nehru and adopted by Congress on 8 August 1942.

Inspired by Gandhi's slogan 'do or die', the Quit India movement turned out to be the biggest civilian uprising in India since the great rebellion of 1857. It was led and orchestrated by lower-ranking Congress leaders, since the top leadership had been swiftly clapped into jail as soon as the 'Quit India' resolution was passed. It began as an urban movement spearheaded by students and workers, which was quickly repressed within a month. In late September 1942 the disturbances spread to the countryside, where large crowds of peasants attacked all symbols of British authority, including revenue offices, police stations, railway lines, post offices and so on. In some instances, arms were looted from captured police stations. British administration collapsed in many districts of Bihar, eastern U.P., western Bengal (especially Midnapur district), Orissa and parts of Bombay province (especially Satara district). Much like the great revolt of 1857, the agrarian dimension of the 1942 movement was multi-class in character even though the smallholding peasantry provided the backbone of resistance in most of the regions that took part in the revolt. Bihar, which was the storm centre of the rebellion, saw strong participation from the caste peasantry as well as tribal people. Parallel governments were set up in the name of the Congress in liberated localities, but overwhelming British military might ultimately prevailed by the spring of 1943, even though some of the underground leaders – Jai Prakash Narain, Ram Manohar Lohia and Aruna Asaf Ali – were not apprehended until later.

The key Muslim-majority provinces of the north-west took little part in the Quit India movement. Right-wing fringe groups like M.S. Golwalkar's Rashtriya Swayamsevak Sangh maintained a studied aloofness, as did right-wing Congress politicians like C. Rajagopalachari. Industrial capitalists, having initially flirted with the Congress, quickly settled down to work in harmony with the colonial state by 1944. The Bombay Plan, propounded by leading Indian industrialists, resonated with the projects of the government's planning and development department set up that year. For communists, despite the opportunity to do some famine relief work and set up progressive cultural organizations like the Indian Progressive Theatre Association, their wartime political posture turned out to be a strategic blunder. The weakening of British power in the eyes of the Quit India rebels had in a sense been an optical illusion. The war had brought about a brief revival of the British empire, certainly the biggest deployment of British military forces on Indian soil. Largely unarmed or poorly armed resistance wilted in the face of the ruthless British onslaught. Yet the martyrs of the Quit India uprising had forced the British raj in India to fall back on its coercive foundations and given the Congress an emotive issue around which to rejuvenate its electoral fortunes at war's end.

An organized armed struggle under the leadership of Netaji Subhas Chandra Bose was launched against the British from across India's north-eastern frontiers. Bose had travelled by submarine from Europe to Asia in early 1943 to lead the Azad Hind Fauj (Indian National Army, INA). Some 40,000 of the 45,000 Indian soldiers of the British Indian Army who had surrendered at Singapore had volunteered to join an army of liberation. To the professional core of the ex-prisoners of war were added civilian recruits from among Indian plantation labourers in Malaya, petty traders in Burma and shopkeepers in Thailand. Punjabi Muslim, Sikh and Pathan professional soldiers mingled with Tamil and Malayali workers in a national army led by a Bengali. An overwhelming majority of more than two million Indian expatriates in South-East Asia responded with great emotional fervour to Bose's call for 'total mobilization', his battle-cry 'Chalo Delhi' and his national greeting 'Jai Hind'.

A few significant features of this movement of resistance deserve emphasis. First, it attacked the kernel of British imperial power, namely the British Indian army, which was the ultimate instrument of colonial control, and sought to replace the loyalty of Indian soldiers to the crown with loyalty to the nationalist cause. Second, unlike the Quit India movement, in which Muslim participation was minimal, the Azad Hind movement was not only characterized by harmony and unity among various religious and linguistic communities but had a very large, and indeed disproportionate, representation of Muslims and Sikhs within its leadership and ranks. Third, this movement saw widespread

Figure 24 An Army of Liberation. Nataji Subhas Chandra Bose and the Indian National
Army in Burma, 1944 (Courtesy of the archives of the Netaji Research Bureau,
Calcutta)

participation by women and included a small but significant women's regiment
named after the Rani of Jhansi – a legendary leader of the 1857 rebellion.

The INA began its march towards Delhi with a ceremonial parade in
September 1943 at the tomb of Bahadur Shah Zafar, the last Mughal emperor,
who had died in exile in Burma. The promised march to the Red Fort of Delhi
was halted at Imphal and Kohima during the monsoon season of 1944.
Although the Indian National Army was militarily defeated in the battles in
north-eastern India and Burma, it underwent a dramatic political resurrection
in the winter of 1945–46. The Congress, Muslim League and other political
groups lauded the heroism of the INA and its leader, who had said: 'The roads
to Delhi are many and Delhi still remains our goal.' When the British made
the grave error of putting on public trial at the Red Fort three officers of
the INA – a Hindu, a Muslim and a Sikh – for waging war against the king-
emperor, the Congress put together a high-powered legal team for their
defence led by Bhulabhai Desai and including Jawaharlal Nehru. Having
shrewdly assessed the public mood, the Congress made the release of the INA
prisoners the main issue in their election campaigns. Although the court martial
sentenced the Red Fort three to deportation for life, the commander-in-chief,

Claude Auchinleck, was compelled under tremendous pressure to release them forthwith.

The final mass movement on an all-India scale took place on the issue of the INA trials in late 1945 and early 1946. Apart from large-scale public protests and Congress's championing of the cause, there was a new dimension to this agitation: it included mutinies, uprisings and dissent within the British Indian armed forces. '[T]he whole country has been roused,' Mahatma Gandhi observed, 'and even the regular forces have been stirred into a new political consciousness and have begun to think in terms of independence.' There were large-scale street protests in Bombay and Calcutta between November 1945 and February 1946. The most serious of the mutinies took place among the ratings of the Royal Indian Navy led by M.S. Khan in Bombay and other ports of western India in February 1946. In street demonstrations the green flag of the Muslim League and the red flag of the communists were occasionally flown together with the Congress and INA tricolor. The communists proved less successful, through these tactics, in rehabilitating themselves with the anti-colonial nationalist movement than the Congress, which turned the INA issue to their electoral advantage. The 'decisive shift' in the British policy on decolonization, Sumit Sarkar has correctly noted, 'came about under mass pressure in the autumn and winter of 1945–46'. Faced with problems at home and unable to muster sufficient forces of coercion or collaboration to put down another Indian movement, the British decided in the spring of 1946 to send out a cabinet mission to discuss the terms and shape of Indian independence.

The remarkable political unity of early 1946 quickly degenerated into serious division and conflict by late 1946 over the all-important question of how power was to be shared among Indians once the British quit. The next two chapters offer an in-depth examination of the forces that led to the partition of India at the moment of decolonization, the colossal human tragedy that it occasioned, and the poisoned legacy of that fateful decision.

16

THE PARTITION OF INDIA AND THE CREATION OF PAKISTAN

The partition of India and the creation of Pakistan form the subject of fierce but lively historical debate. Various theories have been invoked to explain why, in the process of dismantling their raj, the British partitioned India along ostensibly religious lines. Official histories of Pakistan have in the main subscribed to the 'two nation' theory, according to which Indian Muslims were always a distinctive and separate community that had resisted assimilation into their Indian environment. A recurring refrain of historians of mainstream Indian nationalism, on the other hand, has been to blame imperialism for tearing asunder two communities joined by history and tradition – the classical theory of British divide and rule. Both theories, propounded as part and parcel of the ideology of post-colonial nation-states, have had wide popular currency. Yet they raise more questions than they answer. Apart from limiting the terrain of historical study, they have only compounded the problems stemming from the lack of scholarly dialogue across the great divide of 1947. There is now overwhelming evidence to suggest that regardless of whether Muslims were in fact a 'nation', let alone one created by British policies of divide and rule, it was the contradictions and structural peculiarities of Indian society and politics in late colonial India which eventually led to the creation of Pakistan. So it is important to be sensitive to the social and political context which shaped the communitarian discourse on Muslim interests, especially the uses made of the 'two nation' theory by the All-India Muslim League and its leader, Mohammad Ali Jinnah, in the final decade of the British raj in India. There can be no understanding of the larger context of Muslim history in colonial India, of which Jinnah and the League admittedly formed an important part, without accounting for a multitude of other trends that had helped fashion the discourse, and eventually also the politics, of the 'two nation' ideal.

This ideal would have been unimaginable without some of the dominant assumptions underlying the fact of British colonial rule in India. A powerful revisionist school of modern South Asian historiography has been suggesting lately that Indian social tradition, as we know it today, was largely a nineteenth-century British colonial invention. British social enumerators of the later nineteenth century invested the great religions of the subcontinent, Hinduism

Figure 25 Parleys prior to Partition. The Simla Viceregal Lodge, venue of the failed talks of 1945 (Courtesy Ayesha Jalal)

and Islam, with a degree of supra-local significance and cohesion never achieved before. While serving the purpose of subverting the mythology of millennia-old tradition, for instance the 'two nation' theory and its obverse, the 'composite nationality' theory, arguments about the British construction of social identity in South Asia are much in need of analytical disaggregation. For one thing, colonial initiatives may have been more successful in creating political categories out of local religious affiliations than in moulding the mental world of their subject peoples. For another, identities were redefined not simply as a function of skilful social engineering by the colonial masters but also as part of a process of multifaceted resistance against colonial rule.

So were the Muslims of India from the later nineteenth century an artefact of British colonial imagination? To be sure, the definition of the Indian Muslim as an all-India political category for purposes of limited electoral politics triggered all manner of contradictions between Hindu and Muslim as well as Muslim and Muslim, and influenced the course of Muslim politics in the first half of the twentieth century. Yet Muslim social identities in different parts of the subcontinent were being formed by patterns of social and economic relations linked to the fact of British colonial rule, but not wholly shaped by it.

During the nineteenth century Muslim reformist movements with some ideological links with West Asia gave a measure of coherence and articulation to a variety of social and economic discontentments. Some scholars have argued that these movements facilitated the construction of a coherent Indian Muslim identity. Yet Muslim social identities in late nineteenth-century India remained fractured by class, region and the rural–urban divide. The innumerable divisions – doctrinal, sectarian as well as heterodox – in Islam in South Asia even today suggest that the construction of an Indian Muslim identity, much less a coherent one, in the late nineteenth century occurred more in the mind of latter-day scholars than in the actual unfolding of societal rules and relations. A religiously informed cultural identity as a component of a set of multiple identities certainly did not translate automatically into what came to be understood by the late 1920s as communalism and separatism.

It is against the background of changing social identities falling short of effecting grand resolutions on a subcontinental level that the role of British construction, specifically the foisting of the all-India political category of Indian Muslim, acquires special relevance. By the closing decades of the nineteenth century, especially after the great mutiny–rebellion of 1857, British statesmen and officials began perceiving Muslims as a significant and separate political community. Seeing the Muslim lower classes as naturally prone to religious revivalism, and needing a counter to the increasingly assertive Hindu educated classes, the British looked upon the Muslim landed elite as a natural ally. Sections of the Muslim elite were only too eager to encourage this perception. During the 1880s, Sayyid Ahmad Khan, the founder of Aligarh university and the most strident proponent of the merits of a Muslim accommodation with the colonial power, used the argument that there were 'two nations' in India to exhort Muslims to shun the predominantly Hindu Indian National Congress and to impress upon the British the need to view their importance in political rather than in numerical terms. Anxieties about possible Muslim discontent saw the British adopting the principle of maintaining a balance between communities on nominated local government boards. With the extension of the elective principle under Ripon's reforms of 1882–83, the British granted separate electorates to Muslims in local government bodies. Separate electorates were incorporated in the 1909 Morley–Minto reforms, which extended the links between the higher and lower councils.

However, Muslim politics continued to be shaped by local and regional requirements rather than the abstract unity proffered by religious affiliation. Until the turn of the century the narratives on communitarian identity projected by a rapidly expanding press and publications market emphasized culture as difference without elucidating a distinctively Indian Muslim conception of 'nation' and 'nationalism'. Even those subscribing to the ideal of a universal Muslim ummah for political reasons, and scorned by Western observers as Pan-Islamicists, were more anti-colonial than anti-national in orientation. While staying away from the Congress, most Muslims saw no contradiction

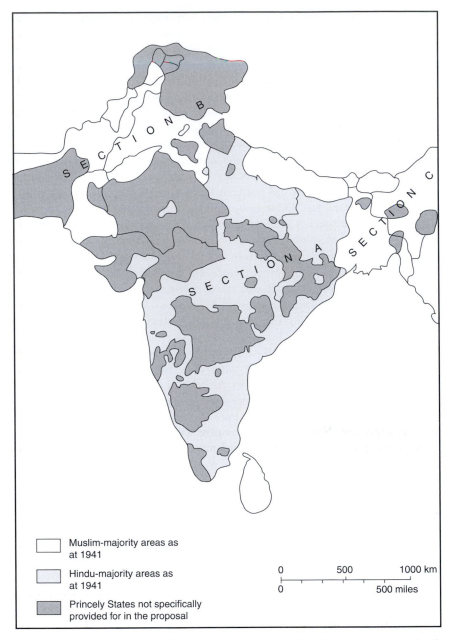

Figure 26 Map of the proposal for a Federational India, 1946 (Source: Ayesha Jalal, *The Sole Spokesman*)

between their extra-territorial loyalties and the forging of a common Indian nationality. The notion of Muslim 'separatism' at a time when the idea of an Indian nation was itself in the process of being forged, negotiated and contested is untenable. It also underplays the exclusionary tendencies in the Hindu majoritarian discourse on the Indian 'nation'. Turning the spotlight on the interplay between class, region and community shows that many competing narratives drawing on affiliations of linguistic and religious community tried contributing to the discourse on the Indian nation. Far from reflecting a neat Hindu–Muslim divide, the nationalist narratives authored by Hindus and Muslims of different regions and classes displayed considerable variety and evoked multiple visions of nationhood. Muslim voices sought location within that emerging discourse on the Indian nation while also seeking political accommodations consistent with their sense of cultural difference.

Within the formal arenas of politics, separate electorates not only survived the constitutional reforms of 1919 but were also actually extended, despite the expressed reservations of its authors. A concession that articulate segments of the Muslim ashraf classes looked upon as a birthright was now difficult to withdraw. If pitting Muslim communitarianism against Indian nationalism had the potential to misfire, playing the region against the centre could secure British imperial interests. The reforms aimed at confining Indian politics to the provinces so that the unitary centre could be kept under the exclusive purview of the British. Politics in provincial and local arenas meshed awkwardly with communally compartmentalized electorates. This structural contradiction was to haunt Muslim politics for the remainder of the colonial period. Instead of lending substance to an all-India Muslim identity or giving rise to a distinctive politics, Muslims were reduced to being a perpetual minority in any constitutional arrangement. Not needing to compete with other Indians, Muslim politicians seeking election in religiously demarcated constituencies could focus wholly on doing down their own co-religionists. Those in the electoral fray – landed notables for the most part – used their local influence and did not need assistance from organized political parties at the centre or in the provinces. This stood in some contrast to the politics of many non-Muslims who, during the first three decades of the twentieth century, saw increasing advantages in allying with the Congress. Despite the existence of an All-India Muslim League since 1906, Muslim politicians in their different regional locales preferred to go it alone.

There is scarcely any evidence to suggest that, in their local and provincial politics, Muslims ever followed the lead of an all-India Muslim political organization until the last decade of British rule. Only when constitutional reforms were on the anvil did Muslims have an incentive to try to cobble together a common front. Working within a restrictive colonial representative system, Muslim politicians at the local and provincial levels often had to make terms with members of other communities. Supra-communal alliances at these levels frequently militated against too close an association with a Muslim

League primarily concerned with promoting the interests of a community defined by religion alone. This became amply evident under the Montagu–Chelmsford reforms of the 1920s. An exclusively Muslim politics held out few attractions in the formal arenas of politics. Separate representation did not guarantee Muslim solidarity, the more so since no single community could dominate the reformed councils under the new constitutional arrangements. So alliances with other communities were forged not only in the United Provinces, where Muslims were in a minority, but also in Punjab and Bengal, where they had bare majorities.

With the provincialization of electoral politics in the 1920s, it was Muslim anxieties about the Turkish Khilafat that served to revive interest at the all-India stage. Yet here was the rub. Instead of cutting themselves adrift from Indian nationalist politics, the Khilafatists rallied to the support of Mohandas Gandhi, hardly the best proof of the Muslim predilection for an exclusively religiously informed politics. After the disintegration of the movement, pro-Khilafat Muslim nationalists like the Ali brothers were rebels without a cause. The Congress was divided down the middle on whether or not to contest elections to the reformed provincial councils. Overshadowed by the Congress and Khilafatist alliance, the Muslim League had become moribund in the 1920s.

During the next round of constitutional negotiations in the early 1930s there was no single all-India Muslim political party which could put forth a plausible claim to speak for all Indian Muslims. Although divided on the issue of separate electorates, Muslim politicians were at one in demanding the right to dominate provinces where they were in a majority. There was much resentment amongst Punjabi and Bengali Muslims over the terms of the Congress–League agreement of 1916 in Lucknow, which in return for weighted representation for minorities had denied them representation based on population proportions. But even as early as 1924, Lala Lajpat Rai, a leading nationalist politician from Punjab and a virulent opponent of separate electorates, had warned that the price for Muslim majority rule would have to be a partition of the province. The same principle might also be extended to Bengal. This was anathema for Muslims in both the provinces. As it was, Congress's inclusionary nationalism based on equal rights of citizenship in an independent India entailed accepting the idea of a singular and homogenous nation, which obfuscated rather than addressed the problem of cultural differences. Inequality in the terms of representation could hardly ensure equality of citizenship.

Anxious to advance their regional interests even at the expense of the community at the all-India level, Muslim politicians in the majority provinces were to clash in louder discord with their co-religionists in the predominantly Hindu provinces, especially once the prospect of full provincial autonomy shifted the pendulum in favour of the majority provinces, Punjab in particular. It was the Punjab Unionists, a supra-communal alliance of Muslim, Hindu and Sikh agriculturalist interests that exercised the most weight in the constitutional dialogue of the 1930s. The Punjabi view of 'Muslim interest', spearheaded by Mian Fazl-i-Husain through the All-India Muslim Conference, found expression in the Communal Award of 1932 and the Government of India Act of 1935 but failed to enthuse Muslims in provinces where they were in a minority. Under the award, Muslims in Punjab and Bengal were not only allowed to retain their separate electorates but granted more seats than any other community in the provincial assemblies. Though it was far from perfect from their point of view, Muslim politicians in these two provinces, as well as their counterparts in the newly created province of Sind and the North West Frontier Province (NWFP), which was elevated to the status of a governor's province, could maximize the gains from provincial autonomy conceded by the 1935 Act. But full autonomy for the provinces dealt a hammer blow to Muslims in the minority provinces. It entailed the elimination of British officials from the provincial councils, which had come to be seen as a safeguard for minority interests.

This was the backdrop against which some Muslim politicians from the minority provinces turned to Mohammad Ali Jinnah. A leading constitutional lawyer who masterminded the Lucknow Pact of 1916, Jinnah had appeared to bid farewell to politics in India after being disenchanted by his Congress colleagues during the controversies surrounding the Nehru report of 1928. By 1934 Jinnah had assumed the mantle of a newly revived All-India Muslim League. The 1935 Act was seen as a prelude to the British eventually agreeing to concede power to Indians at the centre, based on electoral showings in the provinces. If they could somehow counter the adverse effects of the provincialization of politics in the 1920s, Jinnah and his League might win the support of Muslims in the majority provinces. Aided and abetted by their numerically preponderant co-religionists in the north-west and north-east of India, minority-province Muslims could try and extract more at the all-India centre in order to redress their provincial disadvantages. But with the British in no haste to dilute their power at the centre, Muslims in the majority provinces saw no reason to jump onto the All-India Muslim League's bandwagon.

Before the 1936–37 elections, Jinnah and his associates in the League angled for support in the Muslim-majority provinces and also tried striking a deal with the Congress at the all-India level. They were thwarted on both scores. Preoccupied with their own concerns on the eve of full provincial autonomy, politicians in the Muslim provinces had no need for a party existing nowhere but on paper. Unable to prove its following in the Muslim-majority provinces, the League was spurned by the Congress at the centre. The League won an ignominious 4.4 per cent of the total Muslim vote cast. Separate electorates, it was painfully clear, were not prohibitive of variety in the internal politics of a community differentiated by religion. If not for an electoral understanding with a band of influential Muslims in Bengal, who won thirty-nine seats in the provincial assembly, the All-India Muslim League would have come very close to extinction. Even in Bengal the Krishak Praja (Peasants and Tenants) Party

(KPP) leader Fazlul Huq became the leader of the KPP–Muslim League coalition government. Despite a measure of support among urban Muslim Punjabis, the League was categorically rejected by all the Muslim provinces in the northwest. This was ominous. Stirrings of a Muslim revolt against a Congress-led Hindu raj were especially marked in Punjab. If Jinnah and the League were to have any say in the making of India's future constitution, the provincializing trends influencing the articulation of separate identities in Punjab had to be contained.

So it was some consolation that the Muslim League survived oblivion in provinces where Muslims were wholly outnumbered by those categorized as Hindus. It should not have required much political foresight to predict a decent showing for the Congress in the Hindu-majority provinces. But the margins gained by the political mobilization of the early 1920s and 1930s were much wider than could have been predicted. Unanticipated even by its own standards, Congress's victory in the 1937 elections went beyond all expectations. Evidence of the final countdown in the clash between British colonialism and the forces of Indian nationalism, it was based on rather rusty foundations when it came to the nexus between communitarian identities and the 'nation'. Having done so well in its electoral bid, the Congress leadership saw no reason to seek help from outside quarters. There was no space here for Jinnah and the League. And so the party, which claimed to represent the elusive political category of India's Muslim, was out of play both at the centre and in the provinces.

But the Congress too had failed miserably at the hustings in most of the Muslim-majority provinces. A poor comment on the effectiveness of pro-Congress Muslims, this was the straw in the wind that Jinnah had to clutch closely in making his re-entry into all-India politics during the decisive final decade of British colonial rule in India. No ordinary constitutional strategist, Jinnah knew full well that Congress would have a none-too-easy ride trying to rope in the Muslim-majority provinces. The NWFP was the solitary bastion of Congress support in these provinces. What Congress needed to assert its claim to the British Indian centre was a hook into Punjab and Bengal, two provinces that had consistently given it grief but which now would play a key part in charting the route to an independent India. Fiercely attached to their provincial interests, Muslim voters in these provinces opted for regional parties, Unionists in Punjab and the Krishak Praja in Bengal. Not an unexpected consequence of the 1919 reforms, it was countered by the emergence of the Congress as India's premier nationalist party. On Jinnah's reading, this underscored the eventual success of the centre over the provinces. If the League could for once emerge from the political woodwork, it might yet provide a formidable challenge to the Congress.

Even though the electoral arithmetic had produced a disastrous result for the League, there was no disputing the fact that the Indian Muslims, however divided and disorganized, remained a separate political category within the existing constitutional set-up. By adopting causes dear to all Indian Muslims, the All-India Muslim League could continue to pose as the most representative organization of Muslims in majority and minority provinces alike. This required striking just the right sort of balance with the majority provinces – making concessions, to be sure, but taking care to stamp its own authority over them. Backed by the Muslim provinces, the League would not be ignored by the British or the Congress. This might in turn induce the Congress to come to terms with Jinnah and the League.

It was fortuitous that the 1920s and 1930s had seen a distinct hardening of Muslim opposition to a Congress-dominated all-India centre, particularly in Punjab and Bengal. With the Congress in office in eight of British India's eleven provinces, the premiers of Punjab and Bengal, Sikander Hayat Khan of the Unionist party and Fazlul Haq of the Krishak Praja party, thought better to lend support to an all-India Muslim party. Congress rule in the provinces ignited fears of Hindu raj and brought charges of 'atrocities' against Muslim minorities. Seizing his moment with measured grace, Jinnah agreed to represent Punjab and Bengal at the centre and leave the premiers to manage provincial affairs. Perceiving the Congress as near to grabbing the whole cake, Muslims could no longer postpone reckoning with the prospect of an independent India. The federation outlined in the 1935 Act made Muslims uneasy. Both Sikander and Haq could see that a Congress-dominated centre could ride roughshod over the provinces so long as the unitary structure of the colonial state remained intact. Preferring strong provinces and a weak centre, the Muslim-majority provinces disliked the proposed federal arrangement or, at any rate, wanted better assurances of autonomy. An all-India federation offered no consolation to Muslims in provinces where they were in a minority. Separate electorates – even with weighted representation – were simply inadequate. Even if there were to be a miraculous convergence of their identity and politics, Muslim numbers in the federal assembly would be insufficient to override the Congress vote. So long as they remained a minority, Muslims could not expect anything more than a marginal role in settling how power was to be shared in an independent India.

A possible way out of the quandary was to invoke aspects of Sayyid Ahmad Khan's thinking on the subject and assert that Indian Muslims were a nation entitled to equal treatment with the Hindu nation in the distribution of power and patronage. In December 1930 Muhammad Iqbal, the renowned poet and philosopher and a leading proponent of Muslim majority rule in Punjab, had asked the All-India Muslim League's council to endorse the call for the creation of a Muslim state in the north-west of India, including Punjab, Sind, the NWFP and Baluchistan. His ideas were ignored by most Muslim politicians, but gained some momentum in the informal arenas of politics through the medium of the popular press. In 1933 they inspired Chaudhri Rahmat Ali, a student at Cambridge, to invent the word 'Pakistan', etymologically, the 'land of the pure'. 'P' stood for Punjab, 'A' for Afghan (North West Frontier)

Province, 'K' for Kashmir, 'S' for Sind and 'tan' for Baluchistan. Unlike Iqbal's scheme, which was placed strictly within the context of all-India, Rahmat Ali's envisaged a confederation of Muslim states in the subcontinent linked to the 'original Pakistan', including all the Muslim countries in West and Central Asia up to the Bosphorus. Inciting charges of an Islamic conspiracy among sections of the Hindu press, the proposal's irredentist flavour and hint of a massive transfer of Muslim populations from other parts of India made it equally unpalatable to most seasoned Muslim politicians. By the late 1930s Iqbal and Rahmat Ali's ideas had been supplemented by a plethora of Muslim schemes, each looking in its own ingenious way to a solution of a minority community's political dilemma.

Despite differences in emphasis, most of the schemes were predicated on Muslims being a nation and not a minority. A veritable revolt against Hindu majoritarian rule under the Congress banner, Muslim assertions of nationhood were put to the test by the outbreak of war in Europe. Once Congress had stated its conditions for supporting the war effort, namely immediate independence, the viceroy needed some excuse to postpone all constitutional advance for the duration of the war. The League's insistence that it represented all Muslims provided the pretext with which to contest Congress's claim to speak for the whole of India. But in order for the League to press home the advantage, Jinnah had to formulate a demand out of the contradictory requirements of Muslims in the majority and the minority provinces.

So in March 1940, without specifying the exact geographical boundaries, the All-India Muslim League at its annual session in Lahore formally demanded independent Muslim states in the north-west and the north-east of India on the grounds that Indian Muslims were a nation. As Jinnah noted in his address, the term nationalist had become a 'conjurer's trick' in politics. The time had come for Muslims to reject the derogatory label of communalism, once and for all, and advance a vision of nationalism no less valid than that of the Congress. Rising from the ashes of the 1937 electoral débâcle, this was Jinnah and the League's attempt to formally register their claim to speak for all Indian Muslims. An astonishingly bold stance for a vanquished party to take, it drew strength from the rising tide of Muslim antipathy to the prospect of Congress rule at the all-India centre.

Yet nothing could quite detract from the jarring contradictions inherent in the League's posture. The very party claiming to represent all Indian Muslims had staked an apparently separatist demand for independent Muslim states. There was no reference at all in the resolution to a centre, weak or strong, Muslim or Indian. Moreover, there was no mention of either partition or 'Pakistan'. The nub of the League's resolution was that all future constitutional arrangements must be 'reconsidered de novo', since Indian Muslims constituted a 'nation' and not a minority, as had been presumed in the past. In the League's 'considered view', the Muslim-majority provinces in the north-west and the north-east of India should be 'grouped to constitute Independent

States in which the constituent units ... [would] be autonomous and sovereign'. This seemed to suggest an even greater degree of provincial autonomy than already granted under the 1935 Act. Intended as a bait for the Muslim provinces, it was counteracted with the proviso that the 'sovereignty' of these 'Independent States' and also of the constituent units within them would be settled at a later stage. In other words, while there was no going back on the assertion of Muslim nationhood, the demand for separate statehood could be achieved only after protracted negotiations on the quantum of sovereignty and autonomy to be conferred.

This imprecision – together with the lack of any clear reference to a centre – gave Jinnah some breathing space. He had taken care to draft the resolution in such a way that textual ambiguities would not foreclose alternative outcomes. According to the resolution, the frontiers of the 'Independent States' were to be based on the existing boundaries of the Muslim provinces. This would leave Muslims in the minority provinces outside the Muslim 'autonomous and sovereign' areas that would include large non-Muslim minorities in them. Significantly enough, the League envisaged a reciprocal arrangement to protect the interests of both sets of minorities, Muslim and non-Muslim. The fourth paragraph of the resolution refers specifically to 'the constitution' to decide safeguards for minorities inside as well as outside the Muslim states. A constitutional arrangement covering the whole of India had not been ruled out categorically.

H.V. Hodson, the British reforms commissioner, discovered in 1941 that 'every Muslim Leaguer ... interpreted Pakistan as consistent with a confederation of India for common purposes like defence, provided the Hindu and Muslim element therein stood on equal terms'. The Lahore Resolution represented a revolt against minority status, which relegated Muslims to being 'a Cinderella with trade-union rights with a radio in the kitchen but still below-stairs'. Muslims had responded positively to the 'new terminology' invoking nationhood, which 'recognizes that the problem is one of sharing power rather [than of] qualifying the terms on which power is exercised by a majority'. I.I. Chundrigar, a prominent Leaguer from Bombay, explained to his followers that the object of the Lahore Resolution was not to create 'Ulsters', but to achieve 'two nations ... welded into united India on the basis of equality'. And Jinnah himself admitted to Nawab Ismail on 25 November 1941: 'I think Mr. Hodson finally understands as to what our demand is'.

After 1940 Jinnah argued that, as there were at least two identifiable nations in India, a transfer of power would have to involve the dissolution of the unitary centre, which was an artefact of British colonialism. Any reconstitution of that centre would require the agreement of the Muslim-majority provinces as well as the princely states. Once the principle of Muslim provinces being grouped to form a separate state had been conceded, Jinnah was prepared to negotiate whether that state would seek a confederation with the non-Muslim provinces, namely Hindustan, on the basis of equality at the all-India level, or whether, as a sovereign state, it would make treaty arrangements with the rest of India. In either case, the League's demand for a 'Pakistan', the territorial expression of the Muslim claim to nationhood, had to be conceded prior to negotiations determining the shape and powers of the all-India centre.

Since the League claimed to speak for all Indian Muslims, and political geography ensured that the Muslim nation would have citizens straddling the frontiers, Jinnah always maintained that the two main Muslim-majority provinces, Punjab and Bengal, would keep their existing boundaries (and thus their large non-Muslim minorities). The calculation was that a Muslim state built around these two provinces would remain part of a larger all-India whole in which minority Muslims outside the Muslim territory would be protected by the similar position that non-Muslims would have inside it. Jinnah's demand for Pakistan aimed at negotiating a new constitutional arrangement in which Muslims would have an equitable share of power at a centre reconstituted on the basis of a partnership between two essentially sovereign states, Pakistan (representing the Muslim-majority provinces) and Hindustan (representing the Hindu-majority provinces).

This was the strategy of a leader adept at constitutional law but directing a party whose main bases of support were in the Hindu-majority provinces. If they were to have a say in the making of India's constitutional future Jinnah and the League had to prove their support in the Muslim-majority provinces. Such support could not be won by too precise a political programme, since the interests of Muslims in one part of India were different from those of Muslims in others. A socio-economic programme aimed at rousing the Muslim populace was bound to be resisted by the landed oligarchs who dominated local politics and, given the limitations of the franchise, utterly impracticable. With no organizational machinery in the Muslim provinces, Jinnah and the League could not afford to incur the wrath of the landed notables in control of local politics. The best tactic was to build bridges with as many local bigwigs as possible and reserve energies for negotiations at the all-India level.

A glowing prospectus and gnawing organizational weaknesses led Jinnah to make a belated recourse to religion. Hailed by Sarojini Naidu as the 'ambassador of Hindu–Muslim unity', he had often poured scorn on the maulanas, maulvis and mullahs who touted Islam in the bazaars and *mohallas* of Muslim India. Looking for a way to gather together a hopelessly scattered flock, Jinnah's resort to religion had nothing to do with his ideological convictions. This was the most practical way of mobilizing a community divided by politics but defined by religion. By keeping the League's demand for a 'Pakistan' vague and undefined, Jinnah could try to muster up as much Muslim support as possible to block Congress ambitions at the centre.

The remaining years of the war witnessed a spectacular jump in the popularity graph of a 'Pakistan' among most Muslims, whether in the majority or in the minority provinces. Aligarh students popularized the League's creed in British India's remotest villages. Yet popular sentiments for an undefined

demand for a 'Pakistan' did not translate into a matching political organization working for its attainment. Despite Jinnah's undeniable stature, he and
the League's high command fell well short of effecting control over Muslim-
majority province politicians, inside and outside the provincial legislatures, as
well as over the populace at the base. The provincial Leagues in the majority
provinces were riven with divisions and Jinnah had to rest content with gaining the allegiance of whichever combination was temporarily in the ascendancy. Letting his wayward followers make of 'Pakistan' what they pleased,
the Quaid-i-Azam kept his sights on negotiations at the centre. But while this
specifically Muslim demand attracted many Muslims, it further soured relations between the communities in Punjab and Bengal, where the Hindu
Mahasabha had stolen the Congress's thunder during the war period. In
Punjab, Sikh opposition to the League's demand and willingness to ally with
the Congress if necessary greatly accentuated the problems of arriving at
regional political accommodations between different religious communities.
Without the tacit agreement of the non-Muslims in these two provinces,
Jinnah could not palpably claim their undivided territories for 'Pakistan'.

The Cripps Mission of 1942, offering provinces and not communities the
right to opt out of the Indian union, nearly succeeded in bringing out the basic
contradiction in Jinnah's demands. Some Muslim politicians in Punjab and
Bengal could see that the provincial option was incompatible with following
the lead of the Muslim League at the all-India level. But the Cripps Mission
failed and many Muslim politicians for various reasons chose to alienate the
non-Muslims rather than break with the League. A 'Pakistan' that might mean
the division of Punjab and Bengal remained a distant thunder. In 1944 C.R.
Rajagopalachari, a veteran Congress politician from Madras, offered Jinnah a
'Pakistan' carved out of the Muslim-majority districts of Punjab and Bengal.
Such a 'Pakistan' had still to seek common arrangements with the rest of India
on matters to do with defence, communications and commerce. But without
the non-Muslim-majority districts of these two provinces, the League could
not expect to bargain for parity between 'Pakistan' and 'Hindustan'. So
although Pakistan's geographical boundaries in 1947 had been visualized precisely by Rajagopalachari, Jinnah dismissed the scheme as 'offering a shadow
and a husk – a maimed, mutilated and moth-eaten Pakistan, and thus trying to
pass off having met our Pakistan scheme and Muslim demand'.

Cripps and Rajagopalachari had in their different ways put their finger on a
festering sore. 'Pakistan' was anathema for most non-Muslims in the Muslim-
majority provinces. There were repeated warnings from the governors of
Punjab and Bengal, and also Assam. But neither New Delhi nor London cared
to expose the flaw in Jinnah and the League's strategy, namely that 'Pakistan'
could entail partitioning Punjab and Bengal. This allowed Jinnah to concentrate upon building the League's strength in the Muslim-majority province
legislatures. By the time of the first Simla conference in the summer of 1945,
the League was out of office in all the Muslim-majority provinces save Sind.

Jinnah nevertheless had his moment of glory at Simla. The conference failed because the Congress refused to concede his point that the League be allowed to select all the Muslim members to the viceroy's executive council.

Without the Congress's consent, the British could not satisfy Jinnah's demands. This became even more evident once the war was over. New Delhi continued to ignore the gubernatorial exhortations from Punjab and Bengal. For a government based on executive fiat, not a word was issued to dispel the popular perception among Muslims that 'Pakistan' would include most, if not all, of Punjab and Bengal. Congress, for its part, merely reiterated the old line that a solution of the Hindu–Muslim problem would have to await the winning of independence. While neither the British nor the Congress were willing to take the 'Pakistan' demand too seriously, many Muslims thought their best security lay in backing a party strongly advocating the Muslim case in the negotiations to settle the all-important question of how power was to be shared after the British quit India.

In the 1945–46 elections Jinnah and the League won all the Muslim seats to the central assembly, and polled 75 per cent of the total Muslim vote cast in the provincial assembly elections. A remarkable recovery, considering their performance in the 1937 elections, it was nearly as foolproof a step to achieving the substance of the League's demand as might appear at first fight. Electrified by the slogan for a 'Pakistan', the Muslims had not voted for a specific agenda because no agenda had been detailed. No one had a clear idea about the exact meaning of 'Pakistan', let alone its precise geographic boundaries. Local leaders with whom the provincial Leagues struck alliances of convenience had won the elections. These could very well crumble under the pressure of events over which Jinnah and the League had no control. In Punjab the Unionist Party paid the price for having been in office during the war to administer policies inimical to many agriculturalists. With events appearing to move fast at the centre, many local landed notables as well as *pirs* thought it prudent to switch to the League. In Bengal the radical posturing by the Abul Hashim faction of the Muslim League organization and their role in famine relief at a time when many Muslim peasants were victims of profiteering by Hindu traders and landlords had ensured a steady stream of defection from Krishak Praja leaders and activists as well as a groundswell of support for the League. Ignoring such local and regional causes underlying the League's spectacular performance, Jinnah depicted his party's resounding electoral victory as a mandate for a 'Pakistan' built around undivided Punjab and Bengal. But with the Sikhs preparing for a holy war against the Muslims in Punjab and many Hindus doing much the same both here and in Bengal, the claim was not irrefutable. Without solid organizational support in these provinces, there was also nothing the League high command could do to stop Congress from hobnobbing separately with politicians in Muslim-majority provinces. Indeed after the 1946 elections, apart from Bengal, which had a League ministry, Sind was the only province in the north-west where Leaguers were in office. The NWFP

Figure 27 Prime Minister in Waiting. Jawaharlal Nehru as head of the interim government, 1946; seated on his left are Sarat Chandra Bose and Rajendra Prasad
(Courtesy of the archives of the Netaji Research Bureau, Calcutta)

had a Congress ministry and Punjab, the 'corner-stone' of Pakistan, was under
a coalition ministry of Unionists, Congressmen and Panthic Sikhs.

The cabinet mission plan of 1946 for a three-tiered all-India federation
offered Jinnah something worthy of consideration. Compulsory grouping of
provinces at the second tier handed the League a potential centre capable of
disciplining the Muslim provinces and deploying their weight at an all-India
centre confined to dealing only with defence, foreign affairs and communications. But Congress imperatives called for the extension of the centre's powers
so that real authority was vested at the all-India level, not with the group
legislatures as the League demanded. So the mission could only give Jinnah the
choice between an undivided India with a weak federal centre and compulsory
grouping of Muslim and Hindu provinces but without a guarantee of the
Muslim share at the centre, or a sovereign Pakistan stripped of eastern Punjab
and western Bengal (including Calcutta).

On 6 June 1946 Jinnah rejected such a sovereign 'Pakistan', paving the way
for the All-India Muslim League's acceptance of the Mission's plan for a three-
tiered federal arrangement. With the Congress fanning opposition to provincial
grouping among the Frontier Pathans and elsewhere, Jinnah soon realized that
the Mission's proposals would not stick for long after the British withdrawal.
Jawaharlal Nehru's statement of 11 July 1946 after taking over from Maulana

Azad as Congress President, that grouping might not last, alarmed the Muslim League. A 'Pakistan' with its own sovereign centre would alone be capable of controlling the Muslim provinces. But a sovereign Pakistan had to include undivided Punjab and Bengal if it was to receive a large share of the centre's assets (particularly the Indian army). Without some such bargaining weight Jinnah could not hope to negotiate the broader all-India arrangements, which he had always assumed would have to be made.

In a desperate bid to achieve Pakistan, the Muslim League called for a 'Direct Action' day to be observed on 16 August 1946. The 'great Calcutta killing', which began that day and continued until 20 August, left a few thousand Hindus and Muslims dead. In early September the Congress joined an interim government at the centre, while the Muslim League stayed out. After the League joined the interim government in October, the two sets of ministers remained at odds with one another. Meanwhile, relations between religious communities deteriorated sharply in various regions of India. In October, Muslim peasants led by demobilized soldiers attacked Hindu landlords and traders in Noakhali and Tippera districts of east Bengal. Far worse violence was perpetrated against the Muslim minority in neighbouring Bihar in its immediate aftermath. Violence careering out of control at the social base narrowed the options of those negotiating at the centre even further.

By early 1947 London's main priority was to get out of India as quickly as possible before anti-colonial politics became more radicalized than they already were and communal violence reached even more dangerous levels. Throughout the country there were reports of peasant, labour and youth unrest. Poor peasants and sharecroppers rose up in rebellion in certain regions like Telengana and north Bengal. After the rioting in Bengal and Bihar in late 1946, the communal situation was steadily deteriorating in Punjab from January 1947. These myriad conflicts along lines of class and community laid a basis for an understanding between the Congress high command and London. On 20 February 1947 the British prime minister, Clement Attlee, announced that the British would depart from India by 30 June 1948. The Hindu Mahasabha immediately demanded the partition of Punjab and Bengal. The Mahasabha's demand was echoed by the Congress high command in Nehru's statement of 8 March 1947, which called for the partition of Punjab and suggested that the principle of partition might have to be extended to Bengal as well. Mountbatten's arrival as the last viceroy in March hastened the process of British disengagement even further. Mountbatten was minded to withdraw as quickly as possible with the least possible harm to British interests. The Congress leaders Jawaharlal Nehru and Vallabhbhai Patel – their ideological differences notwithstanding – were ready and eager to take power at the British centre at the price of partitioning Bengal and Punjab. 'Beset by Curzon's ghost', the Bengali newsmagazine *Millat* wrote on 11 April 1947, the Congress and the Hindu Mahasabha were performing the role of the matricidal Parashuram of Hindu mythology as they 'together raised a sharpened axe to slice "Mother" into two'.

Figure 28 Walking for Peace. Mahatma Gandhi in Noakhali (Courtesy of the archives of the Netaji Research Bureau, Calcutta)

During April and May 1947 Bengali nationalist leaders Sarat Chandra Bose and Kiran Shankar Roy were able to reach an understanding with Muslim League leaders Husain Shahid Suhrawardy and Abul Hashim on a united and independent Bengal. The scheme received the endorsement of both Gandhi and Jinnah. In fact, as late as 28 May 1947 Mountbatten recorded two alternative broadcast statements in London. Broadcast 'A' was to be used if it appeared probable that Bengal was to be partitioned, and Broadcast 'B' if Bengal was to remain unified, leaving Punjab alone as the candidate for partition. The implacable opposition of Nehru and Patel ensured that broadcast 'B' was discarded on Mountbatten's return to India on 30 May 1947.

On 2 June 1947 Mountbatten unveiled his partition plan to leaders of the Congress and the League. Late that night Jinnah met Mountbatten in an attempt to persuade him not to make the plan public, since the League's council might not accept it. The Viceroy retorted: 'you [Jinnah] will lose Pakistan, probably for good'. Jinnah simply shrugged his soldiers, and said: '[w]hat must be, must be'. 'Mr. Jinnah!' came Mountbatten's threat, 'I do not intend to let you wreck all the work that has gone into this settlement. Since you will not accept for the Muslim League, I will speak for them myself'. At the leaders' meeting the next morning the Quaid-e-Azam was ordered to 'nod

153

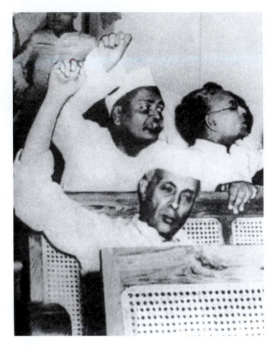

Figure 29 A Tired Vote for Partition. Jawaharlal Nehru raises his hand to vote for partition, June 1947 (Courtesy of the archives of the Nehru Memorial Museum and Library, New Delhi)

[his] head in acquiescence'. The 3 June plan formally presented to the Congress and League leaders and broadcast by Mountbatten later that day virtually decreed partition, leaving a few hollow phrases to keep up the pretence of awaiting 'the decision of the Indian people'. The legislators of the Muslim-majority districts and the remaining districts of both Punjab and Bengal sitting separately were empowered to vote whether or not their provinces should be partitioned. If a simple majority of either part decided in favour of partition, division would take place. The provinces, partitioned or not, would have to choose between joining the existing constituent assembly or a new, i.e. 'Pakistan' constituent assembly.

The charade of ascertaining 'the will of the people' in late June 1947 has left historians with a small advantage. It has put on the record that the majority of legislators in both provinces rejected partition; the decisive votes in favour of partition were cast by east Punjab and west Bengal legislators acting under Congress whip. It now only remained for the British Parliament to pass the necessary legislation to transfer power to two new dominions, which was duly done in July. In a final show of defiance that month Jinnah expressed his desire to convene the Pakistan Constituent Assembly in New Delhi! The Congress leaders would not hear of it. By accepting partition they hoped to

Figure 30 Announcing a Birth. M.A. Jinnah about to make a radio broadcast, June 1947
(Courtesy of the Information Division, Embassy of Pakistan, Washington DC)

have banished the Muslim 'nation' to the north-western and north-eastern extremities of the subcontinent, while riveting central control over the Hindu-majority provinces.

The choice with which Jinnah was presented in the end by the Congress and the British was either an undivided India without any guarantee of the Muslim share of power at the all-India centre or a sovereign Pakistan carved out of the Muslim-majority districts of Punjab and Bengal. Had Jinnah been surer of his following in the Muslim provinces, he might conceivably have decided to work the Mission's plan for an all-India federal structure. In this way he could have prevented the partition of Punjab and Bengal and used the weight of the Muslim provinces to secure safeguards for Indian Muslims in both majority and minority provinces. Jinnah's fears of his own followers, his deep mistrust of the Congress high command, and Mountbatten's decision to move up the date for the final transfer of power from June 1948 to August 1947, left him with little alternative but to acquiesce in the creation of a Pakistan shorn of eastern Punjab and western Bengal (including Calcutta) – the 'maimed, mutilated and moth-eaten' state – which he had rejected out of hand in 1944 and then again in 1946.

A Pakistan without its large non-Muslim minorities in Punjab and Bengal was hardly well placed to demand safeguards for Muslim minorities in the rest

155

Figure 31 The Pity of Partition. Mahatma Gandhi in a pensive mood just outside Calcutta, June 1947 (Courtesy of the archives of the Netaji Research Bureau, Calcutta)

of India. Congress agreed to the principle of partition on the condition that Jinnah and the League accepted it as a final settlement and would not make any further claims on behalf of Muslims in the minority provinces. Moreover, according to the Congress, partition did not entail a division of India into Pakistan and Hindustan as Jinnah had always maintained, but would merely mean that some areas with Muslim majorities had 'opted out' from the 'Union of India' that already existed. Congress's insistence and the British acceptance of the notion that the 'Union of India' would continue to exist without the Muslim-majority areas destroyed the entire basis of the 'two nation' theory as propagated by Jinnah. So the creation of Pakistan, far from being the logical culmination of the theory that there were two nations in India, Hindu and Muslim, was in fact its most decisive political abortion. It was only in an all-India context that the concept of the two nations could have survived the creation of a separate Muslim homeland. Congress's interpretation of partition cast Pakistan in the role of a 'seceding' state, with the added implication that, if it failed to survive, the Muslim areas would have to return to the 'Union of India' severally, not help to recreate it on the basis of two sovereign states.

It was precisely because religion had not been sufficient to bring the Muslim provinces solidly behind an all-India strategy aimed at safeguarding the interests of all Indian Muslims that Jinnah had to abandon his larger political purposes and settle for a truncated Pakistan. This is not to deny that the slogan 'Islam in danger' was a useful rallying cry against the prospect of a Hindu-dominated centre. But the contradictory logic of British constructions – namely the emphasis on provincial and local arenas of politics on the one hand and communally compartmentalized electorates on the other – meant that in the end it was the particularisms of the Muslim provinces rather than a supra-local Islamic sentiment which provided the more important driving force in the making of Pakistan. The Congress leadership's aversion to substantial provincial autonomy as well as the prospect of having to concede a significant share of power at the centre suggests that exclusion, not separatism, might better explain the outcome of 1947.

The dismemberment of the union of India on 14–15 August 1947 was accompanied by the slaughter of hundreds of thousands of innocent Hindus, Muslims and Sikhs as millions stumbled fearfully across the 'shadow lines' separating two post-colonial nation-states. Lord Mountbatten, who never missed an opportunity for self-congratulation, patted himself on the back for having carried out one of 'the greatest administrative operations in history'. As New Delhi took on a festive air before being plunged into a communal carnage, Mahatma Gandhi – the 'father' of the Indian nation – mourned quietly by himself in Calcutta. And, of course, only a British judge could tell for certain where exactly the partitioners' axe was to fall. Radcliffe's award of the precise territorial extents of the two dominions was not made known until at least two days after India and Pakistan had come into being. W.H. Auden did not miss this final irony in the story of Britain's withdrawal from the subcontinent in his poem 'Partition':

> Unbiased at least he was when he arrived on his mission,
> Having never set eyes on this land he was called to partition
> Between two peoples fanatically at odds,
> With their different diets and incompatible gods.
> 'Time,' they had briefed him in London, 'is short. It's too late
> For mutual reconciliation or rational debate:
> The only solution now lies in separation.
> The Viceroy thinks, as you will see from his letter,
> That the less you are seen in his company the better,
> So we've arranged to provide you with other accommodation.
> We can give you four judges, two Moslem and two Hindu,
> To consult with, but the final decision must rest with you.'

Shut up in a lonely mansion, with police night and day
Patrolling the gardens to keep assassins away,
He got down to work, to the task of settling the fate
Of millions. The maps at his disposal were out of date
And the Census Returns almost certainly incorrect,
But there was no time to check them, no time to inspect
Contested areas. The weather was frightfully hot,
And a bout of dysentery kept him constantly on the trot,
But in seven weeks it was done, the frontiers decided,
A continent for better or worse divided.
The next day he sailed for England, where he quickly forgot
The case, as a good lawyer must. Return he would not,
Afraid, as he told his Club, that he might get shot.

17

1947

Memories and meanings

During the closing days of the British raj officials in the imposing secretariat buildings designed by Lutyens resembled apprentice sorcerers who had let loose forces they could barely understand, much less fully control. In 1947 the raj came to its end amidst political and social convulsions in which Hindu and Muslim as well as Muslim and Sikh engaged in an orgy of murder, rape and plunder on an unprecedented scale. Some seventeen million people were shunted across frontiers of a subcontinent ostensibly divided along religious lines for the first time in its history. In the half century that has elapsed India and Pakistan have been to war over the north Indian princely state of Kashmir on two separate occasions. A third war in 1971, preceded by the slaughter of Muslims by Muslims, marked the breakaway of Bangladesh. In 1999 the two neighbours faced the prospect of a fourth war over the Kargil heights in Kashmir, raising the alarming prospect of a nuclear exchange. This bloody baptism of the states that replaced the British raj has wreaked havoc on inter-state relations in the subcontinent. State-sponsored secular nationalism and religious majoritarianism have failed to address the challenge posed by cultural difference in complex societies. There has been a recurrence of centre–region problems in nearly all of South Asia, the denial of regional aspirations in Kashmir and elsewhere, and the ravages of an array of violent social and political conflicts. The legacy of 1947 continues to loom large, both at the domestic and the regional levels. The scars of partition have proven to be deeper than the healing touch of independence from colonial rule.

The sheer magnitude of the events of 1947 has elicited varied interpretations. When clashing emotions have not rendered discussion impossible, the marshalling of contradictory facts has generated bitter controversies. The meanings and memories of 1947 have been suffused by charge and counter-charge of polemicists, whether the apologists of empire, or the embattled pro-pagandists of official nationalism, Indian and Pakistani alike. Until recently the main explanations of why India was partitioned were based on the theory of British divide and rule and arguments about Indian Muslims being a separate and identifiable nation. Neither theory, as we have seen in the last chapter, provides an adequate explanation of the central event in modern South Asian history. Left to statist historians or 'communal' ideologues, debates on the partition and independence of India have drawn upon tortured recollections of displacement, unmitigated terror and the brutal killings and rapes of kith and kin. Invariably viewed through the distorting lens of a politically charged present, these remembrances have tended to harden the lines of hostility across the great divide. A balanced and thoughtful reappraisal of the memories and meanings of 1947 as well as the history and mythology surrounding partition can go a long way in promoting informed dialogue and understanding between the peoples of India, Pakistan and Bangladesh.

There were nearly a hundred million Muslims in the subcontinent, or more than one person in five, at the time India was partitioned. Of these about sixty million were to live in Pakistan, both east and west, making it the largest Muslim state in the world, but a state cut in two by over a thousand miles of Indian territory. Nearly forty million Muslims were left inside India, the largest group of Muslims in a non-Muslim state. These bare facts suggest that if Indian Muslims had a common faith and a shared religiously informed cultural identity, they were in no sense a homogeneous community, especially in their politics. Muslims differed from Muslims on the bases of their regional and local loyalties, language, occupation and economic standing. Ever since the early centuries of Islam in India, Muslims had coexisted and often worked in harmony with followers of other religions. When the British came to power in India, it was certainly not in the face of the organized resistance of Islam; while the British remained in Government House, it was hardly with the organized support of a united Muslim community. Yet when they transferred power in 1947, they did so to two states, in one of which we are invited to believe that an Islamic ideology had become the most important impulse.

There is more than a little that is curious about the claim. Mohammad Ali Jinnah, the man widely credited with the creation of Pakistan, made his mark on Indian politics as an unequivocal protagonist of Hindu–Muslim unity and from 1913 to 1937 stood for a common Congress–League political programme. The triumphant hero of Pakistani hagiography, the monster in the demonology of the less perceptive among Indian and British historians, not to mention the 'lunatic', the 'evil genius' and the 'megalomaniac' in the breathtakingly egotistical utterances of the last viceroy, Jinnah has been until recently acclaimed and denounced in unison for tearing apart the historic unity of the Indian subcontinent. But the result of the end game of the raj was not what Jinnah had been after all along. For a man who liked to describe himself as a 'cold blooded logician', Jinnah avoided any discussion on the logistics of his demand. Indeed at no point during the final decade of the British raj did anyone in the All-India Muslim League give a precise definition to the demand for a 'Pakistan'. While the leaders remained tight-lipped about what Pakistan actually entailed, the followers were allowed to make of it what they wished. Naturally, a host of conflicting shapes and forms, most of them vague, some utopian, others simply fatuous, were given to what was little more than an undefined slogan. Yet if Jinnah did not reveal his real aim or give concrete shape to his notion of Pakistan, he did so with a deliberate purpose. Historians have no excuse to accept the slogan at face value. Jinnah's appeal to religion was not characteristic of his earlier politics, or indeed of his personal convictions. His use of religion was a political tactic, not an ideology to which he was ever committed.

Religion as culture has always been an important element in the identity of Muslims in their varied regional settings. But there has never been any agreement on religion as political ideology. In a context where the local and regional politics of Muslims had never developed within the framework of an all-India Muslim political party, Jinnah and the League could rustle up the semblance of mass support only by bringing the Muslim provincial bosses into line. A precise political programme could not win such support, since what was good for Muslims in one part of India was not good for Muslims in others. A social programme, which might have mobilized the rank and file, held no attractions for the provincial oligarchs who dominated Muslim politics. This is where religion came to Jinnah's rescue, less as a device to be deployed against rival communities, and more as a way of papering over the cracks in the splintered ranks of Muslim India.

In the event, Jinnah's strategy misfired. It had been grounded upon a number of assumptions, many of which proved unsound when it came to the crunch. This shrewd politician underestimated Britain's anxiety to hand over power. He thought he still enjoyed the luxury of a leisurely British timetable. Since a partition of India would clearly damage British interests in some ways, Jinnah assumed London would delay a transfer of power rather than accept it in a hurry. Since Gandhi was implacably opposed to partition, Jinnah assumed Congress would go to great lengths – perhaps even as far as conceding parity – rather than permit it. But Jinnah exaggerated the Mahatma's influence over his erstwhile lieutenants in the Congress High Command, particularly once office at the centre was at stake. Jinnah, of all people, should have understood why the hard men in the Congress, especially Sardar Vallabhbhai Patel and Jawaharlal Nehru, needed a strong unitary centre for India, and realized the high price they would pay to achieve it. Yet the fundamental flaw in Jinnah's strategy was his lack of effective control over his followers in the Muslim-majority provinces. In playing the communal card Jinnah had helped arouse religious passions because, lacking a strong and unified party organization, this was his only trump card against the British, the Congress and even his own recalcitrant allies in the Muslim provinces. Fired by millennial hopes of various sorts, depending on regional and class contexts, the enthusiasts for Pakistan destroyed Jinnah's calculations at the top, which had a very narrow margin for error.

For Jinnah, Pakistan was the means with which to win an equitable share of power for Muslims at the all-India centre. It was not a strategy designed for the benefit of Muslim-majority provinces alone; nor was it in the interests simply of Muslims in the minority provinces. Rather it was the line of a sea-soned politician who, throughout his long career, had set his sights on the all-India stage. Paradoxically, his nationalist sentiments had more in common with those of the Congress high command, an organization in which he had served his political apprenticeship, than with the narrower perspectives of most of his own supporters. Playing for high stakes with an indifferent hand, he could hardly reveal his cards. The appeal to religion proved to be the joker in the pack. This solitary man, who lacked the common touch, had to pretend to be a man of the people; this modern politician with secular leanings had to give the men of religion their due; this dedicated constitutionalist had in the end to threaten his opponents with religiously inspired agitation; and this nationalist, who had dedicated so much of his life to winning for India that strong centre from the colonial masters, ended up by being held responsible for the partition of India and for the creation of a 'maimed, mutilated and moth-eaten' Pakistan, whose Islamic unity has proved to be as fragile as Jinnah – who had for so long and so painstakingly tried to combat the provincial par-ticularisms of the Muslim-majority provinces – must secretly have known. Corroborating evidence that the Quaid-e-Azam never envisaged Islam as ideology to dominate the state of Pakistan can be seen in his address to the first ever meeting of the Pakistani Constituent Assembly on 1 August 1947:

> You are free to go to your temples, you are free to go to your mosques or to any other place of worship in this state of Pakistan ... You may belong to any religion or caste or creed – that has nothing to do with the business of the State ... We are starting with this funda-mental principle that we are all citizens and equal citizens of one State.

Sadly for the man who is still revered by the people of Pakistan as the father of the nation, his ideas that seemed inconvenient were suppressed by ideologues of the post-colonial state. The brazen use of state-controlled education and media since 1947 helped ensure that Jinnah is remembered as the man who gave concrete expression to the vision of an Islamic state. Devoid of historical fact, the partition of India is celebrated as the ultimate victory of Islam in the subcontinent. Few Pakistanis visiting Jinnah's mausoleum have wondered how this great defender of minority rights could have left so many Muslims unprotected in predominantly Hindu India. The time when ignorance was still blissful, however, seems to be running out and more and more Pakistanis are reassessing the memories and meanings of partition as they look agitatedly, if helplessly, at their own fate, held to ransom by Islamic extremists and the predicament of many of their co-religionists in India today.

The gap between meanings and memories of partition has been quite as wide in India. Having successfully appropriated the mantle of the British raj, it was not too difficult for the Congress to lay exclusive claim on the appellation of 'Indian nationalist'. Partha Chatterjee has shown how nationalist thought at its 'moment of arrival', exemplified by Jawaharlal Nehru, became a 'discourse of order' conducted not only in 'a single, consistent, unambiguous voice' but also 'glossing over all earlier contradictions, divergences and differences'. Yet Chatterjee's methodological decision to 'give to nationalist thought its ideological unity by relating it to a form of the post-colonial state' does not leave enough space for the recovery of the contested visions of nationhood and alternative frameworks for the free Indian state. As late as 1945, Gandhi was holding fast to 'the system of Government envisaged in Hind Swaraj' and refusing 'to draw a large scale picture in detail'. If Gandhi's predilection for the small-scale village community led him to refuse to elaborate on the nature of a state on a subcontinental scale, there were plenty of other nationalist models of the state that offered variations on the theme of decentred democracy with room for an interplay between fission and fusion as well as centrifugal and centripetal tendencies. A unitary, post-colonial state was in the end prepared to grant legitimacy to only the one strand of singular nationalism. But it is imperative for historians not to accept the easy conflation between nation and state when no such hyphenated relationship existed until the climactic moment of the post-colonial transition.

In the retrospectively reconstructed narrative of the nationalist past only those Muslims who supported the Congress qualified as 'nationalist Muslims', with little regard to their historically shifting role in colonial and anti-colonial politics. More important, the spectre of a great communal divide, 'finally settled' or 'solved' through the partition of 1947, could conveniently obscure the centre–region contradictions in the rest of India. The lever of a subcontinent-wide conflict between a religious majority and minority enabled the Congress in 1947 not only to cut the Muslim League's contradictory demands to size but also to deploy the powers of the centralized state apparatus it had inherited to assert its authority over the Hindu-majority regions. In the immediate aftermath of independence the proponents of a linguistic reorganization of states, as well as communists fighting for poor peasants' rights in Telengana, could be tarred by the sweeping Nehruvian brush of anti-state terrorism.

There were other benefits that came with a negotiated transfer of power. Through the freshly won control of the official channels of communication the new regime could proudly propagate the myth of how independence was won through Gandhian methods of non-violence, even if it paid little heed to Gandhian values and visions for the future. The revolutionaries who took to the path of armed struggle won much popular veneration but were for decades after independence virtual untouchables so far as official histories and media reportage were concerned. Outside a select company of scholars and intellectuals, the communal holocaust accompanying partition was rarely permitted to challenge the hollowness of the claim of India's non-violent coming to freedom. Among the elite, many Indian Muslims accuse Jinnah and his Pakistan of undermining their socio-economic and political standing in independent India, while the non-Muslim 'majority' hold Pakistan and its principal architect responsible for destroying the sacred unity of Bharatmata or 'mother India'. The situation surrounding Ayodhya, where Hindu majoritarian nationalists sought to build a temple at the alleged birthplace of Ram after razing the sixteenth-century Babri masjid to the ground in 1992, suggests that the real meaning of partition has been lost on Indians quite as much as on the Pakistanis. There is, of course, a major difference. In India the prevalent memory of partition is an acutely negative one, even if the Hindu Mahasabha and the Congress called for it in 1947. Partition seems to be the demon the Bharatiya Janata Party (BJP)-led Hindus wanted to exorcise by felling a mosque and trying to erect Ram's temple in its place. Yet the secular nationalist retrospective view of partition is not that different from that of those whom they denounce as religious 'communalists'.

Notwithstanding a communal holocaust, 1947 was the year British rule was finally terminated and Indians given full responsible government. But as in the case of partition, there is a disjunction between the meanings and the memories attached to the winning of independence on 15 August 1947. For most Indians, independence was won on that day, albeit at the painful but ultimately affordable price of partition. Very few realize, much less question, why their nationalist heroes accepted dominion status rather than the full independence to which they had been committed since the adoption of the Purna Swaraj resolution at Lahore in 1929. More have criticized the decision to accept Pakistan, entailing as it did a total reversal of the Congress policy of acquiring power over a united India. Gandhi's categorical rejection of an independence based on the partition of India lends added weight to this sentiment. A close analysis of the end game reveals that by going along with partition the Congress leadership was able to lay claim to the British unitary centre at New Delhi, pull in the princely states and ensure its triumphant march over three-quarters of India. No mean achievement, especially the integration of the princely states achieved by that man of iron – Vallabhbhai Patel – it was made possible only by compromising on the two main principles of the Indian nationalist creed since the late 1920s – unity and full independence.

If unity and even independence could be compromised, it was easy to dilute Congress's commitment to the socio-economic betterment of the people of India. The assumption of the centralized power of the raj by the Congress professing an ideology of reformist class conciliation, but in fact representing the interests of more specific privileged groups, kept the scales firmly tilted against India's poor. India's 'tryst with destiny' at the midnight hour on 15 August 1947, while it represented in the popular consciousness an achievement second to none in the subcontinent's history, has not eradicated the poverty, discrimination and exploitation of which the nationalists accused the colonialists. Neither the Gandhian dreams of self-sustained village reconstruction, nor the radical objective of rapid socialist development through the instruments of a centralized state have been fulfilled by the configurations that have ruled India since 1947. Even in the twenty-first century, the call for 'inclusive growth' has remained something of an empty slogan. If anything, Congress's inheritance of the colonial state's unitary centre – the glistening prize in the quest of which its leadership took the momentous step of conceding partition and Pakistan – has accentuated centre–state tensions and complicated the task of redressing the socio-economic deprivations of India's teeming multitudes. India's federal dilemma, the threats to its secular ideology, the class, caste and communal conflicts and, above all, military disputes with Pakistan are all directly related to the decisions of expediency taken in 1947.

The memories and meanings of 1947 proved least traumatic for the erstwhile colonial rulers, despite some early manifestations of withdrawal symptoms. Raj nostalgia burst forth on the media screens with aplomb at periodic intervals. Britain's romance with India grew stronger in the aftermath of empire precisely because memories can be selective to the point of distorting the reality. The most acclaimed figure of Britain's grand moment in India at the time of the transfer of power in 1947 is Lord Louis Mountbatten, the last viceroy, who delighted in Hollywood theatrics quite as much as in his royal lineage. Mountbatten's decision to transfer power in August 1947 rather than in June 1948 is attributed to his political acumen, not to his self-serving interest in striking a deal with a Congress leadership that was more anxious to acquire power than uphold the nationalist ideals for which so many freedom fighters in the past had sacrificed their lives. This prince-charming-turned-viceroy never lost an opportunity for self-congratulation. He even claimed laurels for presiding over the agonizing dismemberment of the Punjab and Bengal. In memory of those Hindus, Sikhs and Muslims who perished in their hundreds of thousands, the refugees who in their millions stumbled fearfully across the frontiers of the two states and, above all, the women and children who bore the full brunt of the violence, Mountbatten's contention that he carried out in a matter of months one of 'the greatest administrative operations in history' has to be signposted in the historical archives as the clearest admission of the former colonial masters' dereliction of duty at the moment of India's gravest crisis.

That the dawn of independence came littered with the severed limbs and blood-drenched bodies of innocent men, women and children was a nightmare from which the subcontinent has never fully recovered. The colossal human tragedy of the partition and its continuing aftermath has been better conveyed by the more sensitive creative writers and artists, for example, in Saadat Hasan Manto's short stories and Ritwik Ghatak's films, than by historians. There have been recent, belated attempts by a few historians and anthropologists to capture the experience of pain during the partition. Coming from those who are imbued with a communitarian or fragmentalist perspective, these attempts may be missing a historical nuance or two in their dogged anti-statism. Veena Das has suggested how the Indian state may have impinged on the exercise of choice by raped and abducted women by creating the legal category of 'abducted women' for the purposes of its repatriation programme. While taking a strong and entirely laudable position against the many instances of violence by the post-colonial state, she is curiously silent about the negation of consent and choice at the traumatic, violent moment of abduction and rape. By dramatizing, if not romanticizing, examples of murderers and rapists turned into besotted husbands of their former victims, such as the big bearded Sikh weeping copiously at the border checkpoint, she is presenting a more benign picture of acceptance of raped women by families and kinship communities of victims and perpetrators alike than is warranted by the historical evidence or the cultural context.

In a slightly different vein Gyanendra Pandey, in his effort to write about the experience of partition and challenge colonial and nationalist stereotypes of communal conflict, has treated all violence that was not violence by the state as an undifferentiated category. This has rather disconcerting implications for the recovery of the consciousness of women who were the worst victims of violence at the time of partition. The historians' critique of over-centralized state monoliths of the colonial and post-colonial era must avoid the trap of uncritically celebrating the community or the fragment. The structure and the ideology of the community have to be subjected to the same glare of critical scrutiny as the structure and ideology of the state. Once this is done, the inherent weaknesses of the communitarian mode of analysis in investigations of violence are thrown into sharp relief. Violence intensified communitarian feelings, but was rarely perpetrated by collectivities as a whole. Individuals, even when grouped in armed militias, could settle personal scores in the process of promoting and protecting members of their community. In emphasizing the individual as victim, historians and anthropologists have obfuscated the pivotal role of individuals or, more aptly, banded individuals, as perpetrators.

Implicating entire communities in violence against rival communities provides a very distorted picture of what really happened in 1947, lending an unacceptable degree of legitimacy to the social violence that accompanied the partition of the Punjab. The unprecedented violence in rural Punjab had more to with a fierce scramble over *zar* (wealth), *zameen* (land) and *zan* (women) during a complete collapse of order at the end of empire than with religion as such. The historical evidence makes plain that the vast majority chose not to participate in violence against religiously demarcated rivals, often going against the grain of a supposed communitarian consensus by protecting the victims. Moreover, even when banded individuals resorting to violence consciously adopted the idioms of the discourse and politics of communitarianism, Muslim, Hindu and Sikh, they interpreted them so widely as to disrupt the neat assumptions underpinning the category of 'communal violence'. The best way forward in partition historiography is to investigate the discursive relationship between the social and cultural formation of communities in interaction with political and state-making processes at the local, regional and all-India levels, without treating communities as undifferentiated and homogenous blocks.

Such an approach will go a long way in restoring the subjecthood of subaltern social groups, including women, in the making of history while noting that even their active agency cannot always prevent them from becoming tragic, though not passive, victims of the games of power played by claimants, makers and managers of colonial and post-colonial states.

There are moments, however, when even the most sensitively crafted history of communities and states pales in comparison to the poetic licence of a Faiz Ahmed Faiz, who captured the mood of the times when he wrote the poem 'Freedom's Dawn (August 1947)'

Ye dagh dagh ujala, ye shab-gazida sahar
Vo intizar tha jis-ka, ye vo sahar to nahin,
Ye vo sahar to nahin jis-ki arzu lekar
Chale the yar ke mil-ja egi kahin na kahin
Falak ke dasht men taron ki akhiri manzil,
Kahin to hoga shab-e sust mauk ka sahil,
Kahin to jake rukega safina-e-gham-e-dil.
Jawan lahu ki pur-asrar shahrahon se
Chale jo yar to daman pe itne hath pare;
Diyar-e-husn ki be-sabr khwabgahori se
Pukarti-rahin bahen, badan bulate-rahe;
Bahut aziz thi lekin rukh-e-sahar ki lagan,
Subuk subuk thi tamanna, dabi dabi thi thakan.
Suna hai ho bhi chuka hai firaq-e-zulmat-o-nur
Suna hai ho bhi chuka hai visal-e-manzil-o-gam;
Badal-chuka hai bahut ahl-e-dard ka dastur,
Nishat-e-vasl halal o azab-e-hijr haram.
Jijar ki aag, nazar ki umang, dil ji jalan,
Kisi pe chara-e-hijran ka kuchh asar ni nahin.
Kahan se ai nigar-e-saba, kidhar ko gai?
Abhi charagh-e-sar-e-rah ko kuchh khabar hi nahin;
Abhi girani-e-shab men kami nahin ai,
Najat-e-dida-o-dil ki ghari nahin ai;
Chale-chalo ke vo manzil abhi nahin ai.
(This leprous daybreak, dawn night's fangs have mangled –
This is not that long-looked-for break of day.
Not that clear dawn in quest of which those comrades
Set out, believing that in heaven's wide void
Somewhere must be the stars' last halting place,
Somewhere the verge of night's slow-washing tide,
Somewhere an anchorage for the ship of heartache.
When we set out, we friends, taking youth's secret
Pathways, how many hands plucked at our sleeves!
From beauty's dwellings and their panting casements

167

Soft arms invoked us, flesh cried out to us;
But dearer was the lure of dawn's bright cheek,
Closer her shimmering robe of fairy rays;
Light-winged that longing, feather-light that toil.
But now, word goes, the birth of day from darkness
Is finished, wandering feet stand at their goal;
Our leaders' ways are altering, festive looks
Are all the fashion, discontent reproved; –
And yet this physic still on unslaked eye
Or heart fevered by severance works no cure.
Where did that fine breeze, that the wayside lamp
Has not once felt, blow from – where has it fled?
Night's heaviness is unlessened still, the hour
Of mind and spirit's ransom has not struck;
Let us go on, our goal is not reached yet.)

18

POST-COLONIAL SOUTH ASIA
State and economy, society and politics,
1947 to 1971

Now is the moment when the historical clock ticks past the famous midnight hour of 14–15 August 1947. This chapter aims at breaching the spatial and temporal divide which that moment has come to represent in the domain of scholarship. Despite a much longer shared history, marked by as many commonalities as differences, post-colonial India and Pakistan have for the most part been treated as two starkly antithetical entities. Only a few comparative analysts have risked trespassing across the arbitrary frontiers demarcated at the time of partition. Most have preferred to operate within the contours of independent statehood, even when these fly in the face of overlapping developments rooted in the distant as well as the recent colonial past. Such scholarly deference to the boundaries of post-colonial nation-states in the subcontinent is matched by the attitude of Indian and Pakistani border patrols, who despite firing shots at one another, seem perfectly resigned to the two-way flow of illicit trade in luxury wares, arms and drugs. If a twelve hundred mile-long frontier has served to thwart policing efforts, a millennia-old past persists in unsettling the rigid compartmentalization of historical memory and narration enforced during six decades of state-orchestrated national imaginings. Neither end nor beginning, 1947 has to be seen as intrinsic to the ongoing processes of decolonization while addressing the theme of continuity and change between the colonial and the post-colonial eras.

The overlapping interplay of centralism and regionalism as well as nationalism and religious assertion (both of the communitarian and sectarian varieties) continued to mould the historical experiences of India and Pakistan after independence, albeit with significant variations and modifications. The Congress claimed independence from colonial rule as the triumph of centralism and nationalism. Yet the creation of a Pakistan had underlined the partial success of regionalism and religious communitarianism. In the initial decades of independence, the Congress-dominated Indian centre wedded to an ideology of secular nationalism did better than Islamic Pakistan in containing the forces of regionalism. Not only did the dialectic of centralism and regionalism in India prove more amenable to the setting up of a democratic system but, unlike Pakistan, which came under the dominance of the military and the civil bureaucracy very early on in the day, Congress's inclusionary nationalism appeared to have taken the sting out of the more rebarbative forms of exclusionary communitarianism. It might be tempting to attribute the Congress's achievements in establishing a relatively stable democratic system in India to its ideology of secular nationalism and commitment to centralism. After all, the deployment of Islam as the central tenet of Pakistani nationalism managed to neither curb the forces of regionalism nor piece together the most rudimentary form of a democratic political system.

Yet such a conclusion seems a trifle premature in view of developments in the subsequent decades of independence. Since the mid-1970s, the trappings of democracy and secular nationalism in India have been unable to prevent the centre from coming under increasing pressure from a welter of regional and communitarian groups. If anything, secular and democratic India displayed many of the same stresses and strains during the 1980s and 1990s that made military authoritarian and Islamic Pakistan particularly susceptible to regional resistance. Could it be that post-colonial India and Pakistan continue to grapple with the age-old problem of constant shifts and fluctuations in the balance of power between centre and region?

While the centre has held up in India without the ignominy of a region breaking away from its control, Pakistan in 1971 saw the majority of its population in the eastern wing successfully striking for independence and ushering in the creation of a sovereign state, Bangladesh. A dramatic instance of Pakistan's chronic regional problems, the breakaway of Bangladesh was brought to fruition by India's military intervention. Ever since 1947, regional dissent against central authority has spilled across national boundaries, keeping inter-state relations in perpetual disrepair. In more recent decades, the Indian state's challenges in Punjab, Assam and other north-eastern states, not to mention the perennial problem of Kashmir, the dilemmas presented by Pakistan's provinces of Sind, Baluchistan and the tribal territories in the northwest, and the restiveness among Chakma Buddhists in Bangladesh, all in their different ways have demonstrated the extreme permeability of the borders defining nation-states in the subcontinent.

Why has democratic and secular India done only marginally better than authoritarian and Islamic Pakistan in preventing the recurrence of regional dissidence? The question requires probing not only the structural basis of the two states, but also stripping them of their ideational self-projections. Such a clearing of the decks has multiple advantages. Historically, democracy and its obverse, authoritarianism, secularism and its presumed antithesis, religion, have coexisted if not been thoroughly imbricated. By disturbing the sanguine assumptions underlying conceptions of democracy, authoritarianism, secularism and religion, students of history might gain much by way of nuance and in the process deepen their understanding of these complex but overused terms. Instead of tracing the linear development of democracy and secularism in India and authoritarianism and Islam in Pakistan, the spotlight is best focused on the historical dynamics of the transition from colonialism. This should allow for a better appreciation of the interplay between state consolidation and political processes as it was fashioned and refashioned by the relationship between the two sovereign centres and the various regions.

The modalities of partitioning India effectively precluded its division into two 'successor states'. It was Congress that inherited the unitary central apparatus and international personality of British India. Ignoring Jinnah's vocal protests against Congress seizing the appellation 'India', Mountbatten admitted that he was doing no more than setting up a tent for the government of the newly created Muslim state. The Muslim-majority areas in the north-western and eastern extremities of the subcontinent, constituting Pakistan, were deemed to be merely 'contracting out' of the 'Union of India'. Forced into the role of a state 'seceding' from a continuing sovereign entity, and with Muslim regionalisms showing no signs of receding before an all-powerful Islamic impulse, Pakistan had to somehow register its independent existence. A formidable undertaking, it required building a centre from scratch and con-trolling territories separated by over a thousand miles of Indian territory that had throughout their history resisted the imposition of any outside authority. The different inheritances in the realm of state institutions, especially at the centre, were of critical importance in influencing the nature and direction of historical continuity and change in post-colonial India and Pakistan.

Explanations of India's success in establishing a system of parliamentary democracy have privileged the Congress organization at the expense of other institutions of the post-colonial state. While the Congress as the premier poli-tical party was undoubtedly the main player in the new dispensation, its ability to frame a constitution and enforce central authority over diverse provinces and hitherto nominally independent princely states owed much to the civil bureaucracy, the military and the police. Without these institutional legacies of colonialism, even an organization like the Congress might have baulked at the tasks confronting India in the initial years of independence. By keeping the focus exclusively on the Congress, several Western political scientists have inadvertently helped perpetuate colonial definitions of 'democracy' as mere representation, overlooking the tendencies of bureaucratic authoritarianism that remained embedded in the non-elected institutions of the Indian state. Working in close concert with the Congress, these institutions engaged in a process of state consolidation where legitimacy gained from the formalization of regular elections had frequently to be supplemented with authoritarian methods in the name of preserving law and order in the different regions.

The partnership between the Congress and the non-elected institutions, the civil bureaucracy and the police in particular, facilitated the establishment of a formal democracy within the barely modified structures of British India's uni-tary state system. With a spread of support in the regions and the confidence that comes from having successfully dislodged the colonial rulers, Congress was ready and able to work a Westminster style of parliamentary democracy.

The holding of regular elections lent legitimacy to a multi-party system dominated by the Congress. General elections at five-yearly intervals gave Indian voters the inestimable power to freely choose and depose governments. With the widening of the electoral base, this is a power which a discerning Indian electorate has exercised effectively to oust discredited governments, both at the centre and in the states, in defiance of formidable party organizations enjoying the support of the administrative machinery. Yet electoral verdicts in and of themselves have not sufficiently empowered Indian voters when it has come to shaping the state's social or economic development policies. Political privilege has been far too entrenched at various levels of the polity to permit the elimination of caste, class and gender-based discrimination. In this sense political processes in India have fallen well short of the democratic ideal and may even have served to disguise the authoritarianism inherent within the Indian political economy and state structure. Ruling configurations at the centre have been content with securing support from regional elites who are inclined to further entrench their own political and economic interests, not advance the process of democratization. With only inadequate implementation of the fundamental rights provisions of the Indian constitution, the removal of widespread social inequalities and injustices has remained an unrealized ideal.

Yet there can be no question that India's success in working a system of parliamentary democracy has, over time, greatly assisted the mobilization of ever larger segments of the populace. The more recent assertion of their political muscle by the backward and scheduled castes in several states has spelt important changes on the Indian political scene. Newly empowered middle and lower castes and classes have vigorously challenged the ruling configurations that had dominated the Congress since independence. This democratic result has not been registered at the base without provoking authoritarian responses from the state, usually in conjunction with the social groups ensconced in the executive and legislative institutions. Resistance to this nexus of democratic authoritarianism has given the meaning of democracy a new twist. The possibility of mobilizing electoral support around generalizable symbols like the neat confluence of the Muslim invasion signified by the Babri *masjid* and the birthplace of the great Hindu god, Ram, has been put to effective test by the Bharatiya Janata Party (BJP) since the late 1980s. Equally forcefully, it has provoked one of the stiffest resistances ever by Indian political parties of varying hues and colours to the BJP's perceived intention to dilute the secular credentials of the Indian union. One of the central questions raised by the emergence of a national alternative in a party touting the ideology of Hindutva was whether electoral processes, however democratic, can be allowed to weaken the secular pillars of the Indian state.

A few rules of thumb might help in tracing the historical threads through the different phases of India's post-independence history. Changes in the centre–state dialectic, whether manifested in relations within party organizations or between them and the non-elected institutions, have had a direct bearing on the balance between democratic and authoritarian tendencies within the state structure as well as the larger political system. A distinction between formal democracy – reflected in the phenomenon of regular elections – and substantive democracy – defined as the provision of social opportunities through equitable economic development – is also a useful way to measure the achievements of post-independence India. By the same token, differentiating authoritarianism in its overt and covert manifestations can help in assessing the concrete effects of the close interaction between elected and non-elected institutions at the centre as well as the regions.

The roots of the centre–region tensions in South Asia have less to do with its inherent cultural diversities than with the historical circumstances of the immediate post-colonial period. The trauma of partition in 1947 meant that the first priority of state managers in both India and Pakistan was to set up strong central governments. Such concessions as were made to federalism, whether real or on paper, were handed down from above. With at least fourteen major linguistic groups and some 1652 mother tongues, India's need for a federal system was an imperative rather than simply a matter of political choice. Instead of creating a genuinely federal system, India's early state managers were more anxious to build a state structure capable of ensuring unity. Fears of survival were even greater in Pakistan, where military-bureaucratic dominance combined with an all-pervasive, if ill-defined, Islamic ideology was used to chip away at provincial rights very early on in the post-partition era.

States and provinces in both India and Pakistan were subject to constitutional arrangements borrowed to a great extent from the Government of India Act of 1935. A centrally appointed governor and a cabinet headed by the chief minister appeared to replicate the presidential and prime ministerial equation at the centre. But in actual fact the state governor has been for all practical purposes, like the centrally appointed members of the Indian Administrative Services, an active agent of the centre at the state or provincial level. If the Indian centre feels that a state is not being administered according to the constitution, the elected government headed by the chief minister can be dismissed and the state brought under what is euphemistically known as president's rule. This was done quite often between the late 1950s and the 1980s, until judicial restraints were placed on this executive practice. Central governments in India and Pakistan have constitutional sanction to poach on both the legislative and executive domains of states and provinces respectively. So although federal in form, the Indian and Pakistani state structures have been unitary in substance. Borrowing heavily from the colonial masters in the initial stages, the two state structures became increasingly more centralized.

It has almost become a cliché to ascribe the success of formal democracy in India to the uniqueness of its premier nationalist organization, the Indian National Congress. But India's inheritance of the British raj's unitary centre and its success in warding off international pressures in the first decade of independence were equally, if not more, important in the unravelling of its immediate post-independence experience. Making a virtue out of pragmatism, the Congress leadership, egged on by Sardar Vallabhbhai Patel, moved quickly to appropriate the same Indian civil service which, as Pranab Bardhan has wryly commented, was neither very civil nor service-oriented and had been a consistent target of their attack under colonialism. Renamed the Indian Administrative Services, the old Indian Civil Service (ICS), as well as the Indian police service, an assortment of para-military forces and, on occasion, even the Indian army were deployed to underwrite the centre's authority in areas where the Congress machinery was either weak or riven with factionalism and corruption. The disarray within the Congress was only a few degrees less than dissension within the Muslim League, especially at the state and district levels of the organization. There were remarkable similarities and weaknesses in the dominant political parties of India and Pakistan. What accounted for the success of democracy in one and of authoritarianism in the other was the nature of the links forged by these political parties with the non-elected institutions of state.

Even under Jawaharlal Nehru (prime minister, 1947–64), the dynamics of centre–state relations began shifting the locus of power away from the parliament towards executive authority residing in the hands of the prime minister. Centralization of state authority by Nehru was offset to an extent by the accommodations he made with provincial party bosses. But this prevented the genuine democratization of the state and the premier political party. Although it had an overall organizational advantage over the Muslim League, state and district Congress committees were no less infected by the personality cult of local leaders and no more immune from internal rivalries than in Pakistan. Each successive election saw a broadening of the political base, placing the organizational machinery under greater pressure from newly mobilized social groups. This suggests the deinstitutionalization of the Congress was already well underway before the setback registered in the fourth general elections in 1967. The changing balance of power within the elected institutions was to be reflected in their relationship with the non-elected institutions of the state, the civil bureaucracy in particular. Needing to balance the conflicting interests and demands emanating from various levels of the party organization with the imperatives of state consolidation under Congress auspices, Nehru had no qualms about relying on the civil bureaucracy, the police and the military, when necessary, to buttress central state authority. The spurt in public sector enterprises during the period of the first three development plans (1950–65) created new sources of patronage and greatly aided the cementing of the partnership between the Congress leadership and the non-elected officials of the state. And while Nehru succeeded in stamping his personal imprimatur on the rhetoric behind policy formulation, the Indian state's increasing administrative capacities and deepening interventions into economy and society gave civil bureaucrats considerable discretionary powers *vis-à-vis* elected representatives at various levels of policy implementation.

A new generation of scholars has questioned the earlier conclusions about Nehru's achievement in placing India firmly on the track to democracy. Having been instrumental in Congress's acceptance of power at the British unitary centre, Nehru at the helm of a post-colonial state was not inclined to undermine the exercise of his own authority if this clashed with democratic practice. As early as the 1920s, the Congress had promised federalism based on the linguistic reorganization of existing state boundaries, which were correctly seen to be arbitrary creations for the convenience of colonial administrators. Yet no sooner had independence been won than the Congress under Nehru tried to block the vociferous demands for a reorganization of state boundaries along linguistic lines. On 20 October 1952, Potti Sriramalu – a Gandhian – began a fast unto death unless the centre agreed to the principle of creating a separate state of Andhra based on the eleven Telugu-speaking districts of Madras province. Nehru remained unmoved and on 15 December 1952 Sriramalu died of starvation. This was, ironically enough, the same day that Nehru presented the preamble of his First Five Year Plan for India's development to parliament, describing it as the 'first attempt to create national awareness of the unity of the country'. News of the Telugu leader's death sparked off riots in all eleven Telugu districts of Madras. On 18 December 1952, the central cabinet decided that the state of Andhra would be created. In 1953, the states' reorganization committee was set up and in 1956 its report's implementation began in earnest.

The report provided for fourteen states and six union territories. But it rejected the demand for the reorganization of Bombay and Punjab along linguistic lines. The commission refused to accept the demand to divide Bombay province into Marathi and Gujarati-speaking states because Congress's Gujarati supporters dominated Bombay business while the Marathi-speakers were in a majority. The problem snowballed in the late 1950s. In 1960 there were violent language riots in Bombay. The Marathi speakers finally succeeded in forcing the centre's hand and Gujarat was separated from Maharashtra, which included the city of Bombay. In Punjab there was a long-standing demand for a Punjabi-speaking subah. Even the premier Sikh party, the Akali Dal, was really demanding a state on linguistic rather than religious grounds. But it was not until 1966 that the demand for a Punjabi subah was conceded by the government of Indira Gandhi. But as we shall see shortly, the problem of the Punjab was far from resolved.

In the 1950s Nehru responded to a rebellion in Nagaland by deploying the coercive power of the centralized state, even while expressing some anguish for doing so. The most serious secessionist challenge in the early decades came from the southern state of Tamil Nadu. C.N. Annadurai, founder of the Dravida Munnetra Kazhagam, sought to counterbalance the dominance of the Hindi-speaking north by first promoting a Dravidian nationality and culture and then espousing a strident Tamil nationalism. It was in response to the southern challenge that Nehru proposed his three-language formula. According to this formula, Hindi would be the official language of India, English the link language and regional languages of each state would be compulsory in the school curricula. The completion of the linguistic reorganization of state boundaries in the 1950s and 1960s proved insufficient in alleviating centre–state tensions, which resurfaced during the 1980s with unprecedented intensity as well as simultaneity.

The roots of the problem in Kashmir can also be traced to the early years of Nehru's prime ministership. A princely state with a Hindu ruler and a Muslim-majority populace at the moment of the British transfer of power in 1947, Kashmir has been the most divisive issue in the subcontinent. India and Pakistan have been to war over it in 1948 and 1965 and Kashmir remains the main bone of contention between the two neighbours. The recurring denial of genuine democracy as well as substantive federal autonomy promised soon after independence contributed to acute Kashmiri disenchantment with their status in the Indian union. Threatened by a tribal incursion from Pakistan's North West Frontier Province, Maharaja Hari Singh had signed an Instrument of Accession to India in October 1947. When the first Indo-Pakistan war ended with a United Nations cease-fire resolution in January 1949, some two-thirds of the former princely state was under Indian control and the remaining one-third under Pakistani control. Between 1947 and 1953 the administration of Jammu and Kashmir was in the hands of the popular premier, Sheikh Abdullah, who was the leader of the National Conference. The Delhi Agreement reached between Nehru and Abdullah in 1952 broke down with the latter's arrest in 1953. The terms of autonomy agreed in Delhi had been incorporated into Article 370 of the Indian constitution. During the next two decades these terms were steadily whittled down as Jammu and Kashmir was brought more firmly under the centre's writ and administered by ruling groups willing to do New Delhi's bidding.

Using the carrot-and-stick approach in dealings with his own party leaders, Nehru showed considerable ingenuity and skill in leading the Congress to victory in three successive general elections. Even though each election underscored the limitations of the party's bases of support, Nehru neglected to initiate the kind of reforms that might have offset the processes of organizational disintegration within Congress. Relying on his personal stature in the main, he projected a brand of socialism and commitment to social justice that could appeal to the populace, while taking care to cultivate the support of state officials as well as the fat cats of Indian capitalism. It is noteworthy that India's early development plans borrowed more from the work of the colonial state's development and planning department set up in 1944 than that of the national planning committee of 1938–40. From the mid-1950s onwards India pursued a strategy of capital-goods-led import-substituting industrialization. While it was able to build a heavy industrial base that the planners had envisioned, little progress was made in combating poverty, illiteracy and disease. Indian development planners became engrossed in the task of improving instrumental variables, such as the savings rate, quite forgetting the idioms and intrinsic values that had initially inspired the project of national development. In Amartya Sen's view the Indian obsession with 'means enhancement' and neglect of 'means use' explains to a large extent India's failure to remove chronic malnutrition and hunger and to provide entitlements to basic health and education.

Nehru's death in 1964 plunged the Congress into state party bossism and an oligarchical form of politics. The new prime minister, Lal Bahadur Shastri (1964–66), died prematurely, trying to live down the legacy of his illustrious predecessor. But the problems attending the Congress after Nehru's departure from the Indian political scene were not of Shastri's making. Without the necessary organizational reforms, its limited social support base was turning into a liability, not the asset it had been in the 1937 and 1945–46 elections. To make matters worse still, there were serious divisions in the party organization at the lower levels, which helped fuel a slow but steady downward leakage of power and initiative. Under increasing pressure from members of the Congress state bosses, known as the syndicate, Shastri sought refuge among the notables of the higher civil services. This at least promised to delay if not forestall the attempt by an unrepresentative coterie of regional bosses to turn the Congress party into a vehicle of self-promotion and, in the process, weaken the centre's capacity to secure the interests of its main beneficiaries both within and outside the state structure.

Rule by the Congress state bosses came to an abrupt end with their failure to deliver the vote banks in the 1967 general elections. While scraping through at the centre, the Congress was ousted from power in several states. The challenge of regionalism was now plainly coming from political forces outside the pale of Congress. A simple partnership with the civil bureaucracy was no longer sufficient to maintain Congress hegemony or central authority. Upon being chosen to lead the Congress following Shastri's death in 1966, Indira Gandhi (prime minister, 1966–77, 1980–84) consulted with a kitchen cabinet consisting of skilled bureaucrats. On the electoral front, she decided to up the ante for the Congress by pronouncing in 1969 a populist socio-economic programme. Intermediate castes and classes, especially big farmers and middle to richer peasants, had been providing the principal power base of the opposition to the Congress at the state level in most regions. But there were more radical challenges in the states of West Bengal and Kerala, where left-wing coalitions came to power. The late 1960s also witnessed the Maoist Naxalite movement involving poor peasants and militant students in West Bengal as well as parts of Andhra Pradesh and Bihar. Faced with a variety of challenges, Indira Gandhi set about trying to link the top and bottom layers of agrarian society through renewed efforts to woo the high-caste, old landed elites and advocating the interests of subordinate castes and classes cutting across local and regional arenas. Her populist anti-poverty programme was designed to get the Congress substantial electoral support from scheduled castes and tribes, who also happened to form the bulk of the rural poor. This split the Congress in 1969 but did not rupture its old associations with the civil bureaucracy and sizeable fractions of the industrial capitalist class. Indira Gandhi's socio-economic programme, captured by the ringing slogan '*garibi hatao*' (eliminate poverty) and tactical alliances with populist leaders in the states, proved a resounding success in the general elections of March 1971 and also in the 1972 state assembly elections.

The fifth nationwide reference to the people in India's electoral democracy roughly coincided with the first general election in Pakistan during December 1970 and the military crackdown in March 1971, leading to the secession of its eastern wing by December 1971. This end result of an unhappy union between its two wings shattered the myth about Islam being the sole basis of Pakistan. In the intervening years since independence, the leaders of the new state had concentrated their attention on constructing a new central government apparatus capable of asserting authority over disparate regions through a brazen manipulation of the political process. At the height of Cold War era in the late 1940s and 1950s, when the state structure was still in the process of formation, a combination of domestic, regional and international factors worked to undermine the role of parties and politicians and enhance that of the civil bureaucracy and the military. Pakistan's failure to evolve a democratic political system has been blamed on the organizational weaknesses of the Muslim League. Jinnah's death so soon after its creation has also been a much favoured explanation. But the death of an individual leader, however great, cannot be a sufficient explanation for why Pakistan slipped off the democratic course. A close scrutiny of the historical evidence in any case suggests that, in the immediate aftermath of partition, neither the elected nor the non-elected institutions had a decisive edge. Quite as much as the Muslim League, the civil bureaucracy and the military were a shadow of their counterparts in India. Not only did they lack the necessary pool of skilled manpower, they also suffered from grave infrastructural inadequacies. It was the imperative of building a new centre together with the outbreak of war with India over the north Indian princely state of Kashmir within months of Pakistan's emergence that created the conditions for the dominance of the bureaucracy and the army.

With the division of the military assets of undivided India still incomplete, the Pakistan army was in no position to embark upon a war to liberate Jammu and Kashmir. In setting their sights on wresting this predominantly Muslim princely state from Indian control, the central leadership inadvertently assisted in skewing the relationship between the elected and non-elected institutions of the state. In dire financial straits, the Pakistan central government had to dig more deeply into provincial resources to pay for a defence procurement effort whose costs equalled that of undivided India. The ensuing tussle between the centre and the provinces augured poorly for the political process. With revenue extraction as the primary objective, those at the centre devoted most of their energies to administrative consolidation and expansion rather than building a party-based political system capable of reflecting Pakistan's linguistic and cultural diversities.

As politicians were marginalized or edged out of decision-making, civil servants trained in the colonial tradition of bureaucratic authoritarianism took charge of administering the affairs of the state. The tilting in the balance of power from the political to the administrative arms of the state bent relations between the centre and the provinces out of shape and also provided a pretext for incessant bickering between Punjabis and the non-Punjabis. Greater centralization of the administrative machinery aimed at generating resources for the defence effort entailed poaching on provincial rights. Manned by a team of civil bureaucrats, Punjabis and Urdu-speakers from northern India in the main, the personalized touch given to administrative interventions often worked to the disadvantage of provincial politicians. When they could not be bought or threatened into submission, politicians working in the provincial electoral arenas presented problems for the administration. The decolonization process in Pakistan resulted in one of the more improbable combinations of personalized elements of rule with impersonalized ones. A product of the adjustments between the post-colonial centre and the regions, it has in defining the balance between the political and the administrative arms of the state shaped the course of Pakistan's overt military as well as covert democratic authoritarianism, which has been generally more noxious than the Indian brew.

It was in October 1958 that the Pakistani military high command moved in conjunction with the president and the higher echelons of the civil bureaucracy to directly take over the levers of power. The *coup d'état* had been preceded by a phase of military-bureaucratic dominance that can be traced to as early as 1951, when the first prime minister, Liaquat Ali Khan, was assassinated. A refugee politician from a Muslim minority province of India, Liaquat's exercise of executive authority came to be resented by the predominantly Punjabi federal bureaucracy and army. Moreover, since Bengalis in the eastern wing had an overall majority in the country, any system of representative democracy promised to give them a far greater share of state power than the non-elected institutions and their allies in the political arenas of West Pakistan were ready to countenance. It was only by delaying the drafting of the constitution for nine long years and postponing general elections that the civil-military axis, in conjunction with segments of dominant social classes in the western wing, managed to forestall Bengali dominance. Primarily concerned with raising an effective shield of defence against India, something a resource-crippled state was in no position to guarantee, civil and military officials preferred to bolster their international connections. In doing so they hoped to streamline the administrative machinery and pursue development strategies aimed at creating a political economy of defence rather than one geared to the expansion of social opportunities.

But the very fact of a military takeover suggests that the internal structures of the state were still too fluid and uncertain to ensure the dominance of the civil bureaucracy and the army. The aversion of state functionaries to electoral exercises in the initial decade of Pakistan's independence was linked to the fears of a coalition of political forces led by Bengalis drastically modifying the agendas of the state. This internal battle for supremacy combined with the regional threat from India and pressures from the international capitalist system during the Cold War era to undermine political processes in Pakistan. It was only by curbing and distorting the political process that the early managers of the state were able to exert central authority in a manner consistent with their preferred notions of Pakistan's national interest. So it is necessary to challenge the assumption that the failure of the 'parliamentary system' in Pakistan was the result of the 'power vacuum' created by wayward and venal politicians in command of parties with no effective bases of popular support. By distinguishing between the phases of dominance and actual intervention by the military, it is possible to see why the fragility of political parties in and of itself cannot account for the army high command's decision in 1958 to directly wield state power.

Tinkering with the political process was easier than twisting it to fit the purposes of a state structure where civil and military officials, not politicians, called the shots. As long as Pakistan maintained the façade of a parliamentary system of government, nothing could prevent any number of political configurations from pressing concerns diametrically opposed to those of the non-elected institutions. Only by dismantling a political system that was never really given a chance to function in the first place could the military and the civil bureaucracy assert themselves decisively. Taking advantage of tensions with India and their carefully nurtured nexus with the centres of the international capitalist system in London – and after 1954 in Washington – senior military leaders and bureaucrats opted to consolidate state authority by dispensing with the political process altogether. This might avoid some of the difficulties of electoral mobilization surfacing in India, while outright authoritarianism could release the state from the constraints which acted as an impediment to rapid economic growth – essential if Pakistan was to find the means to sustain a respectable level of security arrangements. The decision to depoliticize Pakistani society was a momentous one. The institutional shift from elected to non-elected institutions in the first decade, which the military intervention of 1958 sought to confirm, endured all manner of experiments: controlled politics, 'populism', outright authoritarianism and even the party-based system of parliamentary democracy in recent decades.

Pakistan remained under a military-cum-bureaucratic dispensation until its disintegration in 1971. During this period state consolidation proceeded apace with a heavy accent on externally driven development planning. Drawing support from a mainly Punjabi army and civil bureaucracy, the military regime of General Mohammed Ayub Khan pursued a strategy of controlled politics aimed at extending differential patronage to carefully vetted segments of society. This form of selective as opposed to mass mobilization was intended to secure the Ayub's regime from threats posed by politicians and parties with provincial bases of support. Ironically enough, the very groups who were virtually disenfranchised from the late 1950s helped engineer Ayub's downfall, while his successor, General Yahya Khan, reaped the whirlwind of regional dissent in eastern Pakistan that the strategy of partial mobilization had been designed to forestall. The Pakistani centre's attempts to assert its unqualified dominance over the provinces had backfired badly. Bengalis in the eastern wing had resented the imposition of Urdu as the official language since the early 1950s. Ayub's 1962 constitution conceded official status for the Bengali language. But even belated concessions in the domain of cultural autonomy could not offset the damage which the dialectic of state construction and political processes had inflicted on relations between the Pakistan centre and the provinces. So it is important to be clear how the decade of Ayub Khan's rule exacerbated an already very estranged relationship between the regions and a newly sovereign centre. Developments that came to a head in the 1960s underlined the limitations of state consolidation under the supervision of the military and the bureaucracy in societies subjected to systematic depoliticization.

Ayub's basic democracies order of 1959 was a transparent attempt at stretching the scope of bureaucratic control into the political arena. Taking its cues from the colonial rulers, Ayub's regime made sure to marginalize the voluble and active groups in urban society – industrial labour and the intelligentsia in particular. He sought to strengthen the state's grip over society by giving the civil bureaucracy a bigger hand in dishing out political and economic patronage. By calling the rural localities directly into the service of the centralizing state, Ayub hoped to exercise his presidential authority without any interference from parties and politicians with provincial bases of support. Dependent on aid and advice from Washington, Ayub and his advisors quickly imbibed the logic of functional inequality and adopted measures to promote growth, not redistribution. Widening regional and class disparities gave fresh impetus to demands for provincial autonomy, especially in east Pakistan, and also in the non-Punjabi provinces in the west, where the consolidation of all four provinces as one unit had given a fillip to Punjabi supremacy over the state apparatus.

The entrenched institutional dominance by a mainly Punjabi army and federal bureaucracy on repeated occasions frustrated attempts to restore democratic processes in Pakistan. After the urban popular upsurge in 1968–69 against an Ayub regime trumpeting its achievements as the 'golden decade' of development, the commander in chief, General Yahya Khan, was in a conciliatory mood. He agreed to hold the first ever national election on the basis of universal adult franchise. But there was no question of letting the future representatives of the people put to the torch interests which the bureaucratic and military nexus had come to acquire through long years of dominating the state structure. As the president and commander in chief, Yahya retained the power to veto any constitutional draft emerging from the national assembly that might prove unacceptable to the higher echelons of the state. The power to veto a

Figure 32 Jai Bangla. Sheikh Mujibur Rahman addressing a rally in Dhaka, March 1971 (Courtesy of the archives of the Ananda Bazaar Patrika, Calcutta)

constitution adopted by a sovereign parliament gave the military high command authority to override parties and politicians. A decade of authoritarianism had made sure that, unlike the late 1940s and early 1950s when state formation was in its incipient phase, the sharing of power between the two wings was not a matter the main political parties could settle on their own. The assertion by the military and the bureaucracy of their corporate interests was by far the bigger obstacle to a negotiated settlement between Mujibur Rahman's Awami League and Zulfikar Ali Bhutto's Pakistan People's Party than the fragmented nature of their social bases of support.

The Bengalis formed just over 50 per cent of the population of undivided Pakistan, but were poorly represented in the two main non-elected institutions of the state – the military and the civil bureaucracy. Since these institutions rose to dominance within the state structure and democratic political processes were aborted in the 1950s, it is possible to see why regional dissidence in Pakistan cannot be understood without reference to the nature of the state. There was, of course, a cultural dimension to the alienation of the Bengalis. They deeply resented the early attempt to impose Urdu as the national language and the 1952 language movement had given the Bengali cause its first martyrs. The strategies of economic development pursued by the military regime of Ayub Khan in the 1960s widened regional disparities. The politics of exclusion and the economics of inequality gave impetus to the Awami League's campaign for provincial autonomy. The clash between the imperatives of the military-bureaucratic state and Bengali politics proved irreconcilable.

In the 1970 elections the Awami League derived mileage from the growing economic disparity between the two wings and the inadequate representation of Bengalis in the two main non-elected institutions of the state. Denied their rightful share of power, Bengalis fared badly when it came to developmental allocations and other forms of state patronage. A more equitable apportioning of power and resources required the acquiescence of the military and the civil bureaucracy as well as their allies in West Pakistan. But with the Awami League's spectacularly strong electoral support confined wholly to the eastern wing, espousing the amorphous interests of western Pakistan was one way the ruling configuration at the centre could stonewall a negotiated settlement that might have prevented the tragic dismemberment of the country. By ordering a brutal military crackdown in March 1971, the central leadership in Pakistan exposed their colonial colours amidst hollow sounding appeals to Islam and national integrity. A common religious bond, abused and distorted to serve the interests of authoritarian rulers, snapped all too easily as the Mukti Bahini (Liberation Army) fought a war of resistance and the army of the Indian state crossed the lines of 1947 to liberate one Muslim majority region from its tormentors in another.

19

POST-COLONIAL SOUTH ASIA

State and economy, society and politics, 1971 to 2010

The early 1970s have been described as an era of populism in India, Pakistan and Bangladesh. Indira Gandhi's success in restoring the Congress party's sagging electoral fortunes with her brand of populism came to be seen as a threat not only by dominant rural groups but also, paradoxically, by the bearers of central state authority. As Nehru seemed to have realized, extending the Congress's social bases of support and the corresponding broadening and deepening of democracy in India could constrain the exercise of authority by the centralized state. But this was a price Indira Gandhi had to pay to keep the Congress slotted in power at the centre. It was not long before she had to face the consequences. Her alliances with populist leaders in the states had only delivered the votes. They had not succeeded in vanquishing the old rural power structures dominated by the syndicate bosses with whom she had parted company. Although they lost the elections, the erstwhile Congress bosses could rely on their middle to richer peasant supporters – many of whom were strategically located in the state police and civil services – to foil a centrally orchestrated populist challenge. As the experience of the Congress ministries in Bihar and Gujarat showed, it was easier to trump the dominant castes and classes at the hustings than to implement populist initiatives on behalf of newly empowered subordinate castes and classes. Stiff resistance by the deposed ruling configurations at the state level not only thwarted the Congress's populist initiatives but also threw up fresh challenges for the party high command from its own rank and file.

The juxtaposition of formal democracy and covert authoritarianism in the heyday of Indira Gandhi's populism reflected a markedly different relationship between centre and region than the one over which Nehru had presided. Opting for more democracy entailed reorganizing the Congress party to consolidate the gains of the new and broader-based electoral alliances. But this meant strengthening popular regional leaders at the expense of the centre, a reversal of fortunes that was untenable without substantially modifying both the party and the state structure. If the Congress party under Nehru had partially mitigated the unitarian strands inherent in the post-colonial Indian state, the institutionalization of shifts in the balance between the high command and

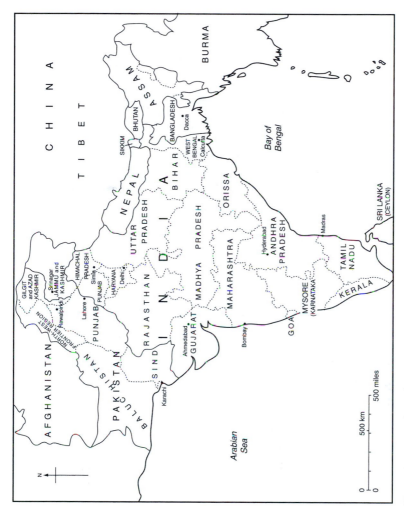

Figure 33 Map of South Asia in 1972

populist state leaders meant conceding more to regional forces than was consistent with the logic of an inclusionary nationalism. So even where her populist venture had registered the best results, for instance in the electorally crucial state of U.P. between 1972 and 1975, Indira Gandhi at the helm of the central executive chose to keep populist leaders at an arm's length. Success at the regional level based on populist mobilization could give Congress politicians like H.N. Bahuguna and Chandreshekar in U.P. and Devraj Urs in Karnataka the means to extract greater concessions for their constituents and, more dangerously, provide them with ammunition to blast their way into power at the

Figure 34 Aristocratic Populists. Indira Gandhi and Zulfiqar Ali Bhutto at Simla, 1972 (Courtesy of the archives of the Ananda Bazaar Patrika, Calcutta)

centre. This was anathema to Indira Gandhi, who reacted by scrapping any semblance of inner party democracy within the Congress. Instead, she preferred to appoint her own loyalists as state and local leaders. Attributed to her insatiable desire for self-aggrandizement in the main, the personalization of power by Indira Gandhi cannot be adequately understood without accounting for the structural contradiction between the exercise of executive power from the centre and the resilience of dominant castes as well as the potential problems which populist power could pose at the level of regional politics and political economies.

Imposing the 'Emergency' of 1975–77 was Indira Gandhi's attempt to ward off both sorts of regional challenges by making the centre the sole repository of supra-local and supra-state populist programmes. Aided by the non-elected institutions of the state, the resort to overt authoritarianism aimed at augmenting central powers against the regions. A workable enough strategy in the short-run, it lacked legitimacy and could not for long withstand concerted opposition from an array of political forces. Even state officials found it difficult to go against the grain of popular opinion, deftly articulated by sections of the press defying censorship, and the burgeoning ranks of Indira Gandhi's political opponents. With members of the civil bureaucracy, the police and the judiciary unwilling to do the bidding of an unpopular government, to say nothing of mounting grievances among the subordinate castes and classes in northern India that had helped fuel Congress's populism since 1969, the brief moment of overt authoritarianism was categorically rejected in the 1977 elections.

The Janata party – a loose conglomeration of regional, left- and right-wing forces united only in their opposition to Indira Gandhi – emerged as the main beneficiary of the polls. Once in power, the Janata, with its regional base confined to the north Indian Hindi heartland, fell prey to its own internal contradictions. Disagreements within its constituent units made certain that the first non-Congress government in India would be tossed to the winds quite as quickly as it had been embraced. After her own electoral defeat in U.P., Indira Gandhi came back into play after winning a bye-election victory in Karnataka, which was then the stronghold of the Congress populist Devraj Urs. But regional patronage was not something a populist seeking power at the apex of the Indian state wanted to encourage. Indira Gandhi's political about-turn – a mere three years after the electorate had rejected her – was based on a careful manipulation of the political scene. Urs was dropped as soon as the subordinate castes, classes and religious minorities in the north began tiring of both the pro-agrarian plank of Janata's predominantly middle to richer caste and class supporters, and the bigotry of traders and merchants in the urban areas who had long been supporters of the Jana Sangh component of the Janata party. With the democratic wheel poised to turn in her favour, Indira Gandhi took to the 1980 elections with alacrity. Not only did she give her opponents a drubbing in key regions, but she was also back in the saddle at the centre, more determined than ever to fight regional dissidence to the bitter end. The problems in Punjab, Assam and, to an extent, also Kashmir were all creations of policies pursued by a Congress-dominated centre. The declining strength of Congress's claim to power at an effectively unitary all-India centre in the 1980s was sought to be offset by substituting populism with implicit, if not explicit, religious majoritarianism.

Pitting 'communalism' against regionalism was a well-tried formula of the colonial state. In 1947 the Congress high command had used it to partition Punjab and Bengal and cut Jinnah and the Muslim League out of any share of power at the all-India centre. In the 1980s the majoritarian card was deployed against regional forces that had emerged to challenge the political centre. The Telegu Desam party, for example, shot to victory in state elections in Andhra Pradesh in 1983. In Punjab the Akali Dal, which until 1966 had been in the vanguard of an agitation for a Punjabi-speaking linguistic state, claimed in the 1970s and the 1980s sovereign national status (though not necessarily a separate state) for the Sikh religious community. The more extreme elements among them acquired sophisticated weapons and launched a violent campaign for the attainment of a separate Sikh homeland – Khalistan. Negotiations between the Indian state and Sikh representatives were fitful; agreements were not implemented and the Punjab became convulsed in waves of terror and counter-terror. A deep psychological alienation was caused by the Indian army's assault on the Golden Temple in June 1984, the assassination of Indira Gandhi by her Sikh bodyguards in October 1984, and the anti-Sikh riots in New Delhi of November 1984.

Riding a sympathy wave following his mother's assassination, Rajiv Gandhi (prime minister, 1985–89) swept the 1984 elections with the help of the Hindu card at a time of widespread regional dissent in the Punjab. Viewing Indian society through the colonial lens that revealed a majority and a minority community based on the religious distinction, the young pilot, who had visions of flying India into the twenty-first century, took a couple of decisions that might have done nineteenth-century viceroys proud. On the one hand, Rajiv Gandhi's government opened the doors of the Ayodhya mosque to Hindu worshippers. On the other, in a curious and ill-advised attempt to placate 'Muslim' opinion after India's judicial system had awarded alimony to Shah Bano, a Muslim widow, he railroaded through parliament a deeply conservative Muslim women's bill. Apart from giving a new meaning to the dialectic of 'communalism' and regionalism, an appeal couched in the idioms of Hindu majoritarianism, only ineffectively balanced by recognition of a particular construct of Muslim 'minority' interest, appeared to give a new lease to the continued exercise of central authority by the Congress. Sabre-rattling against neighbours was another convenient distraction. The 1980s saw one more instance of Indian intervention in a neighbouring country's federal dilemma at a time when New Delhi itself was grappling uncertainly with its multifarious domestic discontents. The opportunity for India's regional projection of its formidable military machine came as the clamour for sovereign nationhood gathered momentum among the Tamil minority of Sri Lanka. Sri Lanka's post-colonial state structure was heavily centralized and the centre came to be dominated by the Sinhalese majority. The problem became particularly acute when Tamils were targeted during riots in the capital city of Colombo in 1983. The Tamils who formed a majority in the northern province of Jaffna, took up arms under the leadership of the Liberation Tigers of Tamil Eelam (LTTE), who demanded a sovereign Tamil state in the northern and the eastern parts of the island. The Indian government initially aided and abetted the Tamil rebels. But the military contingent it sent, ostensibly to enforce an agreement between the Sri Lankan government and the rebels to keep the peace, quickly got embroiled in a war with Tamil guerrillas who refused to be pliable clients.

Meanwhile, the Rajiv Gandhi-led Congress lost one state election after another in the late 1980s, got embroiled in corruption scandals, and missed historic opportunities for negotiated settlements of the problems in the Punjab, Assam and other north-eastern states. The seeds of the post-1989 uprising in Kashmir were also sown in this period. The release of Sheikh Abdullah from prison in 1975 and an agreement with Indira Gandhi had opened the way for two reasonably fair elections in the state, won by the National Conference led by Sheikh Abdullah in 1977 and his son Farooq Abdullah in 1983. The removal of Farooq Abdullah's elected government in 1984, his political deal with Rajiv Gandhi's Congress in order to return to power in 1986, and the royally rigged elections of 1987 led Kashmiris to embark upon a full-fledged campaign aimed at severance of the Indian connection. In 1989 and the early 1990s the popularly backed armed insurgency was orchestrated by the Jammu and Kashmir Liberation Front, which called for a secular and sovereign Kashmir. Kashmiri cultural and linguistic identity appeared to be more potent than Islamic aspirations or pro-Pakistan sentiment in the Vale of Kashmir. In time, however, the balance of firepower among the rebels shifted to the Hizbul Mujahideen, which received more support from Pakistan. The Indian state deployed over 550,000 armed personnel in the early 1990s to severely repress the Kashmiri movement.

By the time the national elections of 1989 came along, it was not the Congress but the Bharatiya Janata Party (BJP) which was poised to do best on the issue of a Hindu *Rashtra* (state), while the newly formed Janata Dal stole the populist thunder. With support from both the BJP and the communists, the Dal was able to form a minority government at the centre under the leadership of V.P. Singh (prime minister, 1989–90). The 1989 electoral verdict pushed the Nehru–Gandhi dynasty to the sidelines for a decade and represented the most decisive success of certain groups influential at the regional level in exercising state power directly from the centre. As in 1977, this was a victory for those dominant in north India's regionally based political economies, but now reaching out to the lower castes and subordinate classes. Outside the Hindi belt the Congress party routed the regional parties, whose electoral gains and agitations had plagued the centre during the 1980s in the southern states. On the face of it, the new configuration of political forces at the centre seemed to have a better chance of reordering priorities, if not the direction, of India's political economy of development. But any economic reorientation privileging the agrarian sector and the big farmers and the middle to richer peasants within it had to contend with the non-elective institutions of the Indian state, the bureaucracy in particular, and the counterweight of powerful industrial capitalist interests. Indeed the Janata Dal had little option but to abandon the fire and fury of its agrarianism and settle down to working within the established parameters of the compromise between formal democracy and covert authoritarianism.

The rise of a Hindu majoritarian politics since the 1980s in India occurred squarely in the context of the many powerful regional challenges to central authority. As ideologies of secularism and socialism lost credibility, the Congress regimes at the centre turned to an implicit, if not explicit, religiously based majoritarianism to parry regional threats. By so doing, they paved the way for the more ideologically committed and organizationally cohesive forces of *Hindutva* – the Bharatiya Janata Party, the Rashtriya Swayamsevak Sangh (RSS) and the Vishwa Hindu Parishad (VHP) – to emerge as major forces on the Indian political scene. Deployed initially *vis-à-vis* a Sikh other in the early 1980s, Hindu majoritarianism increasingly took on anti-Muslim overtones. The symbolic issue that came to the fore was the temple–mosque controversy in Ayodhya, a small town in north India.

Ayodhya was the site of a sixteenth-century mosque named after Babur, the first Mughal emperor. Some extremist Hindu groups, notably the Vishwa Hindu Parishad, began demanding that the Babri masjid be pulled down and a *mandir* to Ram built in its place. The demand was based on the claim that Ram, the mythical hero of the great Hindu epic *Ramayana*, was born exactly on the spot where the mosque stands. On the eve of the 1989 elections the BJP took part in the transportation of 'holy bricks' to Ayodhya and a foundation-laying ceremony for a temple to Ram near the mosque. The Congress government, afraid of losing some Hindu votes, did not stop the ceremony from taking place. Less than a year after the elections, V.P. Singh's decision to implement the recommendations of the Mandal commission to reserve jobs at the centre for backward castes seemed designed to divide the Hindu community by caste and thereby undermine the BJP's electoral project of mobilizing support by playing the Hindu majoritarian card. Its leader, L.K. Advani, responded to the challenge by undertaking a *rath yatra* (a chariot journey). Critics called it a riot *yatra*. After traversing large parts of northern India, Advani threatened to arrive in Ayodhya and start building the temple. The BJP had not only taken on its political rivals but had challenged one of the main ideological foundations of the Indian state. The BJP's attempt to storm the mosque was foiled on that occasion. But two years later, with a BJP government in office in U.P., a large crowd of Hindu 'volunteers' tore down the mosque in the presence of the leaders of the BJP, the RSS and the VHP on 6 December 1992, setting off some of the worst attacks on the Muslim minority in many parts of India.

Although the incident severely damaged the secular façade of the Indian state, it would be a mistake to view religious communalism of the BJP variety as the binary opposite of secular nationalism. Votaries of the centralized post-colonial nation-state have made uses of both ideologies. The promise of Hindutva to shore up central state authority, however, is illusory. Despite the long strides made by the forces of Hindutva in the late 1990s, the heterogeneity of Indian and 'Hindu' society continued to be a formidable obstacle in the way of any easy triumph of religiously based majoritarianism. A renegotiation of the powers of the centre with its varied constituent units would seem to be the most sensible way forward towards the resolution of South Asia's centre–region conflicts. The equation between religion and nation in an intransigent majoritarian vein might only hasten a process of regional fragmentation.

In the domain of political economy the return of the Congress party to power with a working majority in 1991 provided an opportunity for the new government led by P.V. Narasimha Rao (prime minister, 1991–96) to dismantle some of the pillars of what had come to be called the permits, licences and subsidy raj. The initial impetus for the economic reforms came as a result of an acute balance-of-payments crisis in mid-1991, making it necessary to seek an IMF loan and accept certain terms of a stabilization and structural adjustment programme. However, the Indian state was to an extent able to make a virtue out of necessity by removing the many barriers to the entry of firms in the industrial sector. The elaborate system of licensing the use of industrial capacity was virtually abolished and many of the bureaucratic logjams in the path of economic development removed. The economic reforms pursued by the Congress government from June 1991 to May 1996 addressed, however, only the first part of a two-pronged problem facing Indian economic development. The reformers concentrated on redressing the negative effects of over-intervention by the state in certain sectors and removing the more stifling bureaucratic controls on industry. They moved tardily, if at all, to rectify state negligence of critical social sectors, notably, health and education. Neither the economic, free-marketeers' attack nor the cultural, fragmentalist onslaught on development has been sensitive to the potential role state and public action can play in these areas. Amartya Sen and Jean Dreze have made a powerful case for taking the Indian development debate 'well beyond liberalization' to focus on 'expanding social opportunities'. The political costs of pursuing a lop-sided reform process, which contributed to the defeat of the Congress in the 1996 elections, enabled the long-forgotten intrinsic values of development to re-enter the discourse. But the failed institutions of state could not easily be imaginatively refashioned. On the one hand, the privileged but besieged defenders of the centralized monolith resorted to the dangerous course of a bigoted religious majoritarianism propagated by the Bharatiya Janata Party and its followers. On the other, the populism of the 1996 United Front government in New Delhi led by H.D. Deve Gowda (prime minister, 1996–97) and I.K. Gujral (prime minister, 1997–98), of which several regional and left-wing parties were members, displayed deep taints of localism and agrarianism with a rich farmer bias, while proclaiming solidarity with the poor and disadvantaged majority. The successful realization of the idioms of equitable development requires the appropriate instruments, both economic and political, which are yet to be carefully crafted.

While the 'Hindu nationalist' BJP had been regarded as politically untouchable by regional parties until the mid-1990s, the further decline of the Congress party in the general elections of 1998 and 1999 created the conditions for the formation of BJP-led coalition governments at the centre. Atal Behari Vajpayee, the 'moderate' face of the Bharatiya Janata Party, was accepted as prime minister, once the BJP agreed to place the Ayodhya issue as well as its demands for a uniform civil code and the scrapping of Article 370 for Jammu and Kashmir on the back-burner. Regional parties campaigned on local issues and sought more autonomy for the states and a legitimate share of power at a more federal and less unitary centre. Vajpayee became prime minister by deciding not to play King Canute to the rising tide of regional forces. During his campaigns he went to the extent of saying that in a country as diverse as India it would be patently undemocratic to have a single-party government. Even if the BJP won a majority on its own, he added, he would form a coalition. A safe and clever promise, since the BJP did not stand any chance of winning such a majority either in 1998 or 1999.

Sonia Gandhi led the Congress party to its most dismal electoral performance in 1999. In a context where power had seeped down to the regions, her party failed to forge the right regional alliances and made preposterous claims about the Congress's ability to provide India a single-party government. In the 1999 elections the BJP won 182 and the Congress 112 out of the 537 seats up for grabs in the Lok Sabha (House of the People). More than 250 were bagged by a variety of regional parties. On the side of the ruling coalition were parties like the Telegu Desam of Andhra Pradesh led by the pro-economic reform chief minister Chandrababu Naidu; the Dravida Munnetra Kazhagam of Tamil Nadu; the Samata Party of Bihar led by the old socialist George Fernandes, who became defence minister; the regional populist Trinamool Congress of West Bengal and many others. In the opposition benches, too, there were regional parties with lower caste bases of support like the Samajwadi Party and the Bahujan Samaj Party – the latter choosing in 2002 to ally with the BJP in the state of Uttar Pradesh.

If anything, the general elections of 1999 dented the all-India, national pretensions of the Congress and BJP alike. The BJP's bid for power at the centre was facilitated by a pragmatic abandonment of its unitary ideology. But a string of defeats in state elections led the party to fall back on its hard

Hindutva line. The decisive turning point came in Gujarat in 2002, when a murderous attack on a train compartment bringing back Hindu activists from Ayodhya provided the occasion for a state-abetted pogrom against the state's Muslim minority. An election victory in Gujarat close on the heels of the killing of more than 2000 Muslims made certain that the BJP in power failed to learn to accept the reality of its own situation – that it is, all said and done, a large regional party of northern and western India and not especially well equipped to address the myriad class and caste contradictions even within these regions.

During the five years of a BJP-led government in India following 1998, relations with Pakistan were on a rollercoaster. In May 1998 India took the momentous decision to carry out five nuclear tests in the Pokhran desert of Rajasthan, to which Pakistan responded with six blasts in the Chagai hills of Baluchistan. The tit-for-tat nuclear tests in 1998 made the Kashmir conflict an even greater danger for the subcontinent. Prime Minister Atal Behari Vajpayee tried to follow up an irresponsible act with the rhetoric of responsibility and restraint. But the gift of nuclear parity emboldened the Pakistani army high command to engage in military brinkmanship in the Kargil sector, undermining Vajpayee's Lahore diplomatic initiative of February 1999 before the prime minister's bus had started rolling towards the border. The spectre of the Kargil war of the summer of 1999 haunted Indian policy towards Pakistan for a while, resulting in an uncertain policy of diplomatic non-engagement between nuclearized neighbours. Yet, the release of leaders of the Hurriyat conference from prison in the spring 2000, the openness to the short-lived Hizbul Mujahideen ceasefire in summer 2000 and the prime minister's declaration of the Ramzan truce in winter 2000 indicated that the National Democratic Alliance (NDA) government in India was capable of a little more pragmatism and goodwill than its predecessors in an attempt to grasp the Kashmir nettle. These efforts were capped by Prime Minister Vajpayee's invitation to President Pervez Musharraf for talks and the ensuing Agra Summit in mid-July 2001. After hopes having been raised by unprecedented media hype, Kashmir once more proved to be the stumbling-block in the way of putting relations between India and Pakistan on an even keel. A terrorist attack on the Indian parliament in December 2001 contributed to a further downslide in India–Pakistan relations, resulting in political attention and economic resources being directed towards military-strategic objectives rather than social opportunities. The election of a new government led by the People's Democratic Party in Jammu and Kashmir in 2002 inaugurated a 'healing touch' policy in that state. In April 2003 Vajpayee once more took tentative steps towards peace with Pakistan.

Before anything concrete could emerge from this new peace initiative, the National Democratic Alliance led by Vajpayee was defeated by the United Progressive Alliance fashioned by the Congress party in the elections of 2004. The anti-Muslim pogrom may have paid electoral dividends in Gujarat, but it sank the BJP in India as a whole. In addition to revulsion against the Hindu right-wing's misdeeds in Gujarat, the self-congratulatory election plank on the economic front encapsulated by the slogan 'India Shining' also backfired badly. The NDA government had indeed presided over a period of dynamic economic growth and some building of infrastructure. The majority of the populace had not, however, felt the benefits of the glowing macro-economic indicators. The Congress president Sonia Gandhi ran an energetic campaign against the BJP's sins of omission and commission. Upon achieving victory, she gracefully declined to accept the prime ministership and instead anointed Manmohan Singh, who had successfully served as finance minister between 1991 and 1996, as the head of the government.

Reliant on the support of a large contingent of leftist members of parliament, mostly from the Communist Party of India (Marxist), the UPA government was more attentive to challenges of economic justice and social inclusion even while sustaining high rates of economic growth. One example of this was the passage of legislation guaranteeing rural employment for the poor for a minimum of a hundred days in the year. The Congress concordat with the communists began to unravel, however, over the forging of closer ties with the United States of America. This warming of relations had begun in the period of the previous government with the visit of President Bill Clinton to New Delhi in 2000 and was given a further impetus by the successor regimes in both countries. An Indo-US civilian nuclear deal was broached in 2005 and eventually signed and sealed in 2008, leading the communists to angrily withdraw support from the Congress-led government. The Congress not only survived a no-confidence vote in parliament with the help of new backers, but also substantially improved its seat tally in the elections of 2009. A second UPA government led by Manmohan Singh that took office required the support of fewer regional parties.

The comfortable re-election of an incumbent government may give the impression of India's populace being happy with their lot. To be sure, India has been rising at a pace second only to China as Asia recovers in the early twenty-first century the global position it had lost in the late eighteenth. Buoyant economic growth has created a new sense of confidence, and India was able to ride out the global financial crisis of 2008–9 better than most countries of the world. Yet India has a long way to go in assuring access to basic education and health care for the poor, who constitute anything between 30 and 40 per cent of the population. India runs the risk, as Amartya Sen put it, of becoming half-California and half sub-Saharan Africa. Conspicuous consumption by the rich in the major urban centres contrasts sharply with the abject deprivation suffered by tribal peoples in India's rural and forest heartland. A Maoist insurgency grips a very large number of districts in Bihar, Jharkhand, West Bengal, Orissa, Chhattisgarh and Andhra Pradesh. Regional discontent also continues to fester in Kashmir and the north-east.

India's formally democratic spoils system coupled with bureaucratic corruption and inefficiency may have hampered the prospects of equitable economic development and exacerbated disparities between castes, classes and regions. But its effects have been nowhere as devastating as the legacies of military rule in Pakistan – a parallel arms and drugs economy, administrative paralysis and violent social conflict. More than forty years of military authoritarianism in Pakistan have little to show by way of economic development, despite registering on average higher rates of growth than in India prior to the 1990s. An overemphasis on the consumer goods sector, textiles in particular, drew Pakistan more tightly into the net of the international capitalist system than its better endowed neighbour. Heavy dependence on external finances was matched by the concentration of wealth in the hands of those with privileged access to state power. While income disparities widened, the social sectors suffered unconscionable neglect by successive authoritarian regimes. It is true that India's social indicators are not appreciably better than Pakistan's. But this has less to do with the formally democratic or overtly authoritarian character of the regimes that have governed the two countries than with the state–society nexus as a whole. If there is a lesson to be learnt from India's post-colonial experience it is that the paraphernalia of democracy is a necessary but by no means sufficient condition for achieving the goal of development with social justice.

After 1971 both Pakistan and the newly created state of Bangladesh experienced brief phases of parliamentary democracy and populism, followed by lengthy spells of direct or quasi-military rule. In what was left of Pakistan the institutional imbalances within the state structure survived the traumas of dismemberment. With the military and the civil bureaucracy discredited, Pakistan's elected prime minister, Zulfikar Ali Bhutto (1971–77), seemed well poised to start a fresh chapter in its history. But for someone who had served his political apprenticeship in Ayub's government, Bhutto was not about to let the populist appeal of his Pakistan People's Party (PPP) circumscribe his own exercise of state power. His reforms of the military and the civil bureaucracy aimed at enhancing his personal authority, not that of elected institutions such as the parliament, which had for long languished on the margins of the Pakistani political system. Bhutto had promised redistributive reforms for the underprivileged by professing a left-leaning ideology. But once in power he preferred to wield state authority to punish recalcitrant segments of dominant social groups and rewarding those prepared to join the PPP. By packing the party executive with the very landed notables that his agrarian reforms were purportedly targeting, Bhutto considerably watered down his populist platform. The scant respect he showed for civil liberties, indeed for any kind of dissent, earned him the eternal animosity of influential sections of society.

On the issue of provincial rights versus the centre, Bhutto was found badly wanting. In ordering a military crackdown to quell a tribal uprising in

Baluchistan, he gave the army high command an opportunity to claw back the influence it had momentarily appeared to lose in the wake of military defeat at the hands of the country's premier enemy. Not only were the provincial autonomy provisions of the 1973 constitution ignored, but also no headway was made in redefining centre–province relations to better accommodate the social changes in the various regions. Preferring to press the non-elected institutions into his service, and confident of his personal appeal with the floating vote, Bhutto desisted from placing the PPP's organizational machinery on a more effective footing. In 1977 he called elections in the face of mounting resentments against his arbitrary rule. Bhutto's PPP won the elections. But the extent of the sweep gave some credence to the nine-party opposition coalition's charges that the elections had been rigged. Without an effective PPP organization at his disposal, Bhutto was fair game for the military-bureaucratic combine acting in collusion with a cross-section of industrial and commercial groups to oust him from power.

On 5 July 1977 a polarized and fragmented polity sat back and watched Bhutto's hand-picked chief of army staff, General Zia-ul-Haq (military ruler, 1977–88), assuming control of the state apparatus. It soon became clear that the regime had the tacit support of fractions of dominant social classes, landed as well as industrial, who thoroughly disliked Bhutto and his style of governance. Assured of support from the army and a substantial proportion of the bureaucracy, federal as well as provincial, Zia was only too eager to expand his support among these anti-Bhutto elements. While promising elections within ninety days, a promise that was consistently broken over a period of nine years, the general concentrated on winning quick legitimacy by lashing out against the moral turpitude and corruption of Bhutto's government. Appropriating the platform of religious parties like the Jamaat-i-Islami and the Jamiat-ul-Ulema-i-Pakistan, the new military ruler vowed to establish an Islamic social order where virtue and piety would reign supreme. Women became the focal point of Zia-ul-Haq's Islamization programme. In 1979 he passed a series of purportedly Islamic ordinances wildly discriminatory towards women. These blurred the distinction between adultery and rape and called for the evidence of two women to be deemed equivalent to that of one man. Women's groups, notably the Women Action Forum (WAF) showed great courage in opposing these inequitable laws. As Saeeda Gazdar wrote in her poem 'Twelfth of February 1983':

Matami jhandian phar phara rahi thein
Kaneezain baghi ho ghi thein
Do saaw auratain
Charoon tharf say ghiri hui thein
Musala police kai nargai main thein
Anso gas, rifle aur bandooqain
Wireless vainavar jeepain

Haar rastai ki nakabandi thi
Kui panha na thi
Ye larai kudhi larni thi ...
Tum do khatay ho
Hum do crore auratain
Ise zulam aur jabar ke khilaf
Guwahi dein ghien
Jo qanun-e-shahadat ke naam par
Tum ney hamarai saroon pai mara hai
Hum nahin tum
Wajab al-qatal ho
Kay roshni aur sachai kae dushman
Muhabat kay qatal ho.
(The flags of mourning were flapping
the hand-maidens had rebelled
Those two hundred women who came out on the streets
were surrounded on all sides
besieged by armed police.
Tear gas, rifles and guns
wireless vans and jeeps
every path was blockaded
there was no protection
they had to fight themselves ...
You ask for two
We two crores of women
shall testify
against this tyranny and cruelty
hurled at our heads
in the name of the law of evidence
Not us, but you
deserve to be murdered
for being the enemies of light and truth
for being the murderers of love.)

The eloquent defiance of women failed to deter a military ruler anxious to make women – those symbols of Muslim social consciousness – the focal point of a state-sponsored Islamization.

However, it was not the regime's religious credentials but the Soviet invasion of Afghanistan in December 1979 that enabled Zia to use an external threat to Pakistan's survival to consolidate his hold on power. The first step in this direction was to strengthen support within the defence services by drawing them more closely into the day-to-day running of the state and political economy. Unlike Ayub, who relied more on the civil bureaucracy, Zia's only recourse to liberality was in grafting favoured military officials into key

197

positions within the civilian administration as well as in semi-government and autonomous organizations. This was a way of giving the regime's loyalists privileged access to a variety of lucrative business enterprises, an entry point for the more venal into the upper strata of the economy. Together with an emergent *nouveau riche* belonging to the trading classes, the beneficiaries of Zia's patronage in the military have since played a key role in Pakistani politics, certainly in the urban areas.

The disbursement of rewards and privileges by the Zia regime created an even bigger stake for the military in the existing structures of the state and political economy. But this carefully nurtured constituency was still too limited in extent to resolve the regime's dilemma of legitimacy and corresponding search for sufficient social bases of support. Co-opting segments of the dominant socio-economic strata, landlords and nascent commercial and industrial groups, through differential patronage and selective mobilization offered a way out. Using the Islamic notion of the *shoora* or advisory council, Zia readily applied the colonial state's method of conflating representation with selection. It was only after many broken promises that the general agreed to hold non-party-based elections in 1985 to the national and provincial assemblies. By then the regime had garnered enough of a support base through its control over the channels of patronage to feel confident enough to face the electorate. But if there was any doubt in anyone's mind of the military high command's game plan, the passage of the Eighth Amendment by Zia's parliament in exchange for the lifting of martial law should have laid it to rest.

The Eighth Amendment helped to make 1985 a watershed year in the politics of post-1971 Pakistan. A deterrent to martial rule, it was incorporated in the constitution to allow for the continuance of Zia's authoritarian rule with all the democratic paraphernalia. Article 58(b) of this amendment empowered the president to dismiss an elected prime minister and parliament without any obligation to consult with the senate or the Supreme Court. Given the nature of the Pakistani state, the exercise of presidential powers conferred by the clause was inconceivable without the approval of the military high command. With the military as the ultimate overseer, presidents elected by both houses of parliament had no scruples about dismissing national assemblies. After 1985 the Eighth Amendment was used five times until 1996 to oust prime ministers and dissolve elected national and provincial assemblies. Elections were held within the ninety days prescribed in the constitution. However, the significance of repeated references to the people was rendered meaningless when the president acting in league with the military high command could arbitrarily dismiss elected parliaments and prime ministers. The judiciary turned down all except one of the petitions challenging the presidential order. Against a backdrop of rampant corruption, widespread violence and administrative decay, the presidential office served as a convenient decoy for a military command ever ready to exert its will, but loath, until 1999, to assume responsibility for a bankrupt economy and a strife-ridden society.

When Zia vanished into fire and ash in August 1988, the fiscal crisis of the state was visible to all. Not only were revenues failing to keep pace with mounting expenditure but also the trends for the future promised to send the entire country into a tailspin. Zia left other legacies as well. During his military rule Sind had become the main venue of provincial dissidence. Most inadequately represented in the non-elected institutions of the state, Sindhis began to take a powerful stand against Punjabi domination. Rural Sind was transformed during the 1980s into a cauldron of discontent. In urban Sind, where Sindhi speakers were heavily outnumbered by Urdu-speaking *muhajirs* (refugees) and other linguistic groups, the Muhajir Qaumi Mahaz (MQM) made a meteoric entry into Pakistan's political landscape. During the latter half of the 1980s the urban centres of Sind, particularly Karachi and Hyderabad, became battle zones for ferocious conflicts between well-armed rival linguistic communities. Unbridled violence in the informal arenas of politics and the manipulation of *biraderi* or patrilineal kinship ties in the formal arenas of electoral representation were to be key features of the post-Zia era of Pakistani politics.

The removal of the biggest obstacle in their way permitted the judiciary to give a ruling in favour of party-based elections. Held in November 1988, they brought success to Benazir Bhutto (prime minister, 1988–90, 1993–96), who, ever since her father's controversial execution by Zia-ul Haq in 1979, had led the PPP in the movement for the restoration of democracy. With only a third of the popular vote cast, the PPP's emergence as the largest single party in parliament was less than categorical. The beneficiaries of the Zia era, represented by the Pakistan Muslim League led by Nawaz Sharif (prime minister, 1990–93, 1997–99) and packaged by the intelligence services into a coalition of parties called the Islamic Democratic Alliance, made a good showing in Punjab. With Nawaz Sharif as chief minister of Punjab, Benazir's federal government found its options to be far more limited than its promises to the electorate demanded.

The fiscal bankruptcy of the state in any case made it extremely difficult for Benazir, with her support base in Sind, to risk being anything other than a loyal opposition to the pre-existing state structure. Any attempt to enforce changes was likely to meet stringent opposition from a mainly Punjabi military and civil bureaucracy. A state structure geared to high defence expenditure and dominated by the non-elected institutions – namely the military and the civil bureaucracy – cannot easily concede the ascendancy of the elected institutions – parliament in particular. Despite the holding of general elections in 1988, 1990, 1993 and 1997, recurrent dismissals of prime ministers and dissolutions of national assemblies demonstrated the resilence of institutional imbalances within Pakistan's state structure. The army high command's decision to rest content with dominance rather than direct intervention until 1999 was based on a careful calculation of the pros and cons of playing umpire in a highly polarized and violently pulverized political arena.

199

So long as the Eighth Amendment remained in place, constitutional *coups* could be plotted behind the scenes by the intelligence agencies. This was no longer possible once Nawaz Sharif scrapped the Eighth Amendment after winning a thumping two-thirds majority in the February 1997 elections. But Sharif intruded on the military's turf when he sacked the chief of army staff on 12 October 1999. The deposed army chief, General Pervez Musharraf, immediately overthrew the government, dissolving parliament and suspending the constitution. A transitional government headed by the general, including a cabinet and a National Security Council, was established. A pledge was made to hold free and fair elections in October 2002. In June 2001, Musharraf elevated himself to the presidency and, like earlier military autocrats, reiterated his commitment to restore 'genuine' democracy in Pakistan. While initiating reforms aimed at administrative and political decentralization, the general had no intention of relinquishing power.

Musharraf's decision to support the American war on terror after the 11 September 2001 attacks initially appeared to strengthen his domestic position. Despite ferocious opposition from the religious lobby, he promised to curb Islamic militancy and restore Pakistan's image as a moderate member of the international comity of nations. In a controversial referendum in April 2002 Musharraf declared himself elected president for another five years. Elections were held in October 2002, but not before a Legal Framework Order gave Musharraf powers to overrule parliament and change the constitution to create a permanent role for the military in Pakistan's political structure. While state engineering handed victory to the pro-government party, the general's stranglehold on power was met by stolid opposition from the two mainstream political parties led by Benazir Bhutto and Nawaz Sharif and, for different reasons, also from a six-party religious alliance virulently opposed to Musharraf's pro-American policies.

A pragmatic alliance with the USA did not mean abandoning the army's doctrine of 'strategic depth' against India by wresting control over Afghanistan. The crackdown on religious militancy was highly selective. Only sectarian groups threatening the regime's efforts to revitalize the national economy were targeted. Militants serving as proxies for state-sponsored wars in Afghanistan and Kashmir were allowed to function under different nomenclatures. Washington poured billions of dollars in military aid as reward for Musharraf's help in nabbing Arab members of Al-Qaeda. Taking advantage of American distractions with the Iraq war after 2003, the Pakistani Inter-Services Intelligence (ISI) stepped up support for the Afghan Taliban in anticipation of an eventual US pull-out from Afghanistan. This Janus-faced policy jeopardized Pakistan's internal security and undermined Hamid Karzai's precariously placed government in Kabul.

Posturing as the final bastion of liberalism in a nuclearized country threatened by religious extremism, Musharraf doubled up as president and army chief. Denouncing the religious parties as fanatics on the wrong side of history, he swore never to allow Benazir Bhutto and Nawaz Sharif to return to power in Pakistan. A suave senior Citibank executive, Shaukat Aziz, was imported as prime minister to keep relations with international financial institutions on an even keel. As the king's party, the Pakistan Muslim League (PML-Q for Quaid-i-Azam) was entrusted with the task of preventing the opposition from capitalizing on growing popular distress over spiralling prices and widening economic disparities. Musharraf opened up the electronic media as part of his policy of 'enlightened moderation'. It was a double-edged sword. There was a national outcry orchestrated by the media against the killing of the Baluch leader, Akbar Khan Bugti, on Musharraf's orders in August 2006. But the general was more unnerved by the media's wide coverage of the opposition's campaign to force him to give up his military uniform or step down as president. Signs of increasing judicial activism were another source of worry. With an eye on his re-election in November, Musharraf on 9 March 2007 made the colossal error of suspending the chief justice of the Supreme Court, Iftikhar Muhammad Chaudhry. Bar associations across the country rallied behind Justice Chaudhry, insisting he was still the chief justice. As the lawyers' movement gathered momentum with support from the media and opposition parties, urban educated middle classes joined the protests. For the first time in Pakistan's history, the third non-elective institution of the state and the fourth estate were siding with popular political forces.

Adding to the general's woes was the increasing assertiveness of religious extremists at a seminary attached to the Lal Masjid (Red Mosque) in the heart of the nation's capital. The mosque-seminary complex had for decades served as a transit point for ISI-supported militants heading to Afghanistan and Kashmir. After dithering for several months in the face of serious provocation from clerics and students at Lal Masjid that led to questions about his commitment to fighting extremism, Musharraf ordered a full-scale military crackdown. The operation left over a hundred dead, snapping ties between a virulent section of religious militants and their one-time handlers in the state apparatus. Pakistan was rocked by a spate of suicide attacks on military personnel and installations that were claimed by a new organization called the Tehrik-i-Taliban Pakistan (TTP), based in the autonomous north-western tribal areas with known ties to Al-Qaeda.

With the lawyers' movement showing no signs of flagging, Musharraf in a last-ditch attempt declared an emergency on 3 November 2007, clamped down on the press and arrested protesting lawyers and students. It was a losing battle. In October Benazir Bhutto had returned home after eight years, in defiance of Musharraf's advice that for security reasons she ought to come after general elections scheduled for January 2008. Her rapturous welcome procession snaked through Karachi's crowd-filled streets for hours before being hit by twin bomb blasts, killing over 136 people and wounding several hundreds. Benazir survived the trauma but was not so fortunate on 27 December, when she was assassinated after giving a fiery speech against terrorism and dictatorship at a public rally in Rawalpindi's historic Liaquat Bagh. The government blamed her death on the TTP leader, Baitullah Masud, a charge vehemently denied by him and the PPP but, significantly, backed by Washington. Pakistan exploded in an agony of grief as enraged crowds went on a rampage in rural Sind, burning and looting government property. In elections held in February 2008, the PPP emerged as the largest single party but, falling short of an absolute majority, formed a coalition at the centre. Musharraf resigned a few months later and was replaced as president by the late prime minister's tainted husband, Asif Ali Zardari. It was a bitter recompense for the tragic loss of a flawed but charismatic and, for her diehard supporters, endearing populist politician just when a terror-stricken, divided and economically languishing Pakistan most needed the credibility and unifying appeal of Benazir Bhutto's leadership.

After its successful breakaway from Pakistan in 1971, populism in Bangladesh had an even briefer span than in Pakistan. In January 1972 Sheikh Mujibur Rahman (prime minister and president, 1972–75) was released from a prison in Pakistan. Upon returning to Bangladesh he became prime minister in the first Awami League government in the newly independent state of Bangladesh. His populist economic measures included land reforms and the nationalization of the handful of industries in the country. But the ravages of war and the splits in the armed forces reflected by the heroes of the liberation war and repatriates from Pakistan defeated Mujib and the Awami League. Unable to restore a war-torn economy, the government was jolted in 1974 by the woes of hunger from a countryside gripped by famine. Like his counterparts in India and Pakistan, Mujib too began tinkering with authoritarian methods. In early 1975 he announced the setting up of a one-party socialist state. This lost him the support of many of his former backers among the middle classes and the intelligentsia. In August 1975 Mujib and his family were assassinated in a military *coup* believed by many to be linked with the American CIA.

The brutal murder of the country's founding father initiated a brief spell of overt authoritarianism. It was not long before the need for legitimacy became compelling for the new military ruler, General Ziaur Rahman (1975–82). Proof that military regimes do have a patterned response to the twin challenges of administering a civilian population and enjoying legitimacy, Rahman engaged in a form of socio-political engineering reminiscent of Ayub Khan and foreshadowing the tactics of Zia-ul Haq in Pakistan. Elections were first held at the local level, followed by the launching of a state-sponsored political party called the Bangladesh National Party. This created the conditions for Ziaur Rahman's election as president and the inauguration of a subservient parliament. Tensions within the military once again reared their head. In 1982 Ziaur Rahman was assassinated. The advent of another military dictator, General Ershad (1982–90), gave added impetus to the politics of localization and the economics of privatization. Tarred with the brush of corruption, Ershad was unable to withstand pressure from a powerful pro-democracy movement. Since the early 1990s Bangladesh had witnessed a series of general elections, leading to the formation of governments by the Awami League under Mujib's daughter, Sheikh Hasina Wajid and the Bangladesh National Party led by Zia's widow, Khaleda. In December 2008 Sheikh Hasina Wajid led the Awami League and its 'grand alliance' to a sweeping electoral victory. While the daughter of the founding father of Bangladesh returned to the office of prime minister, she assembled a new cabinet with many fresh faces that held promise for the future.

The recent history of Pakistan and, to a lesser extent, of Bangladesh demonstrates just how puerile it would be to presume that military authoritarianism can be brought to an end by the mere holding of elections. During the Cold War era an interplay of domestic, regional and international factors confirmed military dominance in Pakistan. In the late 1970s these same factors reinforced the asymmetry between elected and non-elected institutions in Pakistan and gave rise to similar imbalances within the Bangladeshi state structure. The military-bureaucratic state in both countries extended its patronage to win over significant segments of the dominant socio-economic elite and to localize political horizons in much the same fashion as the colonial state. Elections have been held in both countries in recent years, but the casting of ballots cannot be confused with the full restoration of democracy. Democratic forces in these countries have to overcome a formidable wall of

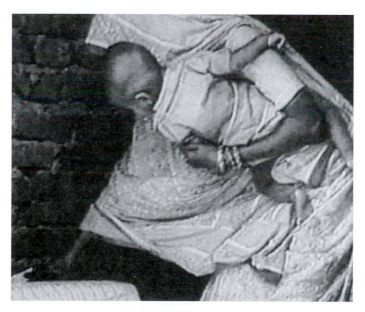

Figure 35 A Secret Ballot. A woman votes in the Indian general elections of 1991 in Madhubani, Bihar (Courtesy of Sugata Bose from his film *Mandir, Masjid, Mandal and Marx: Democracy in India*)

structural obstacles before they can aspire to the boons of even the formal democracy in India.

Despite the differences in the nature of their states and regimes, not to mention the great disparity in size, India, Pakistan and Bangladesh continue to face a common set of social and economic problems. In all three countries one-third of the population continues to be illiterate, even though there have been improvements on this front in Bangladesh and some Indian states since the 1990s. India has an elaborate infrastructure for higher education, but has invested little in primary education. Even though the average life expectancy doubled from a mere 32 years in 1947 to over 64 years six decades later, it remained significantly lower in all three countries than in neighbouring countries like Sri Lanka, Burma and China. The ratio of women to men in the population is dismally low in all three countries – some 93 women to 100 men – evidence of acute discrimination along lines of gender. India shows great regional variation in all of these social indicators – the state of Kerala being a shining exception – suggesting perhaps that social opportunities can be expanded and capabilities enhanced, given the necessary political will. Southern Indian states have done extremely well in the field of information technology. Each of the countries has witnessed increasingly powerful social and cultural movements seeking to rectify the deep-seated imbalances along lines of region, community, class and gender. Yet so long as managers of post-colonial states remain trapped in the colonial mould, valuable resources get frittered away in high defence expenditure occasioned by inter-state hostilities, the potential benefits of a common South Asian market remain unrealized and the promise of social and economic freedom that was supposed to follow on the heels of political independence in 1947 remains a mirage for the majority of the subcontinent's poor and obscure.

20

DECOLONIZING SOUTH ASIAN HISTORY

A view from the new millennium

Transfers of power, however momentous or revolutionary, tend to have an air of anti-climax about them. 'Like the complex electrical system in any large mansion when the owner has fled,' Benedict Anderson has written in *Imagined Communities*, 'the state awaits the new owner's hand at the switch to be very much its old brilliant self again.' Where the inheritance is disputed, it might be added, the festival of lights may have a dark side to it. The capture of state power at the triumphal moment of formal decolonization by forces representing singular nationalism generally brought with it problems of its own in socially and culturally heterogeneous ex-colonies, perhaps nowhere more complex than in South Asia. The new owners of the stately mansions built during the colonial era may have at last laid their hands on the switchboards of the electrical mains; but they soon discovered the short circuits in many of the rooms of the mansion that could easily blow most of the worn fuses. In the absence of effective circuit breakers, whole mansions could easily be plunged into darkness.

To push this metaphor even further, these mansions were not just edifices of brick and mortar, but contained libraries with weighty books. The extent to which anti-colonial nationalist thought was derivative of colonial knowledge is currently a matter of scholarly debate. We have sought to argue in this book that there were many contested visions of nationhood and alternative models of decolonized states in South Asian anti-colonial discourse. These have gained heightened relevance in the new millennium. The historical specificities of the post-colonial political transition generally witnessed the smothering of diversity and the inheritance of colonial structures of state and ideologies of sovereignty by mainstream nationalist elites. But there was a promised difference. Colonial subjects, so long denied and divided along lines of religion, language, tribe or ethnicity, were to be treated to the full-blown rights of equal citizens.

The new occupants of the stately mansions and secretariat buildings busily set about their plans to modernize and streamline 'traditional' and stubbornly intricate societies, deliver a measure of redistributive justice to the inhabitants of huts and shacks, and, in the process, iron out the problem of minorities within political systems which upheld the rule of healthy, democratically elected majorities. Where that failed, modernizing, 'neutral,' post-colonial militaries could always take matters into their iron hand. Meanwhile, the older legacy of the red sandstone and marble palaces of the pre-colonial empires and their regional successor states lay in the desolate isolation of irrelevance, their libraries looted of their treasures and now enriching Orientalist collections of Western museums of learning. In any case, how could the politics and states of those branded 'oriental despots' hold any edifying lessons for post-colonial 'democrats'?

It is now emerging from scholarly research that pre-colonial empires, far from being centralized, bureaucratic autocracies, were flexible, nuanced and overarching suzerainties. Although obviously bereft of modern democratic ideals, these empires and their regional successor states had well-developed political concepts of both individual and communitarian rights as well as political theories of good governance. The emperor merely laid claim to the highest manifestation of sovereignty, leaving the balance to be negotiated with regional sultans and local rajas, merchant institutions, as well as cities and villages. The amount of power actually vested in the different levels of sovereignty was subject to historical shifts, with downward flows and seepages in periods of decentralization and fragmentation. What was non-existent, even in the heyday of pre-colonial empires, was any notion of absolute sovereignty and its concomitant demand of singular allegiance.

The idea of unitary, indivisible sovereignty was a foreign import into Asia and Africa from post-enlightenment Europe. But there was an embargo on the export of rights of citizens of sovereign states to Europe's colonies. This distortion in the international trade in ideas of sovereignty and citizenship had large implications for the quest to achieve freedom and democracy without riding roughshod over legitimate communitarian rights. The colonial state in India claimed to occupy 'neutral' ground above indigenous society which, in its view, could do no better than squabble over the sectional interests of its component parts. Through rigid classificatory schemes employed in colonial censuses and maps, the state made it harder to maintain the peaceful coexistence of multiple social identities, even though colonial constructs never wholly succeeded in shrinking the mental horizons of colonized peoples. Once colonial modernity had redefined 'traditional' social affiliations, the way was open for the construction of divisive political categories that might deflect unified challenges of anti-colonial nationalists. These were not just the larger oppositions such as the one between Hindu and Muslim in India. Colonial powers often preferred to recruit minorities, such as Sikhs in India, in disproportionate numbers into key state institutions such as the military. The problem of assuring minority rights among the subject population became a convenient excuse for the perpetuation of minority, colonial rule.

Late colonialism in India also took to constitutional manoeuvres aimed at directing political attention towards local and provincial arenas to keep central state authority insulated from nationalist challenge. Anti-colonial nationalists, thus, became increasingly suspicious of schemes that threatened 'balkanization' at the moment of decolonization. Minorities came to be seen as only pawns in the end game of colonial empire. A grievous flaw was embedded in this perception. Aspirations for unity among different linguistic and religious communities in anti-colonial politics now came to be replaced by assertions of a singular, 'secular' or 'composite' nationalism. The more far-sighted anti-colonial activists and thinkers had always recognized the imperative of assuring rights of religious, linguistic and other communities and conceding autonomy to diverse regions. 'Particularist' identities, however much they may have been re-invented in the mould of colonial modernity, could not just be wished away but needed to be accommodated within any enlightened view of anti-colonial nationalism. Muhammad Iqbal gave voice to his sense of a distinctive identity when he asserted: 'The light of foreign wisdom does not dazzle me; the collyrium lining my eyelids is the dust of Mecca and Najaf.' Couching his anti-colonialism in an autonomy derived from faith, Iqbal maintained that: 'In slavery, neither swords nor ideas are of any use; but when belief takes its hold, chains are cut loose.'

From another part of the subcontinent, Rabindranath Tagore had tried putting the issue into perspective: 'Where there is genuine difference, it is only by expressing and restraining that difference in its proper place that it is possible to fashion unity. Unity cannot be achieved by issuing legal fiats that everybody is one.' By contrast, Jawaharlal Nehru wrote in 1938 that he looked through a telescope to locate a Hindu–Muslim problem in India and could not spot it. As late as the 1920s, it had been common to forge a common anti-colonial nationalist position through negotiation among diverse religious and linguistic communities. Those who set their sights on the acquisition of power at the helm of a unitary nation-state displayed increasing impatience with articulations of cultural difference and diversity.

In socially heterogeneous colonies there was always the potential for the emergence of multiple contenders for nationhood. As the discourse of main-stream Indian nationalism turned more strident in its insistence on singularity, a sense of unease led some dissenting minorities to couch their own demands in the language of nationalism. Among the proponents of the Indian Muslims' claim to nationhood in the early 1940s there was little enthusiasm for a partitionist solution. Minority claims to nationhood should not necessarily be equated with calls for secession, which may be an option of the last resort when all attempts at negotiating power-sharing arrangements fail. The quest to be recognized as a 'nation' was never the same as its territorial expression in the form of a completely separate 'state'.

Post-colonial South Asian history and historiography showed an inability until very recently to discard colonial definitions of majority and minority based on a system of enumeration privileging the religious distinction, despite being overtaken by events. In military-ruled Pakistan, the denial of democracy led east Pakistan's Bengali majority to claim to be a distinct nation. It is arguable that, as in the 1940s, here too, the initial aim was an equitable share of power, failing which the die was cast in favour of a separate, sovereign state of Bangladesh in 1971. The successful secession of Bangladesh was for quite some time an exceptional occurrence in the history of the post-World War II interstate system. The legitimacy of any given political unit or juridical state has increasingly become a key issue in interlinked campaigns for democratic rights both in its individual and communitarian aspects and for national sovereignty. A social group denied a voice in decision-making within a particular democratic polity may either criticize the quality of such a democracy and seek reforms or question the founding credentials of the state and seek autonomy or secession.

The failure of post-colonial states to assure equal citizenship rights and to deliver on the promise of redistributive justice has brought these entities into some disrepute. As the general concept of the modern, centralized nation-state has been drawn deeper into a crisis of legitimacy, a raging battle has begun between state-sponsored and anti-state nationalisms. As secularism and socialism have increasingly sounded like hollow slogans since the 1980s, centralized states under siege have resorted to majoritarian ideologies, religiously or ethnically defined, in attempts to prevent their own structures from being undermined. The systematic denial of substantive rights of democracy and autonomy by existing states, as the experience of east Pakistan showed, can contribute to the birth of new nations. The rise of Hindu majoritarian 'nationalism' in India was tied to the defence of centralized state authority against a variety of regional as well as caste and class-based challenges even though it did not succeed in dislodging the formal secular ideology of the Indian state.

The clash between majoritarian principles and substantive democracy continues to take an increasingly bloody toll as part of the conflict between incipient nations and juridical states. Instead of the unbending insistence on the singular loyalty of the citizen to the state, the time is overdue to rethink the relevance of multiple and shifting social identities for the cause of democracy. Such identities by their very nature defy capture within unambiguous, permanent or even durable constructs of majority and minority. If the function of democracy is to unsettle permanent or entrenched majorities and democratic processes are meant to ensure that majority support is earned, then the multiplicity of social identities rooted in South Asia's history can only be a boon and not a threat to democratic values and practice. These identities can only flourish within a political and state system based on layered and shared sovereignties. Sovereignty need not be the monolith from the peak of which one flaunts authority and under the weight of which 'the other' is crushed. A realization seems to be dawning in South Asia that borders may be rendered irrelevant, even if it is difficult to redraw them. Identities spilling across the nation-state's frontiers make that change in perspective an urgent necessity. Disenchanted social groups who have, of late, conceived of themselves as 'nations' are unlikely to give up this expression of their new consciousness. But they may yet be invited to form a part of multinational states of union forged from below through negotiation of terms of sovereignty among constituent peoples and nations. That in turn may heal inter-state relations still reeling from the tragedy of partition and improve the prospects of a better South Asia based on mutual understanding and cooperation in the new millennium.

The history of pre-colonial India is replete with instances of rajas, maharajas and maharajadhirajas, shahs and shah-en-shahs reigning in relative peace, having shared out sovereignty along different layers of the subcontinental polity. An emperor was no more than a sovereign at the centre of many sovereigns. It was only when disputes took the form of exclusive possession of territory that there was catastrophic war. The devastating battle of Kurukshetra described in the great epic *Mahabharata* might have been avoided if the Kauravas had agreed to cede five villages to the five Pandava brothers; instead they clung with obduracy to the slogan 'not an inch of soil'.

The then Indian foreign minister, Jaswant Singh, explained that 'conceptual differences' between India and Pakistan had undermined attempts to reach even a joint statement or declaration at the Agra summit of 2001. President Musharraf had insisted that Kashmir must be accepted as the 'core issue' in any dialogue between India and Pakistan. The Indian side had retorted that Kashmir was 'the core of Indian nationhood'. What seems to have doomed the Agra talks were irreconcilable territorial claims put forth by India and Pakistan, an empirical contradiction flowing not from any 'conceptual differences' but a remarkable 'conceptual similarity' shared by the leaders of India and Pakistan on the definition of sovereignty.

South Asians learnt the modern concept of unitary, indivisible sovereignty from their British colonial masters. In 1947, by failing to share sovereignty they ended up dividing the land. Yet it would seem that the British themselves have by now lost faith in the concept of monolithic sovereignty. A drastic redefinition of the idea of sovereignty laid the groundwork for the Good Friday agreement on Northern Ireland and also paved the way for Scottish and Welsh autonomy. An ideational change of this magnitude was not easy to achieve. In a 1993 report titled *Northern Ireland: Sharing Authority*, Brendan O'Leary and his co-authors wrote: ' ... some political theorists, in our view wrongly, believe that sovereignty is indivisible and cannot be shared. To avoid tedious argument we have therefore used the word authority rather than sovereignty throughout – but we will not object if we are read as advocating shared sovereignty.' A conceptual shift needed to precede a breakthrough in the political logjam. The renunciation of absolutist claims to sovereignty over Northern Ireland and the yielding of political space to new democratic arenas hold lessons for attempting to deal with other comparable conflicts. For all the difficulties that beset the power-sharing arrangement in Belfast, instead of building new walls of separation, London and Dublin are engaged in creating joint institutions and forging new spheres of cooperation under the rubric of the European Union. The best political theorists of pre-colonial and anti-colonial South Asia would have seen no cause for tedious argument over the concept of layered and shared sovereignty. There really is no reason why India and Pakistan, beset by the ghosts of Mountbatten and Curzon, should cling to a colonial definition of sovereignty on the question of Kashmir and goad their citizenry in the name of territorial nationalism on to the path of mutually assured destruction. An obsession with territoriality is not just an anachronism in today's globalized world, it is completely out of sync with the best traditions of the subcontinent's own history and political thought. If they are true to themselves, Indians and Pakistanis can do better in crafting a safer and more prosperous future for the peoples of the subcontinent. The need is more pressing than ever today when mounting collateral damage from America's war in Afghanistan is casting a menacing shadow on the subcontinental horizon, blurring national frontiers and gravely impairing the exercise of state sovereignty.

This book – a deliberate act of transgression across the arbitrary lines of 1947 – is a small contribution in that direction. Acts of violence by 'infiltrators' across the border tend to grab the media headlines in an era obsessed with 'terrorism'. Yet the devotional strains of immortal *quawaalis* in the voice of Nusrat Fateh Ali Khan continue to waft across state frontiers in South Asia and beyond. Instead of pointing nuclear-tipped missiles at each other, the peoples of the subcontinent may be able to indulge their shared passion for food and film, music and literature as well as the game of cricket, if they have a better understanding of their common history. There is much to learn and much to leave behind.

GLOSSARY

Adi Granth sacred scripture of the Sikhs containing the teachings of Guru Nanak compiled by Guru Arjan in 1603–4; also known as the Guru Granth Sahib

ahimsa non-violence

ajlaf term used for the lower social orders

Anandamath novel by Bankim Chandra

Arthashastra literally 'science of wealth' or political economy; title of book by Kautilya

Aryavarta land of the Aryas

ashraf (sing. *sharif*) respectable class

ashwamedha yagna horse sacrifice

atmashakti self-strengthening

Bahadur literally 'brave'; honorific title

Bande mataram literally 'hail to the mother'; title of song in Bankim Chandra's novel

Bangamata mother Bengal

bania Hindu trader or moneylender

Bhagavad Gita literally the 'Song of the Lord' which forms the sixth book of the *Mahabharata* containing Krishna's teachings to Arjuna

bhaiachara village brotherhood

bhakti devotion

Bharata name of ancient Hindu king

Bharatavarsha land of Bharata or the lord of Bharat

Bharatmata literally 'mother Bharat'; used to refer to India

bhatta pay bonus

charkha spinning wheel

dhamma ethical way of like

dharma appropriate form of moral and religious obligations in Hinduism

Dharmashastra Hindu law books

211

diku foreigner (Santhal term)

diwan treasurer

diwani right to collect land revenue

dubash literally 'a speaker of two languages'

firangi foreigner

ghazi Muslim warrior of the faith

Hindutva Hindu essence or political identity

hool uprising (Santhal term)

Ibadatkhana place of worship

iqta grant of revenue from land

iqtadars holder of land assignment

jagir land grant from the state in lieu of cash salary or reward for services

jati literally 'birth'; designates sub-caste by occupation

jihad striving for perfection; spiritual endeavour; holy war

jizya tax paid by protected non-Muslims to a Muslim government

kala pani literally 'the dark waters'

kamathabritti habit of a tortoise

karma action or deed; theory of future births being based on quality of actions in the present or previous lives

khadi hand spun and woven cloth

kotwal chief police officer in city or town

madrasah Muslim school of learning originally attached to a mosque

Mahabharata great Hindu epic of ancient India

maharaj title for a great king

Mahatma literally 'great soul'; appellation for Mohandas Gandhi

mansab literally 'rank'

mansabdar holder of a rank; a member of the ruling nobility

mansabdari system of Mughal administration

Marwari member of a Hindu commercial caste

masjid mosque

maulana title given to Muslim religious scholar

maulvi title given to Muslim religious leader

maya doctrine on the illusory nature of life

meghamalhar name of raga in north Indian classical music

moksha theory of salvation or escape from the human cycle of rebirths propounded in the *Upanishad*

mufti expert on Islamic law

mullah title given to Muslim religious leader

murid disciple of a pir

nawab title given to a nobleman or a king

Netaji literally 'revered leader'; title given to Subhas Chandra Bose

nirvana Buddhist notion of the state of enlightenment, signifying release from the human cycle of rebirth

niskama karma disinterested action

nizam rule or ruler

Pandit title given to Hindu religious scholar; also title used for Jawaharlal Nehru

pindaris free riding cavalry

pir saint, living or dead; in Sufism, the spiritual leader and teacher

poligars Telugu-speaking warrior clans

purna swaraj complete independence

qanun-e-shahi imperial edicts or law of the sultans

qasbah small town

qazi Muslim judge

Quaid-i-Azam literally great leader; title given to Mohammed Ali Jinnah

raga melody in north Indian classical music

ragini feminine *raga*

rais a gentleman of respectable position

raiyat peasant cultivator

raiyatwari system of tenure in which cultivators directly paid to the government

raj kingdom, rule or sovereignty

Ram Rajya the rule of the Hindu god, Rama; a kingdom with a benevolent ruler

Ramayana Hindu epic

rashtra state

rupee Indian currency

sabha an association

salaam Muslim greeting

sati a virtuous woman; one who immolates herself on the funeral pyre of her husband

satyagraha literally 'the way of truth'; form of political agitation based on moral pressure pioneered by Gandhi

shagird student

Shaivite followers of Hindu god, Shiva

sharia literally 'a clear path'; set of moral injunctions constituting Islamic law

shetia name of commercial group

shoora advisory council

Shramanik conglomeration of popular religious cults in ancient India

shuddhi purification

sipahi soldier

subah province

subedar governor of a province

Sufi Muslim mystic; the word *sufi* comes from the coarse woollen garment, *suf*, worn by the early mystics of Islam

swadeshi of own country

swaraj self rule

tabligh religious preaching

taluqdar landed aristocrat in Awadh

tanzeem organization

ulema (sing. *alim*) scholar of Islamic jurisprudence; a learned man

ulgulan tribal uprising

Upanishad philosophical and mystical sections of the Vedas

ustad teacher

usuli rationalistic school of Shia jurisprudence

Vaishnavite followers of Hindu god, Vishnu

vakil advocate or lawyer

varna literally 'colour'; caste

Vedas literally 'wisdom' or 'knowledge'; ancient Indian religious scriptures

waqf (*pl.awqaf*) property endowed and held in trust for the welfare of the Muslim community in Islamic law

zamindar loosely used term for landholder, large or small

zamindari system of land revenue administration under which zamindar landlords collected rent from peasants and paid revenue to the (colonial) government

A CHRONOLOGICAL OUTLINE

6500–1750 BCE	The Indus Valley Civilization
1500–1000 BCE	Aryan migrations; the composition of the Vedas
600–500 BCE	The advent of Buddhism and Jainism
326 BCE	Alexander the Great's invasion
322–c. 200 BCE	The Maurya empire
268–231 BCE	Reign of Ashoka
200 BCE–200 CE	Regional polities and diffusion of Sanskritic cultures
320–550 CE	The Gupta empire
455–528 CE	Hun invasions
606–47 CE	Reign of Harshavardhana
700–1200 CE	Regional polities in north and south
712 CE	Arab conquest of Sind
736 CE	The city of Delhi founded by the Tomaras
997–1030 CE	Raids of Mahmud of Ghazni
1022–26	Rajendra Chola's northern campaigns and naval victory over Srivijaya
1030	Al-Beruni's visit
1192	Muhammad Ghuri's victory at Tarain
1206–1526	The Delhi sultanate
1296–1316	Reign of Alauddin Khalji
1325–51	Reign of Muhammad bin Tughlaq
1336–c. 1564	The Vijayanagara kingdom
1345–c. 1500	The Bahmani kingdom
1440–1518	Life of Kabir, *bhakti* saint
1469–1539	Life of Guru Nanak, founder of Sikhism
1486–1533	Life of Chaitnaya, *bhakti* saint
1498	Arrival of Vasco da Gama, the Portuguese, at Calicut
1526	First battle of Panipat and foundation of the Mughal empire
1556	Second battle of Panipat
1556–1605	Reign of Akbar
1619	English East India Company obtains permission to trade in India

1627–58	Reign of Shah Jahan
1658–1707	Reign of Aurangzeb
1730s–1740s	Rise of regional states
1739	Nadir Shah's invasion
1757	Battle of Plassey, beginning of British conquest of Bengal
1760–99	Sultanate of Mysore under Haidar Ali and Tipu Sultan
1761	Third battle of Panipat, Ahmad Shah Abdali's victory over the Marathas
1764	Battle of Buxar
1765	East India Company's acquisition of the *diwani* of Bengal
1770	Great Bengal famine
1770–80s	Resurgence of Maratha power under Mahadaji Sindhia
1790–1839	Reign of Ranjit Singh in Punjab
1793	Permanent settlement of the land revenue with *zamindars* of Bengal
1798–1805	Governor-generalship of Wellesley
1799	Fall of Mysore
1803	Capture of Delhi to the English East India Company
1813	Revision of the Charter Act, ending the company's monopoly of trade
1815	Raja Rammohun Roy's move to Calcutta
1818	Defeat of the Marathas
1818	Foundation of Hindu (later Presidency) College of Calcutta
1828–35	Governor-generalship of Bentinck
1829	Abolition of *sati*
1835	Macaulay's Minute of Education
1839–49	Anglo-Sikh wars and the conquest of Punjab, the first Anglo-Afghan war, the conquest of Sind
1846	Treaty of Amritsar, giving Kashmir to the Dogra ruler of Jammu
1848–56	Governor-generalship of Dalhousie
1855–56	The Santhal *hool* (uprising)
1857	The Great Mutiny and revolt
1858	Deposition and deportation of the last Mughal emperor, Bahadur Shah Zafar
1872	The first all-India census
1875	Foundation of Anglo-Muhammadan Oriental College at Aligarh
1877	Proclamation of Queen Victoria as the Empress of India
1878	The second Anglo-Afghan war
1885	Final conquest of Burma
1885	Foundation of the Indian National Congress
1890s	Famines in western India
1899–1905	Viceroyalty of Curzon

1899–1900	The *Ulgulan* (Great Tumult) led by Birsa Munda
1905–8	The Swadeshi movement
1906	Foundation of the All-India Muslim League
1909	The Morley–Minto reforms, granting separate electorates to Muslims
1911	Revocation of the partition of Bengal and the shift of the capital from Calcutta to Delhi
1913	Rabindranath Tagore wins the Nobel Prize for Literature
1915	Gandhi's return to India from South Africa
1916	The Lucknow Pact between the Congress and the Muslim League
1919	The Montagu–Chelmsford reforms
1919–22	Khilafat and non-co-operation movements led by Gandhi and the Ali Brothers
1929	Passage of the *Purna Swaraj* resolution by the Congress
1930–34	The Civil Disobedience Movement led by Gandhi
1930	Muhammad Iqbal's presidential address to the All-India Muslim League
1932	The Communal Award and the Poona Pact between Gandhi and Ambedkar
1935	Government of India Act
1937	Provincial elections under the 1935 Act
1940	Passage of the Lahore Resolution by the All-India Muslim League led by Mohamed Ali Jinnah; Muslims of India claimed to be a 'nation', not a 'minority'
1940	Individual *Satyagraha* campaign
1942	Launch of the Quit India Movement by Mahatma Gandhi
1943	The great Bengal famine
1943	Netaji Subhas Chandra Bose assumes leadership of the Indian National Army in South-East Asia
1946	Cabinet mission plan for a federal India
1947	Independence and partition
1947–64	Jawaharlal Nehru as Prime Minister of India
1947–49	First India–Pakistan war over Kashmir
1950	India becomes a republic
1958	Pakistan's first military *coup*
1958–69	Military rule of Ayub Khan in Pakistan
1962	India–China war
1965	India–Pakistan war
1966–77, 1980–84	Indira Gandhi as prime minister of India
1971	Emergence of an independent Bangladesh
1972–75	Sheikh Mujibur Rahman as leader of Bangladesh
1972–77	Zulfikar Ali Bhutto as leader of Pakistan
1975–77	'Emergency' in India

1977–88	Zia-ul-Haq's military dictatorship in Pakistan
1984	Crisis in Punjab and assassination of Indira Gandhi
1987	Rigged elections in Jammu and Kashmir
1989	Beginning of insurgency in Kashmir
1991	Beginning of India's economic reforms
1992	Demolition of the Babri Masjid in Ayodhya
1998	Formation of the National Democratic Alliance government in India with Atal Behari Vajpayee of the Bharatiya Janata Party as prime minister
1998	Nuclear tests by India and Pakistan
1999	Limited war in the Kargil sector between India and Pakistan
1999	Military takeover by Pervez Musharraf in Pakistan
2001	Failed Agra summit between India and Pakistan
2003	Tentative peace moves between India and Pakistan
2004	Formation of the United Progressive Alliance government in India with Manmohan Singh of the Indian National Congress as prime minister
2007–8	Assassination of Benazir Bhutto, the downfall of Pervez Musharraf and the formation of a Pakistan People's Party (PPP) government in Pakistan
2008	Landslide victory of the Awami League led by Sheikh Hasina Wajed in Bangladesh general elections
2009	Re-election of the United Progressive Alliance government in India with Manmohan Singh of the Indian National Congress as prime minister

SELECT BIBLIOGRAPHY AND NOTES

A general note on historiographical trends

Among the latest concerns exercising the minds of historians in the academy these days is the challenge of writing histories unfettered by the construct of the modern nation-state. Historians of the South Asian subcontinent have been the most prominent knights-errant in the intellectual endeavour to rescue history from the fetters of the nation. In attempting to do so some influential strands of South Asian historiography run the risk of chaining it to an unspecified and under-theorized, but over-deployed, category of the community. This retreat into the communitarian mode of historical writing is matched by de-centring projects and anti-foundationalist critiques which, in the name of avoiding the snare of metanarratives, would have historians in effect take a vow of silence about global structures of domination. Our interpretative work is based on the premise that it is possible to write critical histories of capitalism and colonialism in South Asia and elucidate the nature of anti-colonial resistance in other than the purely fragmentary mode of historical writing.

The earlier moorings of South Asian historiography have been profoundly shaken by the swirling intellectual currents most commonly identified by the post prefix. These post-modern, post-structural, post-orientalist and post-colonial perspectives have together subverted most of the modernist certitudes, structural rigidities, orientalist stereotypes and colonial vanities that had afflicted South Asian history. The philosophy underlying area studies as it evolved in the USA and, to a lesser extent, in Europe conspired to compartmentalize the study of areas, such as South Asia, South-East Asia, East Asia and West Asia (still referred to as the Middle East in the Western academy), often infusing them with spurious, ahistorical 'religious' and 'cultural' essences and denying peoples of these regions their agency in the making of history. The contribution made by post-Orientalist and post-colonial histories by trespassing across disciplinary frontiers in restoring the subjecthood of subaltern and marginal actors has been, therefore, an altogether welcome development. South Asian history had in some ways been more insular than the rest, constraining its ability to invigorate broader historical arguments. Scholarship on other areas had occasionally managed to break free of the deadweight of modernization theory that burdened area studies to make fresh theoretical interventions on problems, such as the moral economy of the peasant in South-East Asia and science and the sociology of knowledge in East Asia. South Asia's day in the western sun came with the discovery of post-coloniality. Soon enough there emerged signs of hubris in the post-marked histories as well as increasing unease, tension and distance in their relationship with other, often older, radical challenges to historiographical orthodoxies. It had been possible for historians until the mid-1980s to write confidently and concernedly about peasants and labourers in colonial Asia as human beings who lived, worked and died in the context of a political economy of capitalist development that was not especially kind to them. That was before we learnt that rural labourers were produced by colonial discourse and that to utter the phrase 'capitalist development' was to hopelessly succumb to its totalizing power.

The last decade has witnessed a significant shift in historiographical fashion from politics towards discourse, economies towards identities, materiality towards culture, class towards community. Accompanying this shift has been a tendency to celebrate the indigenous authenticity of South Asian religions and cultures in sharp opposition to the universalist claims of European reason, science, modernity and development. Not everyone, of course, chose to subscribe to the fashion of the decade. But their contributions have not always been duly acknowledged in the historiographical literature. In the field of South Asian history the subalternist collective led by Ranajit Guha undoubtedly made an immense impact in highlighting the role of subordinated social groups in anti-colonial resistance. Yet both before and after their intervention many individual historians and social scientists wrote thoughtful and original works on Asian peasant and labour history and addressed the issue of subalternity along lines of class, caste, community and gender. Histories of the kind written by C.A. Bayly focusing on intermediate social groups, such as merchants and service gentry, transformed our understanding of the transition to colonialism and the part played by the colonial state in the reinvention of hierarchy and tradition. New insights were gained into the refashioning of social structures and relations by the linking of economic regions within South Asia to wider capitalist systems. Our understanding of decolonization in South Asia was deepened by analyses of the interplay between the national, communal and regional levels and arenas of politics based on an approach that did not divorce the study of communitarian narratives from processes of state formation.

Prior to the appearance of Edward Said's searing critique of 'orientalism' in 1978, the site of culture had been one of the happiest hunting grounds of anthropologists working on South Asian societies. Anxious not to be tarred by the orientalist brush, a good segment of cultural anthropology reinvented itself in the 1980s as a new historical anthropology, with the professed intention of exposing the nexus between culture and power. Yet, misinterpreting

Said's attack on a spurious comparative method which enabled the occident to brand the orient as the realm of the irrational, the unscientific and the inferior, these historical anthropologists and anthropological historians ended up committing two grave fallacies. First, they failed to notice the dissonance and polyvalence within colonial discourse as it developed over time and imbued it with an ahistorical, monolithic quality. Second, they drew a sharp dichotomy based on a championing of otherness that posed the innocence of local culture against the cunning of universal reason. This also led to a privileging of particular kinds of textualized and oral sources of indigenous knowledge and the abandonment towards them of a critical stance that seemed reserved only for the colonial archives, even as the latter continued to be used as the main repository of the former. The works of historical anthropology that emerged from this re-education and re-orientation were more concerned with cultural representation than political practice and paved the way for the reified notion of irreconcilable cultural difference between Europe and Asia.

It was precisely when the post-structural and post-colonial historical scholarship of *Subaltern Studies* came to be championed by the post-modern and post-orientalist historical anthropology of North America that its radical edge seemed to get blunted. The problem did not stem, as is often asserted, from the invasion of history by the forces of literary and cultural criticism. The insights into post-orientalism and post-colonialism provided by Edward Said and Gayatri Spivak, when drawn with sensitivity to historical complexity and context, have invigorated South Asian historiography. What has also emerged, however, in the name of post-coloniality is a sweeping critique of an ill-defined modernity and, flowing from it, a deep scepticism of the nation-state, of development as its legitimizing ideology and of the justificatory values of science and reason. Since post-colonial nation-states in many instances inherited the centralized structure of colonial predecessors along with their unitary concept of sovereignty, intellectually honest historians are right to seek freedom from their shackles. Yet arguments about cultural specificities and different modernities in South Asia come uncomfortably close to being deployed in favour of a form of socially conservative exclusivism which, in denying the encroachment of universalisms, ends up turning specificity into a value meriting uncritical acclaim. More important, the invitation to resist globalization on the part of some post-colonial intellectuals comes after the prospects of the political practice of resistance have been disabled by their deafening silence about economic and political structures that have a global reach and their decision to operate in a purely communitarian or fragmentary mode. Exulting over the fragment not only erases the individual and leaves class and gender inequities within the fragment unscathed, but also presents little threat to the managers of global capital as well as of centralized post-colonial states. Capital and community, far from being antagonistic forces, have been more often than not deeply imbricated in modern history.

Surely it should be possible to maintain a critical, intellectual stance towards the homogenizing and hegemonizing tendencies of the centralized, colonial and post-colonial nation-states without sliding into mindless anti-statism. A sceptical attitude towards reductionist mega-science surely does not require negating the potential of harnessing science in reducing material deprivations. Questioning the arrogance of the votaries of universal reason need not be premised on a false binary between reason and religion. And taking a stand against the culturally insensitive blockbuster projects of development and the empty boasts of development discourse ought not blind us towards historicizing development as a site of contestation with possibilities of appropriations, resistances and reversals. The adoption of these sharp, yet balanced, perspectives would not have been so difficult if post-colonial scholarship had not compromised with post-modernism and refused to acknowledge that global capitalism and local communitarianism were locked not in an adversarial but in a dialectical relationship. Not just development regimes of nation-states, it must be remembered, but the top echelons of the regime of globalized capital, to borrow a phrase from David Ludden, 'hire historians to make themselves look good'. In addressing the problem of resistance the newest cultural and historical anthropology of South Asia has spoken of ethnographic refusal. What is really called for is unambiguous historiographical refusal, a stern refusal on the part of autonomous intellectuals to do the bidding of the economic structures of power that silently envelop them. The very definition of the intellectual as 'someone whose whole being is staked on a critical sense', as Edward Said puts it, is at issue.

Chapter 1

There has been little agreement among historians as to what might constitute the more important themes and organizing principles around which to write a general history of the subcontinent. Some, like Stanley Wolpert in his *A New History of India* (New York: Oxford University Press, 5th edition, 1997), have avoided facing this problem by being mainly anecdotal and dispensing with the need for an argument drawing on any of the new research of the past two decades. An alternative text, Percival Spear's *A History of India* (Harmondsworth: Penguin, 1979) – elegantly written in the 1960s – told the story of the rise and fall of the British raj and was primarily concerned with the activities of British proconsuls and state institutions as well as Indian elites and their nationalist organizations. A more recent and able work along a similar vein, Judith Brown's *Modern India: the Origins of an Asian Democracy* (Oxford: Oxford University Press, 1985, 1994), also stresses colonial and nationalist institutions and elites and tends to invest these with a teleological lunge towards a Westernized form of democracy. Hermann Kulke and Dietmar Rothermund in *A History of India* (London: Routledge, 1986, reprinted 1996) deal much more extensively with the ancient and medieval periods than the modern one. We are pleased that the publication of the first edition of *Modern South Asia* triggered the production of other general histories, including one by Thomas and Barbara Metcalf and another by David Ludden. We try to offer a unique combination of narrative with synthesis and interpretation, drawing on the best and newest research on South Asian history.

South Asian historiography is much more advanced and nuanced than would be suggested by most of the very general texts and dry factual narratives. It is simply that until 1997 there had been no work of synthesis and interpretation covering the entire spectrum of modern South Asian history and taking full account of the striking new developments in the field. The reader has to turn to two multi-volume series to gain some appreciation of the new research. These are *The New Cambridge History of India* series being published by Cambridge University Press and *The Themes in Indian History* series of Oxford University Press, Delhi. The former consist of single-author volumes that are somewhat uneven in quality, ranging from the excellent to the mediocre. The ones that we recommend are noted under the relevant chapters below. The latter consists of anthologies, each with a long, critical introduction by an editor who is an expert on the theme. These volumes are by and large extremely well done and present a good picture of key historiographical developments in the treatment of major themes.

Among *The New Cambridge History* volumes the one with the broadest sweep is C.A. Bayly's *Indian Society and the Making of the British Empire* (Cambridge: Cambridge University Press, 1988). A masterly synthesis and interpretation of recent research, including his own on the role played by Indian social groups in the transition to colonialism, it ends with a consideration of the aftermath of the 1857 revolt. For a synthesis of work on the more recent period we must turn to Sumit Sarkar's highly regarded *Modern India, 1885–1947* (Madras: Macmillan, 1983). Written in the late 1970s and early 1980s, it has been overtaken by a spate of major research monographs. But it represents an effective compilation of research published until the late 1970s and contains useful sections on the pressures exerted by subordinate social groups on elites, British and Indian alike. Yet the main theme treated in Sarkar's book is the history of Indian nationalism, beginning with the foundation of the Indian National Congress in 1885 and culminating with the winning of independence in 1947. Sarkar chose not to breach the 1947 barrier, an unfortunate decision, given the social, economic and political links between the colonial and post-colonial eras. The first comparative study of the post-colonial history of India, Pakistan and Bangladesh is Ayesha Jalal's *Democracy and Authoritarianism in South Asia: A Comparative and Historical Perspective* (Cambridge: Cambridge University Press, 1995).

Among the major themes in new historical research on South Asian history the best introduction to the work of the subalternist collective is Ranajit Guha and Gayatri Spivak (eds), *Selected Subaltern Studies* (New York: Oxford University Press, 1988). The most important study of intermediate social groups during the transition to colonialism is C.A. Bayly, *Rulers, Townsmen and Bazaars: North Indian Society in the Age of British Expansion* (Cambridge: Cambridge University Press, 1983). On the links between regional economies and social structures within South Asia to wider economic and social systems see the essays by a wide array of historians in Sugata Bose (ed.), *South Asia and World Capitalism* (Delhi: Oxford University Press, 1990); also see C.J. Baker, *An Indian Rural Economy: the Tamilnad Countryside* (Oxford: Oxford University Press, 1984); David Ludden, *Peasant History in South India* (Princeton: Princeton University Press, 1985); and Sugata Bose, *Agrarian Bengal: Economy, Social Structure and Politics, 1919–1947* (Cambridge: Cambridge University Press, 1986) and *The New Cambridge History of India: Peasant Labour and Colonial Capital* (Cambridge: Cambridge University Press, 1993). For an example of analyses of the interplay of national, communal and regional politics and their impact on the nature of decolonization see Ayesha Jalal, *The Sole Spokesman: Jinnah, the Muslim League and the Demand for Pakistan* (Cambridge: Cambridge University Press, 1985 and 1994).

Some of the historiographical debates we have alluded to in this chapter mostly unfolded in the pages of scholarly journals. Those wishing to sample one such exchange may wish to read Gyan Prakash's anti-foundationalist critique 'Writing Post-Orientalist Histories of the Third World: Perspectives from Indian Historiography' in *Comparative Studies in Society and History* (32, 2, 1990), 383–408, and Rosalind O'Hanlon and David Washbrook's forceful response 'After Orientalism' in *CSSH* (34, 1, 1992), 141–67. Some of the North American works of historical anthropology and anthropological history on South Asia since the intellectual stir created by Edward Said's *Orientalism* (New York: Vintage Books, 1978) that have tended to celebrate indigenous knowledge in opposition to a rather monolithic and ahistorical view of colonial discourse include Ronald Inden, *Imagining India* (Chicago: University of Chicago Press, 1990); Nicholas Dirks, *The Hollow Crown* (Cambridge: Cambridge University Press, 1987) and 'Colonial Histories and Native Informants: Biography of an Archive' in Carol Breckenridge and Peter Van der Veer (eds), *Orientalism and the Post-Colonial Predicament* (Delhi: Oxford University Press, 1993); and Gyan Prakash, *Bonded Histories: Genealogies of Labour Servitude in Colonial India* (Cambridge: Cambridge University Press, 1990). There are, however, other currents in South Asian anthropology in North America that explore the problem of cultural identity and difference in more global and trans-national frames. See, for instance, Arjun Appadurai, 'Global Ethnoscapes: Notes and Queries for a Transnational Anthropology' in Richard G. Fox (ed.), *Recapturing Anthropology: Working in the Present* (Santa Fe: School of American Research Press, 1991). For Said's own thoughtful position on modernism and post-modernism as well as nationalism see Edward W. Said, *Culture and Imperialism* (New York: Knopf, 1993) and for Spivak's considered positions and incisive comments on post-colonialism and post-coloniality see Gayatri Spivak, *The Post-Colonial Critic: Interviews, Strategies,*

Dialogues (New York: Routledge, 1990). The communitarian and fragmentalist turn in South Asian studies can be seen in Partha Chatterjee, *The Nation and its Fragments* (Princeton: Princeton University Press, 1993) and Gyanendra Pandey, 'In Defence of the Fragment', *Representations* (37, Winter 1992). For a critical assessment of the new trends in Asian historiography in general and South Asian historiography in particular see Sugata Bose, *Unsettled Frontiers of Asian History* (lecture given at the opening ceremony of ASiA, Asian Studies in Amsterdam, University of Amsterdam, October 1996, published in 1997) and 'Post-Colonial Histories of South Asia: Some Reflections', *Journal of Contemporary History*, (38, 1, 2003), 133–46.

Quotations: The following are the sources of quotations used in this chapter:

G.W.F. Hegel, *The Philosophy of History*, trs. J. Sibree, New York: Dover, 1899, 1956, p. 142.

Mohandas Karamchand Gandhi, *Hind Swaraj*, in *The Collected Works of Mahatma Gandhi, Vol. 10*, New Delhi: Publications Division, Government of India, 1958, first pub. 1908, pp. 22–23.

Bipin Chandra Pal, *The Soul of India: A Constructive Study of Indian Thoughts and Ideals*, 4th edition, Calcutta: Yugayatri Prakashak, 1958, pp. 62–63.

Muhammad Iqbal, 'Tarana-i-Hindi', in 'Bang-e-dara', *Qulliyat-i-Iqbal*, Karachi: Al-Muslim Publishers, n.d., p. 70.

Mohammad Ali Jinnah, cited in Ayesha Jalal, *The Sole Spokesman: Jinnah, the Muslim League and the Demand for Pakistan*, Cambridge: Cambridge University Press, 1985, 1994.

Chapter 2

Allchin, B. and R. (1982). *The Rise of Civilization in India and Pakistan*, Cambridge: Cambridge University Press. A study of the Indus valley civilization.

Basham, A.L. (1954–79). *The Wonder that was India: A Survey of the Culture of the Indian Sub-continent Before the Coming of the Muslims*, London: Sidgwick and Jackson. An accessible cultural history with many questionable assumptions about religious boundaries in ancient India.

Chattopadhyay, B.D., ed. (1988). *Essays in Ancient Indian Economic History*, New Delhi: Munshi Ram Manohar Lal Publishers. An important set of essays put together by one of the leading scholars of ancient and early medieval India.

——(1997). *The Making of Early Medieval India*, Delhi: Oxford University Press. One of the best works on early medieval India.

Kangle, R.P., ed. (1960–65). *The Kautilya Arthashastra*, 3 vols, Bombay: Bombay University Press. The most important text or compilation of texts on statecraft in ancient India.

Kosambi, D.D. (reprint, 1990). *An Introduction to the Study of Indian History*, Bombay: Popular Prakashan. A work for the general reader by the most brilliant historian of material life in ancient India writing in the middle decades of the twentieth century.

Lahiri, Nayanjot (2005). *Finding Forgotten Cities: How the Indus Civilization Was Discovered*, New Delhi: Permanent Black. A riveting account of the archaeoligists' adventure in unearthing the subcontinent's earliest urban settlements.

Majumdar, Ramesh Chandra (1970). *The History and Culture of the Indian People: Vol. 3, The Classical Age*, Bombay: Bharatiya Vidya Bhavan. A useful volume of reference on the cultural history of ancient India.

Raychaudhuri, Hema Chandra (reprint, 1997). *Political History of Ancient India*, Delhi: Oxford University Press. A carefully researched political narrative that has yet to be surpassed several decades after its first publication.

Roy, Kumkum (1994). *The Emergence of Monarchy in Northern India, eighth–fourth centuries B.C. as reflected in Brahmanical Tradition*, Delhi: Oxford University Press. The best study of kingship in pre-Maurya India.

Sastri, K.A. Nilakanta (1955, reprint 1976). *A History of South India from Prehistoric Times to the Fall of Vijayanagara*, Madras: Oxford University Press. A magisterial survey which probably over-emphasizes the degree of centralization in early south Indian kingdoms.

Singh, Upinder (2008). *A History of Ancient and Early Medieval India: from the Stone Age to the Twelfth Century*, New Delhi: Pearson Longman. An authoritative, comprehensive and richly illustrated history of the entire sweep of ancient and early mediaeval Indian history.

Thapar, Romila (1961). *Asoka and the Decline of the Mauryas*, London: Oxford University Press. An excellent monograph.

——(1978). *Ancient Indian Social History: Some Interpretations*, New Delhi: Orient Longman. An important set of interpretive essays.

——(1989). 'Imagined Religious Communities? Ancient History and the Modern Search for a Hindu Identity', *Modern Asian Studies*, 23, 2: 209–31. An essay on the formation of religious identities that is especially strong on the Shramanik traditions of ancient India.

——(2003). *Early India* (Harmondsworth: Penguin). A masterly survey of ancient Indian history by the doyen of ancient Indian historians.

Wheeler, R.E. Mortimer. (1953). *The Indus Valley Civilisation*, Cambridge: Cambridge University Press. An introduction to India's earliest known civilization by a scholar closely involved with archaeological investigations in the area.

Quotations: The following are the sources of quotations used in this chapter:

Jawaharlal Nehru, *The Discovery of India*, Delhi: Oxford University Press, 1996, p. 52.

Subhas Chandra Bose, *The Indian Struggle*, eds Sisir K. Bose and Sugata Bose, Netaji Subhas Chandra Bose *Collected Works Vol. 2*, Calcutta: Netaji Research Bureau, 1997, p. 1.

Romila Thapar, 'Imagined Religious Communities? Ancient History and the Modern Search for a Hindu Identity', *Modern Asian Studies*, 23, 2, 209–31. The quotation appears on p. 216.

Chapter 3

Ahmad, Muhammad Basheer (1941). *The Administration of Justice in Medieval India*, Aligarh: Aligarh Historical Research Institute. A well-researched study of an important topic much neglected in recent scholarship.

Aquil, Raziuddin (2009). *In the Name of Allah: Understanding Islam in Indian History*, Delhi: Penguin. A survey of the history of Islam in India from the thirteenth century onwards.

Bayly, Susan (1986). 'Islam in Southern India: "Purist" or "Syncretic"?', in C.A. Bayly and D.H.A. Kolff (eds), *Two Colonial Empires: Comparative Essays on the History of India and Indonesia in the 19th Century*, Leiden: Martinus Nijhoff Publishers. A sophisticated analysis of Islamic practices in the south Indian cultural environment.

Chaudhuri, K.N. (1990). *Asia before Europe: Economy and Civilization of the Indian Ocean from the Rise of Islam to 1750*, Cambridge: Cambridge University Press. A fascinating study of the *longue durée* in Indian Ocean history drawing on the Braudelian structural approach, Foucauldian human cognitive logic and Cantorian set theory.

Eaton, Richard (1993). *The Rise of Islam and the Bengal Frontier, 1204–1760*, Berkeley: University of California Press. An imaginative argument about the nature of religious conversions, marred by poor grounding in agrarian history and lack of understanding of Bengali sources.

Elliot, H.M. and J. Dowson, eds (1867–77). *The History of India as Told by Its Own Historians*, 8 vols, London: Trubner. The histories of India's 'own' historians are substantially retold in these volumes compiled by these nineteenth-century editors.

Habib, Muhammad and K.A. Nizami, eds (1970, 1982). *A Comprehensive History of India Vol. 5: The Delhi Sultanate*, New Delhi: People's Publishing House. A monumental volume with contributions by some of the most erudite historians of the period of the Sultanate.

Habibullah, A.B.M. (1945). *The Foundation of Muslim Rule in India*, Lahore. A carefully researched book that has stood the test of time.

Husain, Wahed (1934). *Administration of Justice in Medieval India*, Calcutta: Calcutta University Press. An important monograph on a topic much in need of attention from more of today's historians.

Khan, Mohammed Ishaq (1994). *Kashmir's Transition to Islam: The Role of Muslim Rishis (Fifteenth to Eighteenth Century)*, Delhi: Manohar. An important critique of the concept of 'syncretism', this book is as much about Kashmir's contribution to Islam as Kashmir's transition to Islam.

Kufi, Ali ibn Hamid (original 13th c., 1983 ed. N.A. Baloch). *Fathnamah-i-Sind: being the original record of the Arab conquest of Sind* known simply as *Chachnama*. Islamabad: Institute of Islamic History, Culture and Civilization, Islamic University. This early work contains many insights into the nature of conquest and state formation in medieval India.

Rizvi, Saiyid Athar Abbas (1986–92). *A History of Sufism in India*, 2 vols, New Delhi: Munshiram Manoharlal. An encyclopaedic work of reference.

Roy, Asim (1983). *The Islamic Syncretic Tradition in Bengal*, Princeton: Princeton University Press. A pioneering study on Islam in a regional, cultural setting with an original hypothesis about the connection between ecology and the process of conversions.

Schimmel, Annemarie (1975). *Mystical Dimensions of Islam*, Carolina: University of North Carolina Press. An exploration of Sufism by one of the leading authorities on the subject.

Singh, Khushwant (1984). *A History of Sikhism*, 2 vols, Princeton: Princeton University Press. A well-written survey.

Stein, Burton (1989), *Vijayanagar*, in *The New Cambridge History of India*, Cambridge: Cambridge University Press. The best single-volume introduction to the history of this southern kingdom.

Wink, Andre (1990) *Al-Hind – The Making of the Indo-Islamic World*, vol. 1, Leiden: E.J. Brill. A good study of the location of India in the expanding world of Islam between the seventh and the eleventh centuries.

Quotations: The following are the sources of quotations used in this chapter:

Al-Beruni, *India*, trs. E.C. Sachau, New York: Norton, 1971.

Richard Eaton, *The Rise of Islam and the Bengal Frontier, 1204–1760*, Berkeley: University of California Press, p. 281.

Sulaiman in Elliot, H.M. and J. Dowson, eds (1867–77), *The History of India as Told by Its Own Historians, Vol. 1*, London: Trubner, 1867–77, p. 7.

Chapter 4

Abul Fazl, *Ain-i-Akbari. – Akbarnama*. A chronicle of Akbar's reign by his famous friend and courtier.

Alam, Muzaffar and Sanjay Subrahmanyam (2000). *The Mughal State, 1526–1750*, Delhi: Oxford University Press. A valuable collection of articles on the Mughal empire.

Ali, M. Athar (1966). *The Mughal Nobility under Aurangzeb*, Aligarh: Asia Publishing House.

Ahmad, Aziz (1964). *Studies in Islamic Culture in the Indian Subcontinent*, Oxford: Clarendon Press. An important book on the cultural history of Indian Islam.

Asher, Catherine (1992). *Architecture of Mughal India*, in *The New Cambridge History of India*, Cambridge: Cambridge University Press. A well-illustrated introduction to the entire scope of architecture built under Mughal auspices.

Beach, Milo Cleveland (1992). *Mughal and Rajput Painting*, in *The New Cambridge History of India* (Cambridge: Cambridge University Press). An illustrated introduction to the interplay between Mughal and Rajput styles of painting.

Blake, Stephen (1993). *Shahjahanabad: The Sovereign City in Mughal India, 1639–1739*. Cambridge: Cambridge University Press. An insightful study of the urban culture of a Mughal capital.

Dasgupta, Ashin and M.N. Pearson, eds (1987), *India and the Indian Ocean, 1500–1800*, Calcutta: Oxford University Press. An excellent collection of essays on the role of India in the wider networks of Indian Ocean trade.

Habib, Irfan (1963). *The Agrarian System of the Mughal Empire (1556–1707)*, Bombay: Asia Publishing House. A classic study on the subject.

——(1982) *An Atlas of the Mughal Empire*, Delhi: Oxford University Press. An indispensable work of reference

——and Tapan Raychaudhuri, eds (1982). *The Cambridge Economic History of India, Vol. 1, c. 1200–c. 1750*, Cambridge: Cambridge University Press. A useful compilation of research on the economic history of pre-colonial India conducted prior to 1980.

Kling, Blair B. and M.N. Pearson, eds (1979). *The Age of Partnership: Europeans in Asia Before Dominion*, Honolulu: University of Hawaii. An important set of essays on European trade in Asia before colonialism.

Moosvi, Shireen (1987). *The Economy of the Mughal Empire, c. 1595: A Statistical Study*, Delhi: Oxford University Press. A thorough, quantitative examination of the structural composition of the Mughal imperial economy.

Mujeeb, M. (1967). *The Indian Muslims*, London: George Allen and Unwin. A magisterial study with a broad, chronological and thematic sweep.

Pearson, M.N. (1987). *The Portuguese in India*, in *The New Cambridge History of India*, Cambridge: Cambridge University Press. The best single-volume introduction to the economic role of the Portuguese in sixteenth-century India.

Prakash, Om (1988). *The Dutch East India Company and the Economy of Bengal, 1630–1720*, Delhi: Oxford University Press. The best monograph on the Dutch role in seventeenth-century India.

Richards, John F. (1996). *The Mughal Empire*, in *The New Cambridge History of India*, Cambridge: Cambridge University Press. An accessible, single-volume narrative of the history of the Mughal empire.

Rudolph, Susanne (1987). 'State Formation in Asia – Prologomenon to a Comparative Study', *The Journal of Asian Studies*, 46, 4. A very useful overview of the revisionist scholarship on the nature of pre-colonial empires, suggesting that they were flexible suzerainties rather than centralized despotisms.

Russell, Ralph and Khurshidul Islam (1968). *Three Mughal Poets*, Cambridge, MA: Harvard University Press. A delightful introduction to the poetry of the Mughal era.

Subrahmanyam, Sanjay, ed. (1994). *Money and Market in India, 1100–1700*, in *Themes in Indian History*, Delhi: Oxford University Press. An anthology of important articles and chapters of books on this theme with a critical introduction by the editor.

——(1990). *The Political Economy of Commerce: Southern India, 1500–1650*, Cambridge: Cambridge University Press. An excellent monograph.

——(1987). *Improvising Empire: Portuguese Trade and Settlement in the Bay of Bengal, 1500–1700*, Delhi: Oxford University Press. A key work on the Potuguese role in the Indian Ocean region.

Thackston, Wheeler M., trs. and ed. (1996), *The Baburnama: Memoirs of Babar, Prince and Emperor*, New York: Oxford University Press. A very, readable translation of the autobiography of the founder of the Mughal empire.

Quotations: The following are the sources of quotations used in this chapter:

'gunpowder empires': Marshall G.S. Hodgson. *The Venture of Islam: Conscience and History in a World Civilization*, Chicago: Chicago University Press, 1974.

Zahiruddin Babur, *Baburnama*, in Wheeler M. Thackston, trs. and ed., *The Baburnama: Memoirs of Babar, Prince and Emperor*, New York: Oxford University Press, 1966.

Sirhindi cited in Francis Robinson, *Atlas of the Islamic World since 1500*, Oxford: Equinox, 1982, p. 62.

Ashin Dasgupta and M.N. Pearson (eds), *India and the Indian Ocean, 1500–1800*, Calcutta: Oxford University Press, 1987, pp. 28, 39.

Blair B. Kling and M.N. Pearson (eds), *The Age of Partnership: Europeans in Asia Before Dominion*, Honolulu: University of Hawaii, 1979.

Sanjay Subrahmanyam, *The Political Economy of Commerce: Southern India, 1500–1650*, Cambridge: Cambridge University Press, 1990.

Sri Aurobindo, *The Spirit and Form of Indian Polity*, Calcutta: Arya Publishing House, 1947, pp. 86, 89.

Chapter 5

Alam, Muzaffar (1993). *The Crisis of Empire in Mughal North India, Awadh & the Punjab, 1707–1748*, Delhi: Oxford University Press. A superb study of the changing balance in centre–region relations in late Mughal India.

Alavi, Seema (2008). *Islam and Healing: the Loss and Recovery of Indo-Muslim Medicine, 1650–1900*, New Delhi: Permanent Black. An insightful analysis of the Indo-Islamic body politic through a study of *unani* medicine.

Ali, M. Athar (1993). 'The Mughal Polity – a Critique of Revisionist Approaches', *Modern Asian Studies*, 27, 4: 699–710. The objections of the old school to the new revisionism.

Barnett, Richard B. (1980). *North India Between Empires: Awadh, the Mughals, and the British, 1720–1801*, Berkeley: University of California Press. A carefully researched monograph on Awadh between empires.

Bayly, C.A. (1988). *Indian Society and the Making of the British Empire*, in *The New Cambridge History of India*, Cambridge: Cambridge University Press. Chapter 1 of this work of synthesis provides a useful summary of research on the eighteenth century.

——(1990). 'Beating the Boundaries: South Asian History, c. 1700–1850', in Sugata Bose ed., *South Asia and World Capitalism*, Delhi: Oxford University Press. An essay placing developments in eighteenth-century India in a broader inter-regional context.

Bayly, Susan (1989). *Saints, Goddesses and Kings: Muslims and Christians in South Indian Society, 1700–1900*, Cambridge: Cambridge University Press. An insightful social history of the interplay of different religious traditions in the pre-colonial and early colonial periods.

Chandra, Satish (1959). *Parties and Politics at the Mughal Court, 1707–40*, Delhi: People's Publishing House. A thoroughly researched analysis of factions in the court of the later Mughals.

Cole, Juan Ricardo I. (1988). *The Roots of North Indian Shiism in Iran and Iraq: Religion and State in Awadh, 1722–1859*, Berkeley: University of California Press. An excellent monograph on Awadh in the eighteenth and nineteenth centuries.

Dirks, Nicholas (1987). *The Hollow Crown: Ethnohistory of an Indian Kingdom*, Cambridge: Cambridge University Press. An anthropological study of kingship and the politics of caste in the tiny state of Pudukottai in south India.

Gordon, Stewart (1994). *Marathas, Marauders and State Formation in Eighteenth Century India*, Delhi: Oxford University Press. A monograph on state-building by the Marathas from their western Indian base.

Grewal, J.S. (1990). *The Sikhs in the Punjab*, in *The New Cambridge History of India*, Cambridge: Cambridge University Press. A good, single-volume introduction to the history of the Sikhs in the pre-colonial and colonial periods.

Habib, Irfan (1963). *The Agrarian System of Mughal India, 1556–1707*, Bombay: Asia Publishing House. See the important chapter on 'agrarian crisis' in the late seventeenth and early eighteenth centuries and the peasant revolts that are seen to have led to the weakening of the Mughal empire.

Husain, Iqbal (1994). *The Rise and Decline of the Ruhela Chieftaincies in 18th Century India*, Aligarh: Aligarh Muslim University and Delhi: Oxford University Press. A carefully researched monograph on Rohilla state formation.

Khan, Ghulam Hussain (1789, 1832). *Siyar-ul-Mutakharin*, London. One of the key Persian sources on politics and society in eighteenth-century India.

Leonard, Karen (1979). 'The "great firm" theory of the decline of the Mughal empire', *Comparative Studies in Society and History* 21, 3, 151. An important article that sparked a lively debate about the possible role of mercantile and banking groups in the later Mughal era.

Sarkar, Jadunath (1932, reprints 1964–72). *The Fall of the Mughal Empire*, 4 vols, Bombay: Orient Longman. A classic and extremely well written, early twentieth-century study of Mughal decline that has been called into question by more recent historians.

——(reprints 1972–74). *History of Aurangzib: mainly based on Persian sources*, Bombay: Orient Longman. Another important scholarly work of the early twentieth century with an over-emphasis on Aurangzeb's religious bigotry and the Hindu reaction against it.

Sen, S.N. (1923). *The Administrative System of the Marathas*, Calcutta. Another thorough monograph that has stood the test of time.

——(1928). *The Military System of the Marathas*, Calcutta. A masterly study that more than holds its own against more recent work on the Marathas.

Wink, Andre (1986). *Land and Sovereignty in India: Agrarian Society and Politics under the Eighteenth Century Maratha Swarajya*, Cambridge: Cambridge University Press. A research monograph on Maratha state formation which overplays the concept of *fitna* (Arabic) or *fitva* (Marathi), used in the sense of calculated sedition.

Quotations: The following are the sources of quotations used in this chapter:

Syed Muhammad Latif, *History of the Punjab: From the Remotest Antiquity to the Present Time*, Calcutta: Calcutta Central Press Company, 1891, pp. xi, xiii.

C.A. Bayly, *Indian Society and the Making of the British Empire*, in *The New Cambridge History of India*, Cambridge: Cambridge University Press, 1988, p. 13.

Sri Aurobindo, *The Spirit and Form of Indian Polity*, Calcutta: Arya Publishing House, 1947, pp. 77–78, 91

Chapter 6

Bayly, C.A. (1983). *Rulers, Townsmen and Bazaars: North Indian Society in the Age of British Expansion, 1770–1870*, Cambridge: Cambridge University Press. A classic study of the colonial transition with a focus on the role of intermediate social groups, especially merchants and service gentry.

——(1988). *Indian Society and the Making of the British Empire*, in *The New Cambridge History of India*, Cambridge: Cambridge University Press. See chapter 2 for the role of Indian capital in the transition to colonialism.

——(1989). *Imperial Meridian: The British Empire and the World, 1780–1830*, London: Longman. An overview of British nationalism and imperialism in the late eighteenth and early nineteeth centuries.

Chaudhuri, K.N. (1978). *The Trading World of Asia and the English East India Company, 1660-1760*, Cambridge: Cambridge University Press. A very thorough quantitative study of the East India Company's trade.

Fisher, Michael, ed. (1993). *The Politics of British Annexation in India, 1757–1857*, in *Themes in Indian History*, Delhi: Oxford University Press. An anthology of important articles and chapters of books on this theme with a critical introduction by the editor.

Hasan, Mohibbul (1971). *History of Tipu Sultan*, Calcutta: World Press. An important study of the politics of Mysore on the eve of the British conquest.

Khan, Abdul Majed (1969). *The Transition in Bengal, 1756–1775: a Study of Saiyid Muhammad Reza Khan*, Cambridge: Cambridge University Press. A monograph dealing with a crucial moment in Bengal's history.

Marshall, P.J. (1976). *East Indian Fortunes: the British in Bengal in the Eighteenth Century*, Oxford: Clarendon Press. An important monograph on the British role in eighteenth-century Bengal.

——(1988). *Bengal: the British Bridgehead, Eastern India, 1740–1828*, in *The New Cambridge History of India*. Cambridge: Cambridge University Press. A synthesis of research on the British conquest of eastern India.

Nightingale, P. (1970). *Trade and Empire in Western India, 1784–1806*, Cambridge: Cambridge University Press. A monograph on the British move from trade to political dominion in western India.

Sen, Asok (1977). 'A pre-British economic formation in India of the late eighteenth-century', in Barun De (ed.), *Perspectives on Social Sciences*, Calcutta: Center for Studies in Social Sciences. An insightful article on Mysore in the late eighteenth century.

Travers, Robert (2007). *Ideology and Empire in Eighteenth Century India: the British in Bengal 1757–93*, Cambridge: Cambridge University Press. An excellent monograph on the early colonial state.

Tripathi, Amales (1979). *Trade and Finance in the Bengal Presidency, 1793–1833*, Calcutta. An important research monograph on the economic aspects of early company raj.

Quotations: The following are the sources of quotations used in this chapter:

Treaty of Amritsar, quoted in Sumantra Bose, *The Challenge in Kashmir: Democracy, Self-Determination and a Just Peace*, New Delhi, Thousand Oaks and London: Sage, 1997, p. 23.

Chapter 7

Alavi, Seema (1995). *The Sepoys and the Company*, Delhi: Oxford University Press. An important monograph on the relationship between the army and society between 1770 and 1830.

Anderson. Michael R. (1993). 'Islamic Law and the Colonial Encounter in British India', in David Arnold and Peter Robb (eds), *Institutions and Ideologies*, London: Curzon Press. An essay on the connections between religion, law and state in early colonial India.

Bayly, C.A. (1997). *Empire and Information: Political Intelligence and Social Communication in North India, 1780–1880*, Cambridge: Cambridge University Press. An important monograph exploring the complex links between the changing modes of information gathering and the exercise of state power as well as shifts in the theory and practice of governance under colonial rule.

Cohn, Bernard (1996). *Colonialism and its Forms of Knowledge: the British in India*, Princeton: Princeton University Press. A key set of essays by one of the most innovative and stimulating among anthropologists of colonial India.

Derrett, J.D.M. (1968). *Religion, Law and the State in India*, New York: Free Press. A monograph with insights into the changes in the linked domains of religion and law under colonialism.

Fisher, Michael H. (1993), *Indirect Rule in India: Residents and the Residency System, 1764–1857*, Delhi: Oxford University Press. A comprehensive study of the establishment of the company's political ascendancy over India's princely states.

Frykenberg, Robert E., ed. (1969). *Land Control and Social Structure in Indian History*, Madison: University of Wisconsin Press. An edited collection with a number of essays on the early colonial era.

Guha, Ranajit (1963, 1996). *A Rule of Property for Bengal: an Essay on the Idea of Permanent Settlement*, Durham: Duke University Press. A masterly study of the intellectual origins of Bengal's colonial land revenue settlement.

Guha, Sumit (1985). *The Agrarian Economy of the Bombay Deccan, 1818–1941*, Delhi: Oxford University Press. An important regional study of agricultural performance under colonial rule.

Ludden, David (1990). 'World Economy and Village India, 1600–1900: Exploring the Agrarian History of Capitalism', in Sugata Bose (ed.), *South Asia and World Capitalism*, Delhi: Oxford University Press. An essay showing how links were forged between agrarian India and the wider capitalist economy through expanding networks of commodity production.

Morley, William H. (1859). *The Administration of Justice in British India*, London: Williams and Norgate. An important nineteenth-century work on changes in the legal system under company raj.

Siddiqi, Asiya (1973). *Agrarian Change in a Northern Indian State: Uttar Pradesh, 1818–33*, Oxford: Oxford University Press. A key monograph on changes in colonial, financial and agrarian policies and the impact of the 1828–33 depression.

Stein, Burton, ed. (1992). *The Making of Agrarian Policy in British in India, 1770–1790*, in *Themes in Indian History*, Delhi: Oxford University Press. An anthology of important articles and chapters in books on this theme with a critical introduction by the editor.

Washbrook, David (1981). 'Law, State and Agrarian Society in Colonial India', *Modern Asian Studies*, 15, 3. A major article on the clash between the liberal belief in individual enterprise and communitarian principles underlying personal law in colonial India.

——(1990). 'South Asia, the World System and World Capitalism', in Sugata Bose (ed.), *South Asia and World Capitalism*, Delhi: Oxford University Press. An essay showing the points of elision between South Asian history and global history while rejecting the orthodoxies of world-systems analysis.

Quotations: The following are the sources of quotations used in this chapter:

Peter Marshall, *Bengal: the British Bridgehead, Eastern India, 1740–1828*, Cambridge: Cambridge University Press, 1987, p. 101.

C.A. Bayly, *Rulers, Townsmen and Bazaars: North Indian Society in the Age of British Expansion, 1770–1870*, Cambridge: Cambridge University Press, 1983, p. 468.

William J. Jackson, *Tyagaraja: Life and Lyrics*, Madras: Oxford University Press, 1991, p. 355.

Charles Metcalfe, 'infidel ... alcohol', cited in C.A. Bayly, *Indian Society and the Making of the British Empire*, Cambridge: Cambridge University Press, 1988, p. 115.

Chapter 8

Bose, Sugata (1993). *Peasant Labour and Colonial Capital: Rural Bengal since 1770*, in *The New Cambridge History of India*, Cambridge: Cambridge University Press. An interpretation of the interplay between demography, commercialization of agriculture and the structures of agrarian class and community in the long-term history of economic change and peasant resistance.

Chatterjee, Indrani (1999). *Gender, Slavery and Law in Colonial India*, Delhi: Oxford University Press. A monograph on forms of servitude under company raj.

Dale, Stephen Frederic (1980). *Islamic Society on the South Asian Frontier: the Mappilas of Malabar, 1498–1922*, Oxford: Clarendon Press. This study of the long term has some good sections on Mappilla society and politics in the nineteenth century.

Datta, Kalikinkar (reprint 1988). *The Santal Insurrection of 1855–57*, Calcutta: University of Calcutta Press. A monograph on the famous Santal *hool*.

Forbes, Geraldine (1996). *Women in Modern India*, in *The New Cambridge History of India*, Cambridge: Cambridge University. A single-volume introduction to women's history during colonial rule.

Ghosh, Durba (2006). *Sex and the Family in Colonial India: the making of empire*, Cambridge: Cambridge University Press. A monograph on gender relations under company raj.

Guha, Ranajit (1983). *Elementary Aspects of Peasant Insurgency in Colonial India*, Delhi: Oxford University Press. A classic study of peasant consciousness and resistance.

——(1988) 'The Prose of Counter-Insurgency', in Ranajit Guha and Gayatri Chakravorty Spivak (eds), *Selected Subaltern Studies*, New York: Oxford University Press. A seminal critique of the colonial discourse on subaltern insurgency.

Jalal, Ayesha (2008). *Partisans of Allah: Jihad in South Asia*, Cambridge, MA: Harvard University Press. A wide-ranging historical study of the theory and practice of jihad, including the jihad launched by Sayyid Ahmed of Rae Bareilly between 1826 and 1831.

Kopf, David (1969). *British Orientalism and the Bengal Renaissance: the Dynamics of Indian Modernization, 1773–1835*, Berkeley: University of California Press. A monograph on the intellectual currents of British orientalist (in a pre-Saidian sense of the term) scholars and the variety of Indian responses in the early nineteenth century to Western knowledge.

Kumar, Dharma (reprint 1992). *Land and Caste in South India: Agricultural Labourers in Madras Presidency during the Nineteenth Century*, New Delhi: Manohar Publishers. A classic work on agrarian continuity and change under colonial rule.

Ludden, David (1985). *Peasant History in South India*, Princeton: Princeton University Press. This excellent study of a millennium in the peasant history of Tirunelveli district has three chapters on continuity and change in nineteenth century.

Mani, Lata (1989). 'Contentious Traditions: The Debate on *Sati* in Colonial India', in Kumkum Sangari and Sudesh Vaid (eds), *Recasting Women: Essays in Colonial History*, New Delhi: Kali for Women. This article on the nineteenth-century debate on *sati* has become quite central to the contemporary historiographical debate about the nature of social interventions by the colonial state.

Prakash, Gyan, ed. (1990). *Bonded Histories: Genealogies of Labor Servitude in Colonial India*. A critical perspective on the nineteenth-century colonial discourse on freedom.

——(1992). *The World of the Rural Labourer in Colonial India*, in *Themes in Indian History*, Delhi: Oxford University Press. An anthology of important articles and chapters in books on this theme with a critical introduction by the editor.

Ray, Ratnalekha. 1980. *Change in Bengal Agrarian Society, 1760–1850*, Delhi: Oxford University Press. A superb study of agrarian continuity and change under company raj.

Singha, Radhika (1998). *A Despotism of Law: Crime and Justice in Early Colonial India*, Delhi: Oxford University Press. An important study of colonial criminal law in the context of the British conquest of India.

Stokes, Eric (1959). *The English Utilitarians and India*, Oxford: Clarendon Press. A path-breaking intellectual history.

Tod, James (1832, 1880), *Annals and Antiquities of Rajasthan: or the Central and Western Rajpoot States of India*, Madras: Higgins Botham. This encyclopaedic enquiry helped lend substance to principles of hierarchy in Indian rural society.

Washbrook, David (1988). 'Progress and Problems: South Asian Economic and Social History, c.1720 to 1860', *Modern Asian Studies*, 22, 1. An important historiographical essay.

Yang, Anand (1989). *The Limited Raj: Agrarian Relations in Colonial India: Saran District, 1793–1920*, Berkeley: University of California Press. A research monograph on the mechanisms of social control by the colonial state through local landed classes in a district of Bihar.

Quotations: The following are the sources of quotations used in this chapter:

Kalidas Nag and Debajyoti Burman (eds), *The English Works of Rammohun Roy*, Calcutta: Sadharan Brahmo Samaj, 1945–58, part 4, 106–8.

G.M. Young (ed.), *Macaulay, Prose and Poetry*, Cambridge, MA: Harvard University Press, 1952, p. 729.

Chapter 9

Bayly, C.A. (1988) *Indian Society and the Making of the British Empire*, in *The New Cambridge History of India*, Cambridge: Cambridge University Press. See chapter 6 for a discussion of the 1857 rebellion.

Bhadra, Gautam (1988). 'Four Rebels of Eighteen-Fifty-Seven', in Ranajit Guha and Gayatri Chakravorty Spivak, eds, *Selected Subaltern Studies*, New York: Oxford University Press. An excellent article on the variegated leadership of the rebellion.

Chaudhuri, Sashi Bhusan (1955). *Civil Disturbances during British Rule in India, 1765–1857*, Calcutta: World Press. A fine study that places the 1857 revolt in the context of civil uprisings throughout the first century of colonial rule.

——(1957). *Civil Rebellion in the Indian Mutinies*, Calcutta: World Press. This book remains one of the best on the civil dimension of the 1857 revolt.

Dalrymple, William (2008). *The Last Mughal*, London: Bloomsbury. A racy account of the rebellion in Delhi.

Marx, Karl (reprint 1975). *The First Indian War of Independence, 1857–1859*, with F. Engels, Moscow: Progress Publishers. Marx in his jounalistic vein.

Mukherjee, Rudrangshu (1984). *Awadh in Revolt: A Study of Popular Resistance*, Delhi: Oxford University Press. A fine piece of research on one of the storm-centres of the revolt.

Roy Tapti (1996). *A Countryside in Revolt: Bulandshahr District, 1857*, Delhi: Oxford University Press. A carefully researched district-level study of the uprising.

Sen, S.N. (1957). *Eighteen Fifty-Seven*, Delhi: Publications Division, Ministry of Information and Broadcasting, Government of India. A thorough and balanced study of the revolt.

Stokes, Eric (1978). *The Peasant and the Raj: Studies in Agrarian Society and Peasant Rebellion in Colonial India*, Cambridge: Cambridge University Press. A collection of a dozen stylishly written essays including four on the 1857 rebellion.

——(1986). *The Peasant Armed: Indian Revolt of 1857*, ed. C.A. Bayly, Oxford: Clarendon Press. See especially the two excellent chapters on the military course of the rebellion.

Quotations: The following are the sources of quotations used in this chapter:

Maulvi of Faizabad cited in Gautam Bhadra, 'Four Rebels of Eighteen-Fifty-Seven', in Ranajit Guha and Gayatri Chakravorty Spivak (eds), *Selected Subaltern Studies*, New York: Oxford University Press, 1988, p. 171.

Azimgarh proclamation reproduced in Stephen Hay (ed.), *Sources of Indian Tradition, Volume Two: Modern India and Pakistan*, New York: Columbia University Press, 1988, p. 177.

Eric Stokes, *The Peasant and the Raj: Studies in Agrarian Society and Peasant Rebellion in Colonial India*, Cambridge: Cambridge University Press, 1978, p. 184.

Mirza Asadullah Khan Ghalib, *Nawa-e-Sarosh*, compiled by Ghulam Rasul Mehr, Lahore: Sheikh Ghulam Ali and Sons, pp. 530, 308.

Chapter 10

Ali, Imran (1988). *The Punjab Under Imperialism, 1885–1947*, Princeton: Princeton University Press. A detailed monograph on British development policies in Punjab based on colonial archival sources.

Dutt, Romesh C. (1904, 1969). *Economic History of India*, Volume 2: *In the Victorian Age*, New York: A.M. Kelley. The most sustained nationalist critique of colonial economic policies.

Gopal, Sarvepalli (1965). *British Policy in India, 1858–1905*, Cambridge: Cambridge University Press. A study based on the papers of the secretaries of state for India and viceroys of this period.

Guha, Sumit, ed. (1992). *Growth, Stagnation and Decline? Agricultural Productivity in British India*, Delhi: Oxford University Press. An anthology of important articles and chapters of books on this theme with a critical introduction by the editor.

Metcalf, Thomas R. (1964). *The Aftermath of Revolt: India 1857–1870*, Princeton: Princeton University Press. A study of political and economic change under the early crown raj.

——(1997). *Ideologies of the Raj*, in *The New Cambridge History of India*, Cambridge: Cambridge University Press. A useful single-volume introduction to the ideologies underpinning British rule in India.

Naoroji, Dadabhai (1901, 1962). *Poverty and Un-British Rule in India*, Delhi: Publications Division, Government of India. A sophisticated, moderate critique of colonial rule.

Rai, Mridu (2003). *Hindu Rulers, Muslim Subjects: Rights and Religion in Kashmir, 1846–1947*, Princeton: Princeton University Press. An important study of the problem of legitimacy in princely India.

Ray, Rajat Kanta, ed. (1977), 'Political Change in British India', *Indian Economic and Social History Review*, 14, 4: 493–519. A detailed and insightful review essay on the relationship between the colonial state and nationalist politics.

——(1992), *Entrepreneurship and Industry in India, 1800–1947*, Oxford: Oxford University Press. An anthology of important articles and chapters of books on this theme with a critical introduction by the editor.

Roy, Tirthankar (1994). *Artisans and Industrialization: Weavers in Twentieth Century India*, Delhi: Oxford University Press. This book calls into question earlier arguments about deindustrialization.

Sarkar, Sumit (1983). *Modern India, 1885–1947*, Delhi: Macmillan. This general history has some very good sections on state and political economy between 1885 and World War I.

Thorner, Daniel (1962). *Land and Labour in India*, New York: Asia Publishing House. An important work on economic history and political economy.

Tomlinson, B.R. (1993). *The Economy of Modern India, 1860–1970*, in *The New Cambridge History of India*, Cambridge: Cambridge University Press. A very useful single-volume introduction to the economy history of modern India.

Quotations: The following are the sources of quotations used in this chapter:

'counterpoise ... natives' and 'Sikh ... need': Hiralal Singh, *Problems and Policies of British in India*, Bombay, 1963, pp. 140, 142.

Rajat Kanta Ray, 'Political Change in British India', *Indian Economic and Social History Review*, 14, 4, Oct–Dec 1977, p. 5030.

Ramabai Ranade (ed.), *Miscellaneous Writings of the late Hon'ble Mr. Justice M.G. Ranade*, Delhi: Sahitya Akademi, 1992, p. 180.

Chapter 11

Ahmad, Rafiuddin (1981). *The Bengal Muslims, 1871–1906: a Quest for Identity*, New York: Oxford University Press. A study of the process of redefinition of Bengali Muslim identity.

Arnold, David (1988). 'Touching the Body: Perspectives on the Indian Plague, 1896 to 1900', in Ranajit Guha and Gayatri Chakravorty Spivak (eds), *Selected Subaltern Studies*, Delhi: Oxford University Press. A critique of the nexus between modern medicine and the colonial state.

——and Ramchandra Guha (eds) (1995). *Nature, Culture, Imperialism: Essays on the Environmental History of South Asia*, Delhi: Oxford University Press. An excellent collection of wide-ranging essays on the subject; see especially the introduction by the editors and Neeladri Bhattacharya's essay 'Pastoralists in a Colonial World' on late nineteenth-century Punjab.

Bayly, C.A. (1975). *The Local Roots of Indian Politics: Allahabad, 1880–1920*, Oxford: Clarendon Press. A research monograph on the origins of nationalist politics in a key urban centre of north India.

Bose, Sugata (1997). 'Nation as Mother: Representations and Contestations of India in Bengali Literature and Culture', in Sugata Bose and Ayesha Jalal (eds), *Nationalism, Democracy and Development: State and Politics in India*, Delhi: Oxford University Press. A re-examination of the relationship of nationalist thought and colonial knowledge along the boundaries of the 'nation' with the categories of gender, class, religious community, linguistic region as well as the 'state'.

Bose, Sugata (2007). 'The Spirit and Form of an Ethical Polity: A Meditation on Aurobindo's Thought', *Modern Intellectual History*, 4, 1: 129–44. An essay on the history of ideas in the Swadeshi era.

Chandravarkar, Rajnarayan (1994). *The Origins of Industrial Capitalism in India*, Cambridge: Cambridge University Press. A study of industrialization and the social history of labour in the Bombay textile mills sector.

Chakrabarti, Hiren (1992). *Political Protest in Bengal: Boycott and Terrorism, 1905–18*, Calcutta: Papyrus. An excellent, but little-known, study of the Swadeshi movement and its aftermath.

Chakrabarty, Dipesh (1989). *Rethinking Working Class History: Bengal, 1890–1940*, Princeton: Princeton University Press. A major study of the culture and consciousness of jute mill workers in the industrial belt around Calcutta.

Chatterjee, Partha (1986, 1993), *Nationalist Thought and the Colonial World: a Derivative Discourse?* London: Zed Press and Minneapolis: University of Minnesota Press. This path-breaking book has a chapter on the 'moment of departure', exemplified by the late nineteenth-century novelist Bankim Chandra Chattopadhyay.

——(1994). *The Nation and its Fragments*, Princeton: Princeton University Press. A key set of essays arguing the autonomy of nationalist thought in an inner spiritual domain seen to be distinct from an outer material sphere.

——(1997). 'Our Modernity', in Partha Chatterjee, *The Present History of West Bengal: Essays in Political Criticism*, Delhi: Oxford University Press. An essay on the difference of the colonial variant from the norms and claims of European modernity.

Deshpande, Prachi (2007). *Creative Pasts: Historical Memory and Identity in Western India, 1700–1960*, New York: Columbia University Press. A subtle exploration of history and identity in Maharashtra.

Fox, Richard (1985). *Lions of the Punjab: Culture in the Making*, Berkeley: University of California Press. An excellent historical anthropology of the shifts in Sikh identity during colonial rule.

Freitag, Sandria (1989). *Collective Action and Community: Public Arenas and the Emergence of Communalism in North India*. A study of the origins of 'communalism' in the collective activities with new forms of popular participation since the later nineteenth century.

Gallagher, John, Gordon Johnson and Anil Seal, eds (1973). *Locality, Province and Nation*, Cambridge: Cambridge University Press. A set of essays on the local and national politics in the late nineteenth and early twentieth centuries.

Ghose, Aurobindo (1974). *New Lamps for Old*. Pondicherry: Sri Aurobindo Ashram. Six important essays written in 1894 criticizing moderate nationalism.

Guha-Thakurta, Tapati (1992). *The Making of a New 'Indian' Art: Artists, Aesthetics and Nationalism in Bengal, c. 1850–1920*, Cambridge: Cambridge University Press. A fine monograph on the relationship between art and nationalism.

Hardiman, David, ed. (1992). *Peasant Resistance in India, 1858–1914*, Delhi: Oxford University Press. An anthology of important articles and chapters of books on this theme with a critical introduction by the editor.

Hardy, Peter (1972). *The Muslims of British India*, Cambridge: Cambridge University Press. This major study contains important chapters on Muslim society and politics in the late nineteenth and early twentieth centuries.

Haynes, Douglas (1991). *Rhetoric and Ritual in Colonial India: the Shaping of a Public Culture in Surat City, 1852–1928*. A monograph focusing on the merchant groups of a western Indian port city.

Hossain, Rokeya Sakhawat (1981). *Sultana's Dream and Selections from The Secluded Ones*, edited and translated by Roushan Jahan, New York: The Feminist Press at the City University of New York. An edition of the author's fascinating 1906 tract and other writings.

Jalal, Ayesha (1997). 'Exploding Communalism: the Politics of Muslim Identity in South Asia', in Sugata Bose and Ayesha Jalal (eds), *Nationalism, Democracy and Development: State and Politics in India*, Delhi: Oxford University Press. Drawing a distinction between a religiously informed cultural identity and the politics of cultural nationalism, this essay provides a critique of the dominant historical and political discourse on 'communalism'.

——(2000). *Self and Sovereignty: Individual and Community in South Asian Islam since 1850*, London: Routledge. This book examines the shifts in Muslim thought and politics in response to colonial rule in India through to the period of decolonization and partition.

Jones, Kenneth W. (1976), *Arya Dharm: Hindu Consciousness in 19th-Century Punjab*, Berkeley: University of California Press. A monograph on the Arya Samaj.

Kaviraj, Sudipta (1995). *The Unhappy Consciousness: Bankimchandra Chattopadhyay and the Formation of Nationalist Discourse in India*, Delhi: Oxford University Press. Another meditation on Bankim to be read with Partha Chatterjee's chapter in *Nationalist Thought*.

Kozlowski, Gregory C. (1986). *Muslim Endowments and Society in British India*, Cambridge: Cambridge University Press. A monograph that sheds useful light on the changing nature of property and charity in colonial India.

Kumar, Ravinder (1968). *Western India in the Nineteenth Century: A Study in the Social History of Maharashtra*, London: Routledge. A monograph making a strong argument about the disruptive impact of colonial rule on Indian society.

Lelyveld, David (1977). *Aligarh's First Generation*, Princeton: Princeton University Press. An intellectual and social history of north India's *ashraf* elite in the mid to late nineteenth century.

Metcalf, Barbara Daly (1982). *Islamic Revival in British India: Deoband, 1860–1900*, Princeton: Princeton University Press. A monograph on the Deoband school of Muslim religious scholars and scholarship.

Mir, Farina (2010). *The Social Space of Language: Vernacular Culture in British Colonial Punjab*, Berkeley: University of California Press. A nuanced study of language, religion and power through an analysis of many versions of Punjab's most famous folk tale.

Mitter, Partha (1994). *Art and Nationalism in Colonial India, 1850–1922: Occidental Orientations*, Cambridge: Cambridge University Press. A richly illustrated and insightful book that can be read profitably alongside Tapati Guha-Thakurta's *The Making of a New Indian Art*.

Murshid, Tazeen (1996). *The Sacred and the Secular*, Delhi: Oxford University Press. A study of Muslim society and politics in Bengal from 1877 to 1977.

Oberoi, Harjot (1994). *The Construction of Religious Boundaries: Culture, Identity and Diversity in the Sikh Tradition*, Delhi: Oxford University Press. This work of historical anthropology has some good chapters on the Singh Sabhas of the late nineteenth century.

239

O'Hanlon, Rosalind (1985). *Caste, Conflict, and Ideology: Mahatma Jotirao Phule and Low Caste Protest in Nineteenth-Century Western India*, Cambridge: Cambridge University Press. An excellent study of a non-Brahman movement and its leader.

Pandey, Gyanendra (1990). *The Construction of Communalism in Colonial North India*, Delhi: Oxford University Press. An important monograph showing the shared genealogy of the ideologies of nationalism and communalism.

Ray, Rajat Kanta (1984). *Social Conflict and Political Unrest in Bengal, 1875–1927*, Delhi: Oxford University Press. A well-researched monograph on Bengali society and politics.

Robinson, Francis (1974). *Separatism Among Indian Muslims: The Politics of United Provinces Muslims, 1860–1923*, Cambridge: Cambridge University Press. A carefully researched account of U.P. Muslim politics.

Sarkar, Sumit (1973). *The Swadeshi Movement in Bengal, 1903–1908*. New Delhi: People's Publishing House. A fine study of the Swadeshi movement.

Tagore, Rabindranath (1917). *Nationalism*, London: Macmillan. Three critical lectures on nationalism in Japan, the West and India.

Washbrook, David (1976). *The Emergence of Provincial Politics: The Madras Presidency, 1870–1920*, Cambridge: Cambridge University Press. A major political study of south India.

Zutshi, Chitralekha (2003). *Languages of Belonging: Islam, Community and the State in Kashmir, 1880s to 1950s*, New York: Oxford University Press. A skilful study of regional patriotism and religious identity in Kashmir.

Quotations: The following are the sources of quotations used in this chapter:

Ramabai Ranade (ed.), *Miscellaneous Writings of the late Hon'ble Mr. Justice M.G. Ranade*, Delhi: Sahitya Akademi, 1992, p. 190.

V.C. Joshi (ed.), *Lala Lajpat Rai: Writings and Speeches, Vol. 1*, Delhi: University Publishers, 1966, p. 47.

Aurobindo Ghose, 'New Lamps for Old', in Haridas Mukherjee and Uma Mukherjee, *Sri Aurobindo's Political Thought (1893–1908)*, Calcutta: Firma K.L. Mukhopadhyay, 1958, pp. 103–4.

Kulliyat-e-Akbar Allahabadi, Vol. 1, Delhi: n.d., p. 95.

Aurobindo Ghose, 'Rishi Bankimchandra', in *Bande Mataram*, 16 April, 1907, cited in Sugata Bose, 'Nation as Mother', in Sugata Bose and Ayesha Jalal (eds), *Nationalism, Democracy and Development*, Delhi: Oxford University Press, p. 52.

Sri Aurobindo, *The Spirit and Form of Indian Polity*, Calcutta: Arya Publishing House, 1947, p. 77–78, 91.

Bipin Chandra Pal, 'New India', in *New India*, August 12, 1901.

Mohamed Ali, 'The Communal Patriot', February 1912, in Afzal Iqbal (ed.), *Writings and Speeches of Maulana Mohamed Ali*, Lahore: 1987, pp. 75–77.

Bipin Chandra Pal, *The Soul of India: a Constructive Study of Indian Thought and Ideals*, 4th edn, Calcutta: Yugayatri Prakashak, 1958, pp. 62–63, 65, 68, 92.

Chapters 12 and 13

Amin, Shahid (1988). 'Gandhi as Mahatma: Gorakhpur District, Eastern U.P. 1921–22', in Ranajit Guha and Gayatri Chakravorty Spivak (eds), *Selected Subaltern Studies*,

New York: Oxford University Press. An evocative essay on popular perceptions of the Mahatma and the role of rumour in the spread of his message.

——(1995). *Event, Metaphor, Memory: Chauri Chaura, 1922–1992*, Delhi: Oxford University Press. An imaginative retelling of an event that came to be treated as an aberration in the official story of Gandhian nationalism.

Balachandaran, G. (1996). *John Bullions' Empire: Britain's Gold Problem and India Between the Wars*. Richmond and Surrey: Curzon. An important study of finance in the late colonial era.

Birla, Ritu (2009). *Stages of Capital: Law, Culture and Market Governance in Late Colonial India*, Durham, NC: Duke University Press. A deft analysis of the discourse of colonial capitalism.

Bose, Sugata and Kris Manjapra, eds (2010).*Cosmopolitan Thought Zones: South Asia and the Global Circulation of Ideas*, London: Palgrave Macmillan. A collection of essays on cosmopolitanism and universalism in the age of anti-colonial nationalism.

Brown, Judith M. (1972). *Gandhi's Rise to Power: Indian Politics 1915–22*, Cambridge: Cambridge University Press. A political analysis of Gandhi's assumption of the leadership of the Indian National Congress.

Chatterjee, Partha (1986, 1993). *Nationalist Thought and the Colonial World: a Derivative Discourse?* Minneapolis: University of Minnesota Press. See the chapter on the 'moment of manouevre' exemplified by Gandhi.

Hardiman, David (1981). *Peasant Nationalists of Gujarat: Kheda District*, Delhi: Oxford University Press. A probing analysis of Gandhian movements in Kheda district.

Hasan, Mushirul, ed. (1979). *Nationalism and Communal Politics in India, 1916–1928*, Delhi: Manohar. A carefully researched monograph covering the rise and decline of the Khilafat movement.

——(1981). *Communal and Pan-Islamic Trends in Colonial India*, Delhi: Manohar. A collection of essays on aspects of Muslim politics.

Jalal, Ayesha (2000). *Self and Sovereignty: Individual and Community in South Asian Islam since 1850*, London: Routledge. This book examines the shifts in Muslim thought and politics in response to colonial rule in India through to the period of decolonization and partition; see chapter 5 for the Khilafat movement.

Jeffrey, Robin, ed. (1978). *People, Princes and Paramount Power: Society and Politics in the Indian Princely States*, Delhi: Oxford University Press. A set of articles on princely India.

Manjapra, Kris (2010). *M.N. Roy: Marxism and Colonial Cosmopolitanism*, Delhi: Routledge. An incisive intellectual and political biography.

Minault, Gail (1982). *The Khilafat Movement: Religious Symbolism and Political Mobilizationin India*, New York: Columbia University Press.

Nanda, B.R. (1989). *Gandhi: Pan-Islamism, Imperialism and Nationalism in India*, Delhi: Oxford University Press. An anecdotal history of the 1915–25 decade critical of the pro-Khilafat Muslims.

Nandy, Ashish (1983). *The Intimate Enemy: Loss and Recovery of Self under Colonialism*, Delhi: Oxford University Press. A subtle, psychological analysis of the meaning of the colonial experience, with insights into the nature of Gandhian resistance.

Nehru, Jawaharlal (1962). *An Autobiography with Musings on Recent Events in India*. Bombay: Allied Publishers. This well-written autobiography contains many insights into India's freedom movement.

Page, David (1982). *Prelude to Partition: The Indian Muslims and the Imperial System of Control 1920–1932*, Oxford: Oxford University Press. See this work for the political conflicts that emerged after the collapse of the non-cooperation and Khilafat movement.

Pandey, Gyanendra (1979). *The Ascendancy of the Congress in Uttar Pradesh, 1926–1934*. A monograph on nationalist politics in U.P. in the 1920s and 1930s.

Siddiqui, Majid Hayat (1978). *Agrarian Unrest in North India: The United Provinces, 1918–1922*, Delhi: Vikas. An excellent study of peasant politics and mass nationalism.

Tejani, Shabnum (2008). *Indian Secularism: A Social and Intellectual History 1890–1950*. Bloomington: Indiana University Press. A monograph on religion and politics with particular reference to western India.

Tomlinson, B.R. (1979). *The Political Economy of the Raj, 1914–1947: the Economics of Decolonization in India*, London: Macmillan. A study of the changing economic relations between metropolis and colony after World War I.

Quotations: The following are the sources of quotations used in these chapters:

Hira Singh: 'I ... plainly'. L/MIL/5/825, Part 4, folio 570, India Office Records, London, cited in Sugata Bose, 'Black Pepper, Red Pepper: Waging War for King and Country, 1914–45' (mimeograph).

Mohandas Gandhi, *Hind Swaraj*, in *The Collected Works of Mahatma Gandhi*, vol.10, New Delhi: Government of India, Publications Division, 1958–78, pp. 15, 16, 57; vol. 18, pp. 132–33.

Mahatma Gandhi, *Young India 1919–1922*, Madras: S. Ganesan, 1922, cited in Sugata Bose, 'Nation, Reason and Religion: India's Independence in International Perspective', G.M. Trevelyan Lecture, University of Cambridge, 26 November, 1997, *Economic and Political Weekly*, 1–8 August, 1998.

Rabindranath Tagore, 'The Call of Truth', *Modern Review*, 30, 4 (1921), p. 430.

Rajat Kanta Ray, 'Political Change in British India', *Indian Economic and Social History Review*, 14, 4, Oct–Dec 1977.

Afzal Iqbal (ed.), *Select Writings and Speeches of Mohamed Ali*, Lahore: 1987, p. 356.

Sisir Kumar Bose and Sugata Bose (eds), *The Essential Writings of Netaji Subhas Chandra Bose*, Calcutta: Netaji Research Bureau and Delhi: Oxford University Press, 1997, p. 86.

Chapters 14 and 15

Bagchi, Amiya (1969). *Private Investment in India, 1900–39*, Cambridge: Cambridge University Press. This classic study based on thorough research has good sections on the Depression era.

Baker, C.J. (1984). *An Indian Rural Economy: the Tamilnad Countryside*, Oxford: Oxford University Press. A masterly study of the Tamilnad rural economy from the late nineteenth century to the 1950s, with particular emphasis on the Depression decade.

Bose, Sugata (1986). *Agrarian Bengal: Economy, Social Structure and Politics, 1919–1947*, Cambridge: Cambridge University Press. This study focuses on the ways in which the international economic crisis of the 1930s affected the region's economy, society and politics.

——(1990). 'Starvation amidst Plenty: the Making of Famine in Bengal, Honan and Tonkin, 1942–45', *Modern Asian Studies*. A comparative essay on three great wartime famines, including the Bengal famine of 1943.

Brown, Judith (1977). *Gandhi and Civil Disobedience: The Mahatma in Indian Politics, 1928–34*, Cambridge: Cambridge University Press. A sequel to *Gandhi's Rise to Power*.

Desai A.R., ed. (1979). *Peasant Struggles in India*, Bombay: Oxford University Press. This book contains a number of useful chapters on popular movements of the 1930s and 1940s.

Fay, Peter Ward (1994). *The Forgotten Army: India's Armed Struggle for Independence, 1942–45*. A study of the Indian National Army.

Gordon, Leonard (1990). *Brothers Against the Raj: a Biography of Indian Nationalist Sarat and Subhas Chandra Bose*, New York: Columbia University Press. This monumental biography has strong chapters on nationalist politics in the 1930s and 1940s.

Greenough, Paul R. (1982). *Prosperity and Misery in Modern Bengal: the Famine of 1943–1944*, New York: Oxford University Press. A social and cultural history of the great famine.

Low, D.A., ed. (1977). *Congress and the Raj: Facets of the Indian Struggle, 1917–47*, London: Arnold-Heinemann. This collection has some good articles on mass movements of the 1930 and 1940s, including the Quit India Movement of 1942.

Markovits, Claude (1985). *Indian Business and Nationalist Politics, 1931–1939: The Indigenous Capitalist Class and the Rise of Congress Party*, Cambridge: Cambridge University Press. An important study of the business–politics nexus in the 1930s.

Menon, Dilip M. (1994). *Caste, Nationalism and Communism in South India, Malabar, 1900–1948*, Cambridge: Cambridge University Press. A study of Kerala politics, with especially strong chapters on the 1930s and 1940s.

Omvedt, Gail (1994). *Dalits and Democratic Revolution: Dr. Ambedkar and the Dalit Movement in Colonial India*, New Delhi; Thousand Oaks: Sage Publications. A sensitive study of the movement and its leader.

Ray, Rajat Kanta (1979). *Industrialization in India: Growth and Conflict in the Private Corporate Sector, 1914–1947*, Delhi: Oxford University Press. This study can be read alongside Amiya Bagchi's *Private Investment in India, 1900–1939*.

Rothermund, Dietmar (1992). *India and the Great Depression, 1929–1939*. New Delhi: Manohar Publications. An overview of India's experience of the world crisis.

Sen, Amartya (1981). *Poverty and Famines: An Essay in Entitlement and Deprivation*, Oxford: Clarendon Press. This valuable work of theory has a chapter on the Bengal famine of 1943 and another on the Bangladesh famine of 1974.

Quotations: The following are the sources of quotations used in these chapters:

'We … difficult'. The district magistrate of Midnapur to the chief secretary, 12 June 1930, Government of Bengal, Political Confidential File 434–1930 (West Bengal State Archives), cited in Sugata Bose, *Agrarian Bengal*, Cambridge: Cambridge University Press, p. 238.

Winston Churchill quoted in Brian Porter, *The Lion's Share: A Short History of British Imperialism*, London: Longman, 1984, p. 298.

Jawaharlal Nehru, *Selected Works of Jawaharlal Nehru*, vol. 7, New Delhi: Orient Longman, 1975, p. 182.

Subhas Chandra Bose, *The Indian Struggle, 1920 to 1942*, ed. Sisir K. Bose and Sugata Bose, Calcutta: Netaji Research Bureau.

M.A. Jinnah, 'Most ... states'. Speech at 24th session of the All-India Muslim League at Bombay, April, 1936, cited in Ayesha Jalal, *The Sole Spokesman*, Cambridge: Cambridge University Press, p. 20.

Mohandas Gandhi, *The Collected Works of Mahatma Gandhi*, vol. 76, New Delhi: Government of India, Publications Division, 1958–78, pp. 87, 105, 114, 120, 242, 381. Sisir Kumar Bose and Sugata Bose (eds), *The Essential Writings of Netaji Subhas Chandra Bose*, Calcutta: Netaji Research Bureau and Delhi: Oxford University Press, 1997, pp. 17, 316.

Sumit Sarkar, *Modern India*, Delhi: Macmillan, p. 418.

Chapters 16 and 17

Chatterjee, Partha (1986, 1993). *Nationalist Thought and the Colonial World: a Derivative Discourse?* Minneapolis: University of Minnesota Press. See the chapter on the 'moment of arrival' exemplified by Jawaharlal Nehru.

Das, Veena (1995). *Critical Events: An Anthropological Perspective on Contemporary India*, Delhi: Oxford University Press. Chapter 3 of this book provides a sharp critique of the post-colonial state's repatriation programme for 'abducted women'.

Das, Suranjan (1993). *Communal Riots in Bengal*, Delhi: Oxford University Press. A study of episodes of Hindu–Muslim violence in the first half of the twentieth century.

Gilmartin, David (1988). *Empire and Islam: Punjab and the Making of Pakistan*, Berkeley: University of California Press.

Hasan, Mushirul, ed. (1993). *India's Partition: Process, Strategy and Mobilization, Themes in Indian History*, Delhi: Oxford University Press. An anthology of articles, stories and selected primary documents on this theme with a critical introduction by the editor. See, for example, Asim Roy's review article on the high politics of partition and Leonard Gordon's on Bengal.

Low, Donald Anthony, ed. (1991). *The Political Inheritance of Pakistan*, London: Macmillan. A collection of essays on politics in the provinces that became part of Pakistan.

Jalal, Ayesha (1985, 1994). *The Sole Spokesman: Jinnah, the Muslim League and the Demand for Pakistan*, Cambridge: Cambridge University Press. A study of the aims and strategy of Jinnah and the All-India Muslim League that brings out the divergence in the interests of Muslims in majority and minority provinces.

——(1996). 'Secularists, Subalterns and the Stigma of Communalism: Partition Historiography Revisited', *Indian Economic and Social History Review*, 33, 1, 93–103. A review article containing a critical appraisal of Mushirul Hasan's *India's Partition* and Gyanendra Pandey's 'The Prose of Otherness'.

Mansergh, N., E.W.R. Lumby and Penderel Moon, eds (1970–83), *Constitutional Relations Between Britain and India: The Transfer of Power 1942–7*, 12 vols, London: Her Majesty's Stationery Office. A very important collection of primary documents.

Manto, Saadat Hasan (1997). *Back Milk: A Collection of Short Stories*, translated and with an introduction by Hamid Jalal, Lahore: Sang-e-Meal Publications. A new edition of the earliest translations of Manto's gripping stories, many of which are set against the backdrop of the human tragedy that accompanied partition.

Nair, Neeti (2011). *Changing Homelands: Hindu Politics and the Partition of India*, Cambridge, MA: Harvard University Press. A key monograph on the politics of Punjabi Hindus in the first half of the twentieth century.

Naim, C.M., ed. (1979). *Iqbal, Jinnah and Pakistan: The Vision and the Reality*. Syracuse: University of Syracuse Press. A study of ideological currents in the Pakistan movement.

Pandey, Gyanendra (1994). 'The Prose of Otherness', in David Arnold and David Hardiman (eds), *Subaltern Studies VIII: Essays in Honour of Ranajit Guha*, Delhi: Oxford University Press. A critical essay on partition historiography.

Talbot, Ian (1988). *Punjab and the Raj, 1849–1947*, New Delhi: Manohar. The later chapters of this study contain useful material on Muslim politics in the Punjab.

——(1996). *Freedom's Cry: the Popular Dimension in the Pakistan Movement and Partition Experience in North-West India*, Karachi: Oxford University Press. A study of the politics and experience of partition.

Wolpert, Stanley (1984). *Jinnah of Pakistan*, New York: Oxford University Press. Biography that misses by a wide mark the real political aims of Jinnah and the Muslim League.

Quotations: The following are the sources of quotations used in these chapters:

M.A. Jinnah's presidential address to the All-India Muslim League at Lahore, 22 March 1940, cited in Ayesha Jalal, 'Exploding Communalism', in Sugata Bose and Ayesha Jalal (eds), *Nationalism, Democracy and Development*, Delhi: Oxford University Press, p. 92.

Lahore Resolution of the All-India Muslim League cited in Ayesha Jalal, *The Sole Spokesmen*, pp. 57–59.

H.V. Hodson cited in Ayesha Jalal, *The Sole Spokesman*, Cambridge: Cambridge University Press, 1985 and 1994, p. 70.

I.I. Chundrigar, cited in Ayesha Jalal, *The Sole Spokesman*, p. 70.

M.A. Jinnah to Nawab Ismail, 25 November 1941, cited in Ayesha Jalal, *The Sole Spokesman*, p.71.

M.A. Jinnah on the Rajagopalachari formula in an address to the Council of the All-India Muslim League at Lahore, 30 July 1944, cited in Ayesha Jalal, *The Sole Spokesman*, p. 121. *Millat*, 11 April 1947, cited in Sugata Bose, 'Nation as Mother', in Bose and Jalal (eds), *Nationalism, Democracy and Development*, pp. 51, 75.

Jinnah–Mountbatten conversation, 2 June 1947, recorded in Alan Campbell-Johnson, *Mission with Mountbatten*, 2nd edn, Connecticut, 1971, p. 103, and cited in Ayesha Jalal, *The Sole Spokesman*, pp. 284–85.

'Shadow Lines', title of Amitav Ghosh's novel *The Shadow Lines*, Harmondsworth: Penguin, 1988.

W.H. Auden, 'Partition', in *The Collected Poems of W.H. Auden*, edited by Edward Mendelson, London: Faber and Faber, 1994, pp. 803–4.

M.A. Jinnah's speech to the first meeting of the Pakistan Constituent Assembly at Karachi, 11 August 1947, in M.A. Jinnah, *Speeches as Governor-General of Pakistan, 1947–48*. Karachi: n.d. and cited in Ayesha Jalal, *Democracy and Authoritarianism in South Asia*, Cambridge: Cambridge University Press, 1995, p. 234.

Partha Chatterjee, *Nationalist Thought and the Colonial World*, London: Zed Press and Minneapolis: University of Minnesota Press, 1986 and 1993, pp. 49–51.

Gandhi to Jawaharlal Nehru, 5 October 1945, in Jawaharlal Nehru, *A Bunch of Old Letters*, Delhi: Oxford University Press, centenary edn, 1989, pp. 505–6.

Mountbatten's address to the Indian Constituent Assembly at New Delhi, 15 August 1947, in *Time Only to Look Forward: Speeches of Rear Admiral The Earl Mountbatten of Burma*, London: 1949, cited in Ayesha Jalal, *The Sole Spokesman*, p. 293.

Faiz Ahmed Faiz, 'Freedoms Dawn' (August 1947) in *Poems by Faiz*, translated by Victor Kiernan London: George Allen and Unwin, 1971, pp. 123–27.

Chapters 18 and 19

Alavi, Hamza (1973). 'The State in Post-Colonial Societies: Pakistan and Bangladesh', in K. Gough and H.P. Sharma (eds), *Imperialism and Revolution in South Asia*, New York. An important essay on the class-state nexus.

Bardhan, Pranab (1985). *The Political Economy of Development in India*, Delhi: Oxford University Press. An argument about the relationship between three dominant proprietary classes in the Indian state.

Basu, Amrita (1992). *Two Faces of Protest: Contrasting Modes of Women's Activism in India*, Berkeley: University of California Press. A study of women's politics in Maharashtra and West Bengal.

Basu, Amrita and Srirupa Roy (eds) (2007). *Violence and Democracy in India*, Calcutta/New York: Seagull Books. A collection of essays on the nexus between violence and democracy in India.

Betielle, Andre (1992). *The Backward Classes in Contemporary India*, Delhi: Oxford University Press. An important sociological perspective on the politics of the backward classes.

Bose, Sugata (1997). 'Instruments and Idioms of Colonial and National Development: India's Historical Experience in Comparative Perspective', in Frederick Cooper and Randall Packard (eds), *International Development and the Social Sciences*, Berkeley: University of California Press. An essay exploring the continuities and paradigm shifts in development knowledge and practice in late colonial and post-colonial India.

Bose, Sugata and Ayesha Jalal (eds) (1997). *Nationalism, Democracy and Development: State and Politics in India*, Delhi: Oxford University Press. A collection of essays by Amartya Sen, David Washbrook, Sugata Bose, Ayesha Jalal, Sumantra Bose, Jayati Ghosh and Pranab Bhardan that takes issue with cultural critiques of modernity and nationalism while delineating the structural and ideological aspects of the late colonial and post-colonial state in India.

Bose, Sumantra (2003). *Kashmir: Roots of Conflict, Paths to Peace*, Cambridge, MA: Harvard University Press. A study informed by theory and based on field research in Kashmir on the makings of the subcontinent's deepest political crisis and what could be the building-blocks for a peace-building framework.

Brass, Paul (1990). *The Politics of India since Independence*, in *The New Cambridge History of India*, IV.1, Cambridge: Cambridge University Press. A single-volume introduction to Indian politics.

Byres, Terence, ed. (1993). *The State and Development Planning in India*, Delhi: Oxford University Press. A set of essays from a variety of perspectives with an introduction by the editor.

Chakrabarty, Sukhamoy (1987). *Development Planning: The Indian Experience*, Delhi: Oxford University Press. A perspective on Indian development planning by a leading economist actively involved in the process.

Choudhury, R.A., Shama Ghamkar and Aurobindo Ghose (1990). *The Indian Economy and its Performance since Independence*, Delhi: Oxford University Press. A collection of essays assessing India's economic performance.

Dreze, Jean and Amartya Sen (1995). *India: Economic Development and Social Opportunity*, Delhi: Oxford University Press. An important contribution to the development debate in India calling for an alternative development strategy based on expanding social opportunities.

Frankel, Francine R. (1978). *India's Political Economy, 1947–1977*, Princeton: Princeton University Press. A carefully researched monograph with insights into Nehruvian reformist class conciliation and the nature of Indira Gandhi's populism.

Frankel, Francine R. and M.S.A. Rao, eds (1989 and 1990). *Dominance and State Power in Modern India: Decline of a Social Order*, 2 vols, Delhi: Oxford University Press. A collection of essays exploring the domination–resistance dialectic along class and caste lines in various regions of India.

Guha, Ramachandra (2007). *India after Gandhi: the History of the World's Largest Democracy*, Delhi: Picador. A panoramic view of the unfolding of sixty years of India's political history since independence.

Herring, Ronald (1983). *Land to the Tiller: The Political Economy of Agrarian Reform in South Asia*, New Haven: Yale University Press. A definitive study of the obstacles in the path of land reform.

Jahan, Rounaq (1977). *Pakistan: Failure in National Integration*, Dhaka: 1977, 2nd edn. A study of the break-up of Pakistan.

Jalal, Ayesha (1990). *The State of Martial Rule: the Origins of Pakistan's Political Economy of Defence*, Cambridge: Cambridge University Press. A study of the rise to dominance of military-bureaucratic institutions within the Pakistani state structure in the broader context of regional rivalries and the international Cold War.

——(1995). *Democracy and Authoritarianism in South Asia: A Comparative and Historical Perspective*, Cambridge: Cambridge University Press. A comparative study of state structures and political processes, political economy, centre–region relations as well as ideology and culture in post-colonial India, Pakistan and Bangladesh.

Kohli, Atul, ed. (1988). *India Democracy: An Analysis of Changing State–Society Relations*, Princeton: Princeton University Press. A collection of essays on many facets of Indian politics, including an especially incisive one by Paul Brass on the making of the Punjab crisis.

Kothari, Rajni (1988). *State against Democracy: In Search of Humane Governance*, New Delhi: Konark. A critical analysis of increasingly anti-democratic tendencies of the Indian state.

Ludden, David (1992). 'India's Development Regime', in Nicholas Dirks (ed.), *Colonialism and Culture*, Ann Arbor: Michigan University Press, pp. 247–87. A historical perspective on Indian development.

——ed. (1996). *Making India Hindu*, Delhi: Oxford University Press. A collection of essays by historians, anthropologists and political scientists addressing the phenomenon of Hindu nationalism and communalism (also published under the title *Contesting the Nation* by the University of Pennsylvania Press).

Misra, B.B. (1986). *Government and Bureaucracy in India, 1947–1976*, Delhi: Oxford University Press. An insightful study of the contradiction between India's rule-bound institutions and a society accustomed to more personalized forms of governance.

Rose, Leo O. and Richard Sisson (1990). *War and Secession: Pakistan, India and the Creation of Bangladesh*, Berkeley: University of California Press. A study of the political processes and conflicts leading to the Bangladesh war of 1971.

Rudolph, Lloyd and Susanne Hoeber (1987). *In Pursuit of Lakshmi: the Political Economy of the Indian State*, Chicago: Chicago University Press. A study of India's political economy with insights into the role of agrarian demand groups described as 'bullock capitalists'.

Schendel, Willem Van (2009). *A History of Bangladesh*, Cambridge: Cambridge University Press. A useful overview of the modern history of Bangladesh.

Sen, Amanya (1989). 'Indian Development: Lessons and Non-Lessons', *Daedalus*, 118, 4. A perceptive evaluation of the successes and failures of India's development efforts.

Sobhan, Rehman (1993). *Bangladesh: Problems of Governance*, New Delhi. An insightful introduction to the nature of the state, politics and economy of Bangladesh.

Talbot, Ian (1998). *Pakistan: A Modern History*, London: Hurst. An overview of Pakistan's post-colonial history.

Vanaik, Achin (1990). *The Painful Transition: Bourgeois Democracy in India*, London: Zed Press. A rigorous analysis of the shifting class bases of support of the Congress during Indira Gandhi's populism.

Quotations: The following are the sources of quotations used in these chapters:

Saeeda Gazdar, 'Twelfth of February 1983', in Rukhsana Ahmad (trs.), *Beyond Belief: Contemporary Feminist Urdu Poetry*, Lahore: Asr Publications, pp. 18–21.

Chapter 20

Quotations: The following are the sources of quotations used in this chapter:

Benedict Anderson, *Imagined Communities: Reflections on the Origin and Spread of Nationalism*, London: Verso, 1991, p. 160.

Muhammad Iqbal, 'Bal-e-Jabriel', in *Kulliyat-I-Iqbal*, Karachi: Al-Muslim Publishers, n.d., p. 34.

Muhammad Iqbal, 'Bang-e-Dara', in *Kulliyat-I-Iqbal*, Karachi: Al-Muslim Publishers, n.d., p. 221.

Rabindranath Tagore, 'Bharatbarsher Itihas', *Bharatbarsha* in *Rabindra Rachanabali*, vol. 4. Viswa-Bharati: Shantiniketan, 1965, p. 381.

'Through the telescope', Jawaharlal Nehru, quoted in M.A. Jinnah to Jawaharlal Nehru, 17 March 1938, in Jawaharlal Nehru, *A Bunch of Old Letters*, Delhi: Oxford University Press, 1989, centenary edn, p. 278.

'Some political theorists … sovereignty', Brendan O'Leary, Tom Lyne, Jim Marshall and Bob Rowthorn, *Northern Ireland: Sharing Authority* (London: Institute for Public Policy Research, 1993), p. 136.

INDEX

Page numbers in *italics* denotes an illustration

Taylor & Francis

eBooks

FOR LIBRARIES

ORDER YOUR
FREE 30 DAY
INSTITUTIONAL
TRIAL TODAY!

Over 22,000 eBook titles in the Humanities,
Social Sciences, STM and Law from some of the
world's leading imprints.

Choose from a range of subject packages or create your own!

Benefits for **you**

▶ Free MARC records
▶ COUNTER-compliant usage statistics
▶ Flexible purchase and pricing options

Benefits for your **user**

▶ Off-site, anytime access via Athens or referring URL
▶ Print or copy pages or chapters
▶ Full content search
▶ Bookmark, highlight and annotate text
▶ Access to thousands of pages of quality research
   at the click of a button

For more information, pricing enquiries or to order
a free trial, contact your local online sales team.

UK and Rest of World: **online.sales@tandf.co.uk**

US, Canada and Latin America:
e-reference@taylorandfrancis.com

www.ebooksubscriptions.com

ALPSP Award for
BEST eBOOK
PUBLISHER
2009 Finalist
sponsored by

Taylor & Francis eBooks
Taylor & Francis Group

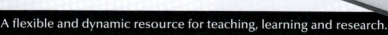A flexible and dynamic resource for teaching, learning and research.

www.routledge.com/asianstudies

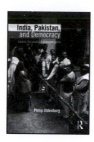

India, Pakistan, and Democracy

Solving the Puzzle of Divergent Paths

Philip Oldenburg, Columbia University, USA

'This fine book, full of insight and wisdom, reflects Philip Oldenburg's long scholarly engagement with the study of South Asian politics, and offers a magisterial synthesis of a wide literature in developing what will surely stand as the definitive comparative analysis of the political systems of India and Pakistan.' - *John Harriss, School for International Studies, Simon Fraser University, Canada*

The question of why some countries have democratic regimes and others do not is a significant issue in comparative politics. This book looks at India and Pakistan, two countries with clearly contrasting political regime histories, and presents an argument on why India is a democracy and Pakistan is not. Focusing on the specificities and the nuances of each state system, the author examines in detail the balance of authority and power between popular or elected politicians and the state apparatus through substantial historical analysis.

Providing a comparative analysis of the political systems of India and Pakistan as well as a historical overview of the two countries, this textbook constitutes essential reading for students of South Asian History and Politics. It is a useful and balanced introduction to the politics of India and Pakistan.

July 2010: 278pp
Pb: 978-0-415-78019-3

For more information and to order a copy visit
www.routledge.com/9780415780193

Available from all good bookshops

www.routledge.com/history

The Ideal Companion to Modern South Asia

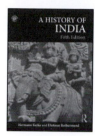

A History of India
5ᵗʰ Edition

Hermann Kulke, University of Kiel, Germany and **Dietmar Rothermund**, University of Heidelberg, Germany

A History of India presents the grand sweep of Indian history from antiquity to the present in a compact and readable survey. The authors examine the major political, economic, social and cultural forces which have shaped the history of the Indian subcontinent. Providing an authoritative and detailed account, **Hermann Kulke** and **Dietmar Rothermund** emphasise and analyse the structural pattern of Indian history.

Revised throughout, the fifth edition of this highly accessible book brings the history of India up to date to consider, for example, the elections of 2009. In addition a great deal more material on cultural history, art and architecture has been included in the book, including 20 new illustrations.

Heavily illustrated with notes and glossary, this is an attractive and useful student guide to Indian history.

April 2010: 246x174: 368pp
Pb: 978-0-415-48543-2

For more information and to order a copy visit
www.routledge.com/9780415485432

Available from all good bookshops

www.routledge.com/asianstudies

Understanding India's New Political Economy

A Great Transformation?

Edited by **Sanjay Ruparelia, Sanjay Reddy, John Harriss, Stuart Corbridge**

A number of large-scale transformations have shaped the economy, polity and society of India over the past quarter century. This book provides a detailed account of three that are of particular importance: the advent of liberal economic reform, the ascendance of Hindu cultural nationalism, and the empowerment of historically subordinate classes through popular democratic mobilizations.

Filling a gap in existing literature, the book goes beyond looking at the transformations in isolation, managing to:

• Explain the empirical linkages between these three phenomena
• Provide an account that integrates the insights of separate disciplinary perspectives
• Explain their distinct but possibly related causes and the likely consequences of these central transformations taken together

By seeking to explain the causal relationships between these central transformations through a coordinated conversation across different disciplines, the dynamics of India's new political economy are captured. Chapters focus on the political, economic and social aspects of India in their current and historical context. The contributors use new empirical research to discuss how India's multidimensional story of economic growth, social welfare and democratic deepening is likely to develop. This is an essential text for students and researchers of India's political economy and the growth economies of Asia.

March 2011: 288pp
Pb: 978-0-415-59811-8

For more information and to order a copy visit
www.routledge.com/9780415598118

Available from all good bookshops